Pilgrim's Process

Essays from a Theological Journey

DAVID R. PEEL

RESOURCE *Publications* · Eugene, Oregon

PILGRIM'S PROCESS
Essays from a Theological Journey

Resource Publications
An Imprint of Wipf and Stock Publishers
199 W. 8th Ave., Suite 3
Eugene, OR 97401

www.wipfandstock.com

PAPERBACK ISBN: 978-1-6667-0916-2
HARDCOVER ISBN: 978-1-6667-0917-9
EBOOK ISBN: 978-1-6667-0918-6

08/24/21

Pilgrim's Process

To
Clyde Binfield
Edgar Jones
Schubert Ogden
David Pailin
Ronald Preston

Along with the many other colleagues and teachers whose wisdom as well as constructive and critical guidance supported my theological journey.

"A great teacher does not impart facts; a great teacher instils an attitude, an approach, a way of observing, a way of responding."

—Neville Cardus

"I have felt as a theologian, written as a theologian . . . all other subjects in my mind are connected with theology, and subordinate to it."

—F.D. Maurice

"What must the truth have been and be if that is how it looked to people who thought and wrote like that?"

—Leonard Hodgson

"Ultimately human life is ensconced in mystery, and this must properly qualify and relativize all our theological claims."

—Gordon Kaufman

"Any theology which cannot help us cope with dynamic change is useless."

—Ronald Preston

"Children of God we all in fact are, ever were, and ever shall be, even apart from the event of Jesus Christ, although the decisive significance of Jesus, which Christians acknowledge by confessing him to be "the Christ," is that he is the revelation to all humankind of this great fact about each and every one of us."

—Schubert Ogden

"We must develop a new theological understanding of nature which will teach us to read nature — from matter to human beings — as God's sign language, so that we may learn to hear and see, taste and feel God in all things and all things in God."

—Jürgen Moltmann

Contents

Preface

THE GENESIS OF THIS book can be traced to comments made by two friends in connection with *Crucicentric, Congregational, and Catholic,* my study of the theology of Alan Sell. One wished he might have learned more about my theological position from reading the exposition of Sell's thinking; the other wanted to know what I planned to write next, noting that I might follow Sell's strategy of bringing together individual essays to form a book. Upon reflection I concluded that one friend's suggested strategy might enable me to fulfil the other's wish.

This book brings together essays written during my career. Some have already been published distant from a mainstream readership; others appear here for the first time. In the opening chapter I map out my theological journey. Then in chapters 2–8 I illustrate it. The book ends with a short retrospective postscript. The essays remain as originally written save for some minor alterations to correct mistakes, reduce repetition to a minimum, or comply with the required house-style.

The topics addressed are wide-ranging: the need for the church to address honestly the questions and issues of each age; the crucial importance of theology in the church's life; the use of the Bible; the nature and *raison d'être* of the church and its ministry; unfinished issues for the churches following the Great Ejectment; and the preparation of ordained ministers. I am found doing theology in conversation with other Reformed theologians, e.g. P.T. Forsyth, Lesslie Newbigin, Alan Sell, and Colin Gunton. My theology belongs to the tradition of *revisionary* theology (some call it "liberal" or "progressive"). I draw upon insights from a variety of thinkers, including Friedrich Schleiermacher, Reinhold Niebuhr, Paul Tillich, Jürgen Moltmann, Gordon Kaufman, Walter Brueggemann, and Schubert Ogden. Although I am wedded to a part of the Reformed tradition, my theological journey has taken me in ecumenical and hence catholic directions.

The journey spans a life-time. Along the way countless people have helped me with comments upon my work. They know who they are, but any attempt to list them all is nigh on impossible. I am grateful for their stimulation. Without the help of the staff of the following libraries my theological task would have been much harder: Dr. Williams's, London; John Rylands, Manchester; Luther King House, Manchester; Manchester University; and Westminster College, Cambridge. I am grateful that John Durell and Alison Hall proof-read the text prior to submission. Any remaining mistakes are my responsibility not theirs. Yet again I am indebted to my wife, Pat, who typed the manuscript. I am also grateful to Wipf & Stock for the efficient way in which they have taken the manuscript through the various stages of publication.

I have used inclusive language in this book, but I have not made any attempt to alter or point out the use of non-inclusive language by those whom I quote. They were children of their time; we are now without excuse.

As you read about my theological journey I hope your own theological thinking will be stimulated. God's claim upon us is absolute, not our claims about God: when we do theology with this truth firmly in view we start out on a journey towards an adequate theology, albeit one that is always incomplete.

Abbreviations

BCC	British Council of Churches
CCEW	Congregational Church in England and Wales
C of E	Church of England
CUEW	Congregational Union of England and Wales
GEAR	Group for Evangelism and Renewal within the United Reformed Church
JURCHS	Journal of the United Reformed Church History Society
NEOC	North East Oecumenical Course
SCM	Student Christian Movement
SPCK	Society for Promoting Christian Knowledge
UK	United Kingdom
URC	United Reformed Church
USA	United States of America
WARC	World Alliance of Reformed Churches
WCC	World Council of Churches

Acknowledgments

THE AUTHOR AND PUBLISHER are grateful to those named for permission to reprint the following essays:

David Steers, editor of *Faith and Freedom* for "Can You Not Read 'The Signs of the Times'?," originally published in *Faith and Freedom* 43.1/2 127/128 (Spring/Summer 1990) 43–50.

Louise Ault of the United Reformed Church Communications Department for "P.T. Forsyth on Ministry: A Model for our Time?," originally published in *P.T. Forsyth: Theologian for a New Millennium,* edited by Alan P. F. Sell. London: United Reformed Church, 1999.

Charlie Cuthbert, Marketing & Digital Coordinator of Authentic Media Ltd. for "The Theological Legacy of Lesslie Newbigin," originally published in a book from the Studies in Christian History and Thought series, edited by Anna Robbins and entitled *Ecumenical and Eclectic: Studies in Honour of Alan P.F. Sell.* Milton Keynes: Paternoster, 2007. Paternoster is an imprint of Authentic Media Ltd.

Martin Camroux of the Free to Believe network for "*Sola Scriptura*: The Achilles Heel of Reformed Theology?," originally produced as a booklet by Free to Believe, June 2012.

Robert Pope, editor of *JURCHS* for "Some Unfinished Business from the Great Ejectment of 1662," originally published in JURCHS 9.3 (November 2013) 171–84.

All biblical quotations are taken from the New Revised Standard Version.

1

Theological Autobiography

CHRISTIAN THEOLOGY IS A distinctive way of thinking. It scrutinizes expressions of Christian witness to assess their adequacy. Thereby it reveals itself as a *critical* discipline. It asks two fundamental questions. First, is the Christian witness under investigation congruent with the Jesus tradition, as it has flowed through the Christian tradition from its origins in the earliest New Testament witness to Jesus? Secondly, is it credible today? Christian theology however does not just examine Christian praxis to ascertain whether it is actually Christian and cuts ice in the modern world. It also comes into play whenever Christian thought and practice is revised so that more adequate examples of Christian witness are generated. As theology carries out this *constructive* task we are reminded that all examples of Christian praxis are historically conditioned. None can be granted absolute status. Christianity has been an evolving phenomenon, taking shape at the interface of the Christian tradition and the questions, issues, problems, and possibilities of particular times and places. When unfaithful mutations of the Christian tradition have taken place it has been theology's task to call them out and suggest more adequate examples of Christian praxis. In good theology criticism always leads to construction.

This book illustrates one person's theological journey. As I consider thinkers whose theologies have influenced me or the church tradition in which I stand, or try to understand what church history has to teach us today, or attempt to discover good practice in ministry, I will be providing examples of my own critical and constructive approach to theology. The following *theological* autobiography puts the book's chapters in context. It explains not only why certain essays were written but also relates the material in this book chronologically to my other writings.

FORMATIVE YEARS (1949–62)

I was born on 25 July 1949 at The Victoria Hospital in Keighley, then in the West Riding of Yorkshire, the only child of Arthur Blakey and Marjorie, née Jackson, Peel. We lived with my Mother's parents in the Highfield area of the town, just below the hospital, high up from its bustling center, and in a Victorian terraced house. I have only a distant memory of Grandma Jackson. She died when I was very young, but Grandpa Jackson played an important part in my childhood. He was working-class, a fitter of industrial machinery for the woolen industry, a friend to many in need, and generous to a fault, but deeply suspicious of institutional religion due to what he regarded as its inherent tendency towards hypocrisy. Irvine Peel, my other Grandfather, was a very tall, austere figure. He ran a draper's shop in the town centre, thereby bringing an element of lower middle-class influence into the family. His business, however, was not very profitable and my father had to leave Keighley Boys' Grammar School to take up an apprenticeship in the telecommunications side of the Post Office rather than go to university. I would become the first member of the family to enter Higher Education. Grandma Peel also died when I was very young, thus leaving me with few memories of her. Both my grandfathers died when I was a teenager: my Father and I found Grandpa Peel dead when we returned from a holiday, and I witnessed Grandpa Jackson's life drain away during a lengthy and difficult battle with cancer. Their deaths left a mark on me: I learned that life has to be understood and then lived in the light of the undeniable fact that we are all born terminally ill, and that departure from this life is easier for some than it is for others.

My father served in the Royal Signals during World War II. He never saw active service, spending most of his time at Catterick Garrison teaching service personnel to use land telephones, and apparently also playing a great deal of rugby and cricket. He met my mother in the primary department of the Sunday School at Devonshire Street Congregational Church in Keighley, neither of them remembering a time when they did not know each other. They married at the end of the War when my father returned to the Post Office; he would eventually serve on the Board of the North East Area of British Telecom. My mother left her work as a solicitor's clerk before I was born to care for her house-bound mother. Our life centered upon

Devonshire Street Church: my father was the Scoutmaster and my mother the Cubmistress, both sang in the choir, and my father became a Deacon and eventually the Church Secretary. When I was young I seldom saw my father mid-week. He worked in Bradford, only arriving home just before my bedtime, and quite often he then rushed out to attend meetings or lead Church activities. I found myself more in my grandfather's company than his; this explains why Grandpa Jackson became so influential in my life.

I have few early memories, a fact sometimes attributed to a happy childhood. I attended Highfield Primary School, a stone's throw from where I was born, and St. Andrew's Church of England Junior School. Both my father and grandfather encouraged my love of sport: rugby in the winter and cricket in the summer. I was a better rugby player than cricketer, but always more attracted to cricket than rugby, with our regular visits to watch Yorkshire County Cricket Club setting the foundations for a life-time interest in the sport. Far more significant for my development was my love of the countryside. I was blessed with living surrounded by some great scenery: the Yorkshire Dales—a trip to Swaledale on the occasion of my father conducting worship at Keld left a great impression upon me and was the root of a subsequent involvement in a rural mission project there; the Pennine moors—my bedroom window looked out on to the Brontë Country; and well within daily reach the East Yorkshire Wolds and the Coast, with Scarborough, the jewel in the crown and venue of the annual cricket festival which I still enjoy attending. At Junior School the nature table was a great attraction. I watched seeds sprout, frog-spawn turn into tadpoles, and learned to identify common animals, birds, and flowers. Also my grandfather taught me the rudiments of gardening, a pastime that I still enjoy. When I learned about the life and beliefs of Albert Schweitzer in Sunday School, I was able to make instant connections with his commitment to the principle of "reverence for life." It seems that I had a greater ability to "read" nature in my early years than to read books. Only additional coaching in English enabled me to get selected for Keighley Boys' Grammar School.

Some of the crucial foundation stones for my theology were laid down before I had a clue about what theology involves. First, through the natural world I became intuitively aware of God. Before I could get round to search for God, God was revealed to me, as the Apostle Paul puts it, "through the things he has made" (Rom.1: 20). When awestruck by the view from the graveyard at Keld I knew that the Psalmist's testimony is true: "The heavens are telling the glory of God; and the firmament proclaims his handiwork" (Ps. 19: 1). Much later I came to see that the "mysterium tremendum et fascinans" (Rudolf Otto) I was encountering through nature in an existentially certain way needed conceptualizing coherently if I was going to make sense of my experience. I continue to find what Peter Berger, the American sociologist, calls "*signals of transcendence* within the empirically given human situation";[1] or, to use the terminology of Ian T. Ramsey, on largely unplanned occasions I experience "cosmic disclosures in which I am aware of being acted upon, of something (someone) bearing actively upon me."[2] I can now see that all my theological endeavors have been directed to a common end, one of making sense of what I have been led to believe is faith-endowing religious experience. I have thus been engaged in a task of exploring religion, what Schleiermacher calls "sense and taste for the Infinite."[3]

Secondly, my life has always been centred within a Christian community: I was baptized and raised in Devonshire Street Congregational Church. My relationship, however, with the institutional church has been nuanced for as long as I can remember: I have loved and hated it in equal measure. At its best what was said of the early Christians is in evidence: "See how they love one another";[4] while at its worst it often becomes beset by petty wrangling and rank bad behavior, thus no different from any other all too human organization. It can certainly be what Lesslie Newbigin describes as "the place where the reign of God is actually present and at work in the midst of history, and where the mission of Jesus is being accomplished,"[5] but it can also descend into an inward-looking and self-serving community. I experienced both faces of the church very early in life, and I continue to do so.

Thirdly, from an early age I became fascinated by Jesus of Nazareth. Through teachers at school as well as at church the Gospel stories about Jesus were opened up for me in ways that made becoming a follower of Jesus an attractive option. Seeds were sown that later turned into a commitment to a vision of God revealed through the life, death, and resurrection of Jesus. In the God *re-presented* for us in Jesus I have experienced a "love so amazing, so divine" which, as Isaac Watts testifies, "demands my soul, my life, my all."[6] A connection is thus made between the *original* revelation of God I have encountered through nature and the *special* revelation of God in the Christ event. I have never been able to accept exclusively Christocentric views of salvation since my faith has been generated in an important sense outside as well as inside the Christian community: God is not the tribal

1. Berger, *Rumour*, 70.

2. Ramsay, *Models*, 62. On "disclosure situations" see also Ramsay, *Religious Language*, 11–48.

3. Schleiermacher, *On Religion*, 39.

4. Tertullian, *Apology*, 39.

5. Newbigin, *Open Secret*, 60.

6. From Isaac Watts' hymn "When I survey the wondrous Cross" found in *Rejoice and Sing*, no.217.

deity of Christians but the creator and redeemer of the entire world. If I had been brought up inside a Muslim family the likelihood is that my experience of "signals of transcendence" would have been interpreted through Islamic teaching. The issues surrounding the relationship between Christianity and the other world faiths not surprisingly therefore have been of great interest to me in my theological explorations.

Fourthly, it follows that the Bible is of fundamental importance for me. It remains my sole access to the early church's witness to Jesus. Without the New Testament we would have no knowledge of Jesus or what his early followers claimed about him; without the Old Testament we would not know much about the religion of Jesus and hence be unaware of the Jewish context in which his life, teaching, death, and resurrection needs to be understood. I am grateful therefore that I was given at an early age an appreciation of the Bible; but as I came to work out how the Bible plays a crucial role in Christian theology it increasingly became clear that I could not accept the way some Christians use it. I once thought that with the acceptance of biblical criticism "fundamentalism" would become as peripheral to the Christian church as "flat-earth" theories are to geology, but actually the reverse seems to be the case in some parts of the church.

Fifthly, by the time I left Junior School I had discovered the ecumenical divide that then existed between "Church" and "Chapel." It became apparent that the way we Congregationalists did things was different from the Anglican practices that underpinned the religious life of my school. Not only did "us and them" attitudes surface from time to time, but the frequent visits to the neighbouring parish church left me feeling uneasily aware of being a Nonconformist. Moreover, when I heard some of "us" talking in very disparaging tones about Roman Catholics I couldn't help but think that the ancient Protestant versus Catholic feuds I was learning about in English history were not finally over. Thankfully, sufficient Christian adults were around who suggested that all such hostilities were decidedly un-Christian. Looking back I can now recognize the emergence of a positive ecumenical outlook during that first encounter with the Church of England.

Sixthly, my first day at Junior School drew my attention to the deep-seated inequalities in society. The entire new intake was lined up in the school hall. A teacher walked past us, occasionally directing individuals to move into an adjacent classroom. About a quarter of the class was "chosen," but I was not among them. Those who had been selected became beneficiaries of new shoes courtesy either of the State or a charity—I'm not sure which. In fact, they got shoes the like of which I had never seen before: I was very jealous since they gave an unfair advantage in the break-time football games! When I got home after school I learned that the shoes were actually clogs which had been given to children who had not got adequate footwear because their parents were poor, and that I should be grateful for what I had rather than be jealous about what the other children had received. But why were they poor? That was a question I had to put down for further investigation. Liberal politics were once at the heart of the Nonconformist outlook, with a stress on individuals trying to better themselves, coupled with commitment to improving the lot of the disadvantaged. After the War however the Labour Party had largely replaced the Liberals. It created the Welfare State and espoused a commitment to end inequality. I missed out on the clogs, but the experience made me receptive at a later stage to many of the principles of democratic socialism.

SECONDARY EDUCATION (1962–68)

My time at Keighley Boys' Grammar School, later to be called Keighley School, when a co-educational, comprehensive era was ushered in, proved to be a mixed experience. The school had notable former pupils, historians Herbert Butterfield and Asa Briggs among the best known. It took me a long time to settle down. I had left behind important friends, some who had "failed" the Eleven Plus exams and two others whose parents had sent them to fee-paying schools. I became proficient on the sports field long before I fulfilled my educational potential with outstanding GCE "O" Level results. The only blot on that early academic profile concerned the low pass grade I received for English Language. The teaching I received, especially in the Sixth Form, was of very mixed quality, a far cry from the much higher standards our children later received at an inner-city Sixth Form College in Manchester. Events beyond my control largely contributed to what undoubtedly was under-achievement at "A" Level: a serious leg injury (which also put paid to a promising rugby career) and a debilitating bout of glandular fever that derailed my Sixth Form studies.

I was placed under great pressure to study science at "A" Level. It was partly self-imposed, stemming from a desire to know more about the natural world—how things had got to where they are now, what they are made of, and how they work. Also, externally, the challenge to engage in what Harold Wilson, the then Prime Minister, had called "the white-hot technological revolution" had been enthusiastically put before us. A subject combination of English literature, history, and geography might have been an option were it not for my noted weakness with the English Language; a poor French teacher had meant that the study of languages was never to become one of my greatest pleasures; and further work in chemistry, mathematics, and physics therefore seemed to make the most sense. While I am not totally sad about the choice I made, I deeply regret having being part of an educational system which necessitates such an early degree of specialization.

Away from my studies involvement in church life gathered pace. Attracted largely by the provisions being made for young people I became a member of Knowle Park Congregational Church. John M. Marsh, its minister, was a great encouragement, and I gained a great deal from being set free from the at times divisive atmosphere of the congregation in which I had grown up. This period of church life seemed dominated by theological exploration and discussions about the shape the church needed to attain if it were to become a credible and effective witness in the turbulent 1960s. The CCEW produced *A Declaration of Faith* in 1967 following a lengthy consultation process among its congregations.[7] It thereby engendered a process of theological discussion throughout the denomination that arguably was as significant and important as the excellent end-product. The publication of *Honest to God* also generated widespread theological discussion in the churches, shocking many who felt that their doctrinal foundations were being attacked but liberating those for whom the doctrines of Christian orthodoxy had become problematical.[8] Lay people took up opportunities to meet together in house groups using study material like *Church Without Walls* and *The People Next Door*. Many of these groups were made up of people drawn from different Christian denominations. Theological discussion, once the preserve of the ordained, was taking place in a refreshing way amongst rank and file Christian disciples.[9] I was glad to be involved in it and it contributed immensely to my early theological development. I found a new and exciting world opening up for me. The roots of a liberal, revisionist approach to theology were being firmly established.

The religious education teaching at school left a lot to be desired. It was reduced too often to periods of private study caused by the sole specialist teacher's bouts of illness. He was an Anglican clergyman whose pedagogical

7. The document can be found in Thompson, *Stating The Gospel*, 198–247.

8. Robinson, *Honest to God*. When I came to read the book, well after the heated debate it generated had died down, I found that it encouraged me to read for myself the German theologians the book introduces. See also Robinson and Edwards, *The Honest to God Debate* for an analysis and interpretation of the subsequent discussion. I never could quite understand what all the fuss was about.

9. A very important book for me (and others) at this time was Gibbs and Morton, *God's Frozen People*. As a Congregationalist, its vision of the central role to be played by lay-education in the church's life needed no *theoretical* justification, although I have continued to regret how many church members do not feel the need to engage in the lay-education opportunities that are available. See also Gibbs and Morton, *God's Lively People*.

performance was sufficient to put those he taught off Christianity for life. He belonged to the tough love school of education. When he took us on Paul's journeys around the Mediterranean we learned more about the places the Apostle visited than the gospel he proclaimed and lived out. Setting to one side his Thomas Cook style approach, though, he left me with an insight of enduring importance, namely, that Christianity in essence is a movement and only by practical necessity an institution. So often, however, the primary missiological purpose of the church gets swallowed up by the all-consuming requirement to keep the institution going. I have found it helpful to reformulate a program made famous by Rudolf Bultmann by arguing that there comes a time when churches need to engage in the process of de-institutionalization and missionary re-envisaging if faithfulness to the gospel is to be followed.[10] Very early in my church involvement I felt that such a time had arrived. Subsequent experiences have done little to alter my judgment.

It very quickly became apparent to me that the relationship between theology and science has had a fraught history. Some of my teachers were hostile towards religion and since the predominant religion in Western culture is Christianity their atheism involved a dislike of the church. Their presence in School Assemblies stood out because of their non-participation in the communal religious aspects. On the other hand, Frank Trenouth, my chemistry teacher, was a devout Anglican. Whatever intellectual problems his colleagues had about belief in God clearly had not prevented him from enthusiastic involvement at his local parish church. He had brought together two worlds that others find incompatible: one which poses huge challenges to orthodox patterns of believing, rooted as they often are in problematical expressions of *super*naturalism; the other which promotes the idea that everything in the world, including our experience of it, is irreducible to *natural* phenomena. Much of my initial theological investigation involved trying to bring together the two "worlds" which I found myself inhabiting: science and religion.

My church world began to expand. I became involved in gatherings of regional and national Congregational Youth, meeting a wider range of Christian young people and having my horizons broadened by conference speakers and denominational leaders. My parents were regular participants at The Congregational Forum, an annual holiday conference held at The Hayes Conference Centre in Derbyshire. From 1965 onwards the event became a regular part of my summer. It was at Forum that I caught an ecumenical vision from an address delivered by John Huxtable, then the General Secretary of the

---

10. I tried to fill out what this might involve in my *Encountering Church*.

CCEW. I still share much of that vision, though I no longer believe it contains the necessity for the denominations to be organically united. The God-given genius of Christianity lies partly in its ability to morph into different forms appropriate to different contexts. Christian diversity will never be contained within a single *organic* structure. In 1968 I experienced first hand more of the riches of that diversity at a work camp organized by the WCC at Åsa in Sweden and at a BCC Youth Conference in Edinburgh. While in Sweden I was able to visit the General Assembly of the WCC which was taking place at Uppsala. The urgent themes of world poverty and racism were central to an agenda that was increasingly influenced by the churches of the Two-Third's World. At Uppsala I also came to realize that my Christian thinking ought not to be centered solely upon theoretical questions concerned with the context of Christian believing; I also had to address the call placed on all our lives by the cries of the poor, disadvantaged, and oppressed. These practical concerns found expression in my commitment to democratic socialism and engagement with the World Development Movement. They provided a foundation upon which I would later make a positive response to the challenges of the various theologies of liberation.

My visit to Uppsala started a decade of involvement with the WCC. I was a steward at its subsequent Assembly at Nairobi, Kenya (1975) and co-leader of the stewards at the Conference on Faith, Science and the Future at the Massachusetts Institute of Technology (1979). My theological horizons were thereby broadened and a strong ecumenical commitment evolved. Later in the 1980s, when attempts to further the cause of visible church union in England ground to a halt, that commitment would be severely challenged.

FROM CHEMISTRY TO THEOLOGY (1968–71)

After a careers counseling session the idea was kindled that I should read social science at University. It seemed appropriate: it fitted my burgeoning interest in wanting to benefit less fortunate people and my general social concerns and commitments, and it also was a *science*, albeit one whose status as such was and still is questioned by many natural scientists. Very few universities at the time offered social science courses; most did not expect applications from students with a natural science background; and competition for places was very high. Given my disappointing "A" Level results it was hardly surprising that I was denied a route into the social sciences and consequently I decided to adopt the default position of reading chemistry at the University of London through Sir John Cass College.

Initially, I enjoyed devoting my time to my favorite school subject with the help of good teachers. Class sizes were usually very small and the education style surprisingly relaxed and intimate, though we sometimes joined with other students from other colleges for rather more formal lectures in larger groups at more prestigious venues like Imperial, King's or Queen Mary Colleges. I found lodgings in Tottenham, sharing a room with Alan Catt, a geography student from Deal in Kent. We got on well together and both played in the College rugby team. Alan was living proof, if ever I needed it, that an individual does not have to possess explicit religious commitment to be a genuinely decent person. At this point in my life I had come to realize that my church membership set me apart from most of my contemporaries. Although I recognized that overall the Christian denominations were in serious numerical decline, I privately held the thought that if local churches really got their acts together the tide could easily be turned. The power of secularization had not yet impacted upon me.

I found my early days in London disorienting and lonely, but once I met up with established friends from the Congregational Youth network at Kensington Chapel I began to enjoy being in London. My Sundays revolved around the Eden Fellowship which met after the evening service. I benefitted greatly from worship conducted by Caryl Micklem, whose liturgical style and structure rubbed off on me more than anything I was later taught in worship courses at theological college.[11] Of greater significance was meeting Patricia Evelyn Burton. From early 1969 onwards we went out together, enjoying the London theatres and concert halls. We married in the summer of 1971.

Music has always been part of my life, but it was not until my time in London that I discovered how much it can become a vehicle for experiencing transcendence. I found myself addressed by God in the concert hall, not just through nature and worship. That remains the case even though I still appreciate the art of good preaching. Neville Cardus, doyen of cricket writers and music critic, speaks for many:

> Often I have listened to *Gerontius* in the cathedrals of the West of England and at the end, after "Softly and gently, dear ransomed soul, In my most loving arms I now enfold thee . . . Swiftly shall pass thy night of trial here. And I shall come and wake thee on the morrow"—these words to music of a hushed peace that seemed there and then to ease all human hurt and apprehension; and I have scarcely been able to see in front of me

11. For Caryl Micklem see Binfield and Taylor, *Who They Were.*

because of mist of tears. But I have been aware of, sitting next to me, many a gaitered divine, apparently unaffected; and I am what an orthodox Christian would call an unbeliever.[12]

Cardus may well have been the "The Great Romantic,"[13] but Samuel Taylor Coleridge most certainly had a point when he sought to distinguish "understanding" from "knowing." By "understanding" Coleridge meant "the 'science of phenomena' . . . the kind of thinking that separates, analyses, measures, classifies, knows in terms of cause and effect, is concerned with means rather than ends."[14] "Reason," on the other hand he maintained, is "a 'conscious self-knowledge', an intuition of ourselves as related to the whole as a living reality, . . . a knowing that is religious (and poetic), a seeing that goes beyond space and time, . . . the 'organ of the supersensuous', the faculty of the infinite, the knowledge of the infinite, the knowledge of 'the laws of the whole considered as one'."[15] Central to my intellectual development during undergraduate studies was learning how to hold together what Coleridge helpfully distinguishes.

There is a world of difference however between a "distinction" and a "separation." While some scientists ignore what Coleridge means by "reason," preferring to view everything in terms of what he calls "understanding," many Christians are guilty of the reverse. Through my science studies I was introduced to the quantum world, that arena of indeterminacy at the sub-atomic level, where notions of "probability," "randomness," "uncertainty," and "openness" govern our understanding of reality. It became implausible according to this world view to conceive God as a kind of Mr Fixit who from eternity had created a world whose every moment has been known to him in advance, or one who acts as a *deus ex machina* when things get in a mess. "Understanding" and "reason" need holding together for a *full* appreciation of the world, our place within it, and our responsibilities towards it. Simon Barnes is right when he says: "You impoverish yourself if you accept only science, just as you impoverish yourself—perhaps more greatly—by ignoring science."[16]

After my first term at university I became a hostelman at New College in West Hampstead, one of the Congregational (and later URC) theological colleges. I relished life in a student community with a firm Christian base. As time went on I found my life centering on the church more than the

---

12. Cardus, *Second Innings*, 129–30.

13. The title of Duncan Hamilton's biography of Cardus.

14. Welch, "Samuel Taylor Coleridge," 8.

15. Welch, "Samuel Taylor Coleridge," 9.

16. Barnes, *Meaning of Birds*, 74.

laboratory. Involvement with Congregational Youth increased when I became its Honorary Secretary and my theological reading was stepped up. Two individuals influenced me greatly during these years: Donald Hilton, the CCEW Youth Secretary[17] and Charles Duthie, the Principal of New College.[18] Donald presented a model of Christian ministry that I found enormously attractive and he was to preach the "Charge to the Minister" at my ordination. "Charlie," on the other hand, supplied me with endless suggestions about appropriate reading for somebody now living at the interface of science and religion. He introduced me for example to the sermons of Paul Tillich, the writings of Pierre Teilhard de Chardin, and the theology of Nels Ferré who was making interesting use of process philosophy in his theology. I also found myself increasingly associating with the New College theological students, some of whom have remained firm friends; and by the end of my second undergraduate year I knew I was not destined for a chemistry career: I had "felt" a calling to Christian ministry, which was duly tested by the Church, with the result that I was accepted as a student at The Congregational College, Manchester.

During the university vacations I returned home to Keighley. I found jobs to earn much-needed cash: working in a mill, tending to graves in a cemetery, and delivering the Christmas post. Each job provided me with useful experience, particularly my time in the mill. I recall the hot, noisy conditions, wondering how anyone could cope with such an environment for a life-time. The mill, though, provided me with an important opportunity to work alongside Pakistani operatives, among the first Asian immigrants who had made their home in the West Riding. They had been brought over to England to work the night shifts, doing tasks usually undertaken by women. Factory legislation prevented women from night working; local men would not do "women's work"; so the immigrant workforces enabled the mill-owners to run their machines night as well as day. I got on well with men whose hard work was proportional to their poor English; but my Urdu was much worse. I admired their devotion to prayer and they introduced me to their cuisine. I have been saddened to observe the racism which has been generated towards the Asian communities who have found their home in Yorkshire, even from within Christian churches.

At meals in the New College dining hall I sat at a table next to a wall upon which was fixed a portrait of P.T. Forsyth, whom Alan Sell rates as "*The*

---

17. Hilton was Moderator of the URC General Assembly(1993–4). His "Address to Assembly," entitled "To follow truth, and thus . . . An elliptical faith," is underpinned with theology that is music to my ears.

18. For Duthie see Sell, *Hinterland Theology*, 500–562.

British Reformed theologian of the twentieth century."[19] Forsyth's *Lectures on the Church and Sacraments* made a great impression on me. They contributed to the more positive view of the church which developed as I experienced in London a quality of worship and preaching I had seldom encountered before. I also enjoyed in London as well as Manchester being among people who wanted to talk theology, not just because it is an interesting pastime, but because of the need to construct a Christian narrative that is as vital for our personal development as it is for Christian mission. Edgar Jones, my theological college Principal, used to say that if we strip the institutional church of all that it does for the social benefit of its members we come near to the heart of a faithful church. Only theological awareness will enable it then to be a credible and relevant witness in contemporary society. As Chapter 2 indicates it has been a repeated concern of mine that the church reads "the signs of the times" (Matt 16: 3) and responds in appropriate ways.

Forsyth challenged me to get to the heart of what is involved in being a Christian community, but I have never been satisfied with the overly cross-centered and clearly exclusivist underpinnings of his ecclesiology. I also had similar misgivings about Dietrich Bonhoeffer's suggestive contribution to Christian ecclesiology.[20] The universal scope of the redemptive activity of God ought not to be reduced in such a way that all those who lived before Jesus or outside the stream of consciousness flowing from him are inevitably denied access to it. Nor have I ever warmed to the ultra-Calvinist strand that has been around in parts of Nonconformist tradition. Some views of the doctrine of the atonement which have been drawn from it, for example, presuppose a picture of a God I find unworthy of our belief. As I headed to Manchester to prepare for stipendiary ministry another burning theological question was now forming in my mind: How can we talk about the saving significance of the Christ event without reducing God to the tribal deity of Christians?

19. Sell, *Enlightenment*, 259. Italics mine.

20. I later came to the conclusion that the basic clues for understanding Bonhoeffer's idea of "religionless Christianity," made popular through his *Letters and Papers from Prison*, are located in his first published work, *Sanctorum Communio*. Bonhoeffer's ecclesiology is far from being as *avant-garde* as some claim: it is thoroughly grounded in a typically neo-orthodox rejection of "religion" as the all too human distortion of the faith-community which was called into being by the saving work of Jesus Christ: "Communion with God exists only through Christ, but Christ is present only in his church, hence there is communion with God only in the church" (*Sanctorum Communio*, 116).

PREPARATION FOR ORDINATION (1971–75)

Manchester (1971–74)

We found our time in Manchester quite difficult. I was one of the few married students at a college which had no accommodation on site for married students and showed little foresight about the need for it. I was totally reliant for funding from a bursary, but unlike resident single students I did not benefit from having my accommodation paid. We struggled financially which explains why we were never able to attend the Hallé orchestra—nor was it Yorkshire prejudice that prevented me watching cricket at Old Trafford. Pat had felt a level of welcome at New College that was not replicated for her during our three years at the Congregational College. Nor did I feel a need to repeat the undergraduate experience so much in evidence.

My course was demanding: the University of Manchester BD degree, plus College pastoralia courses and regular Sunday visits to local churches to conduct worship. After years of studying science I was more adept at tackling theories, working through equations, and plotting graphs than reading books and writing essays. Also the Manchester BD is a second degree, which assumes students have a working knowledge of the biblical languages before studying prescribed biblical texts and also presupposes preparatory knowledge the likes of which I would have had, if, say, I had taken a survey course in church history before specializing in one particular period of it. Learning biblical Greek consumed much of my energy in a first year that I was relieved to complete unscathed. By the second year I had got into my stride and, contrary to many others' experience, I found tackling Hebrew less difficult than learning Greek. My final year turned out to be hugely rewarding and enjoyable: I had moved from being a scientist to becoming a theologian.

I appreciated the thorough introduction to the Bible I received at Manchester. Sometimes I felt that not enough attention was paid to the historical critical method, particularly when we were preparing for in-house examinations on the English text of the Bible, but the scene was set for what has been a life-time's fascination with scripture. When I conducted worship a few years ago someone who hadn't heard me preach for a while remarked that he'd forgotten how biblical I was. In the churches I ministered in I put a great deal of effort into helping church members appreciate individual biblical books, not least some of the least well-known ones. Edgar Jones, an excellent Old Testament teacher, guaranteed that I would never succumb to Marcionite tendencies—it is one of the downsides of lectionary use that very often the Old Testament is not heard in public worship. He kindled in me a love of the Jewish scriptures that has remained with me to this day. But in biblical studies I could not help asking questions such as: "If there is a "consensus of scholarly opinion" on the question of the historicity of the Gospels, why do so many New Testament scholars come to such different conclusions about the historical Jesus?" or "If that's what you think Paul meant, was he correct to think so?" Questions concerning the authority of the Bible were also never far from my theological concerns when I left Manchester. One of the biblical scholars who most helped me frame and answer such questions was James Barr, Professor of Semitic Languages and Literature when I studied at the University of Manchester. But oddly he never taught me in person.[21] My attempt to tackle the issues surrounding our use of the Bible in the contemporary church is found in Chapter 6.

The teacher who undoubtedly influenced my theological development the most during my Manchester period was David Pailin, a Methodist who encouraged me to face up to difficult questions in an honest fashion.[22] He helped me confirm Charles Duthie's hunch that, akin to Nels Ferré, I might find process philosophy helpful. His lectures on the panentheistic model for conceiving God's relationship with the world[23] and on the dipolar structure of the concept of God[24] were eureka moments on my intellectual journey. In writing an essay for him I was intensely stimulated and helped by Schubert M. Ogden's, *The Reality of God and Other Essays.* Not only was Ogden shortly to supervise my year of post-graduate study in the USA but his theology would become the subject of my doctoral studies under Pailin's supervision. Three other teachers made a positive impact upon me at the University of Manchester. Raymond Plant's course on Hegel[25] provided me with a philosophical background to set in context the theologies of Jürgen Moltmann and Wolfhart Pannenberg, the so-called "theologians of hope." His lectures were a model of good communication, displaying a commendable ability to make the most complex of thinkers intelligible. Secondly, Ronald Preston, the Anglican social ethicist, introduced me to the

21. Barr's, *Bible and The Modern World* was a landmark book for me.

22. I attended various courses taught by Pailin, the contents of which eventually found their way into his published books. See the bibliography.

23. See Pailin, *Groundwork*, 123–29 and *God and the Processes of Reality*, 76–95. For a thorough investigation of the different ways in which the concept of panentheism can be construed and an analysis of its strengths and weaknesses see Clayton and Peacocke, *In Whom We Live and Move and Have Our Being.*

24. See Pailin, *Groundwork*, 147–51 and *God and the Processes of Reality*, 57–75.

25. See Plant, *Hegel.* Plant, under the title Lord Plant of Highfield, became an active Labour peer in the House of Lords.

writings of Reinhold Niebuhr, thereby enabling me to see the importance of acknowledging the corporate as well as individual origins of human wrong-doing. *Moral Man and Immoral Society* and *The Children of Light and The Children of Darkness* made a significant impression on me, but it was not until researching *Reforming Theology* that I got round to Niebuhr's Gifford Lectures.[26] Then I fully came to appreciate the profundity of his analysis of the human condition, even if his view of sin however has subsequently been subjected to penetrating feminist critique.[27] Thirdly, Henry Rack prompted an exploration of religion in Manchester during Queen Victoria's reign. His course revealed how little church history I knew. I came to appreciate in particular the importance and significance of Congregationalism in English civic life. Given that the teachers who influenced me the most during my Manchester period included two Anglicans and two Methodists I can say that the Manchester BD was an *ecumenical* experience within a *secular* university.

While preparing for ministry in Manchester I particularly enjoyed the regular contact we had with local churches. I conducted worship on most Sundays during term time and undertook more extensive student pastorates in the summer vacations. I learned a great deal from being involved with Friary Congregational Church, Nottingham (1972) and the Stockport Group of United Reformed Churches (1973–4), where the constructive and critical comments of ministers and church members were often the difference between merely having an experience on a pastoral placement and actually receiving a pastoral education.[28] I was grateful overall for what the College and University offered me in Manchester as I prepared for ministry. When it was decided that I should spend my fourth year in the USA it was inevitable that I would miss some parts of the standard curriculum, particularly those final year courses that had a particular bearing on the more practical aspects of ministry. It now seems strange that a Congregationalist could leave theological college without having covered in depth Reformation history or the theology of John Calvin. Fortunately some of those "gaps" were attended to later, only leaving me with regrets that more had not been attempted at Manchester to help us integrate academic study with training in practical skills.

---

26. See Niebuhr, *Nature and Destiny.*

27. See for example Hampson, *Theology and Feminism,* 116–26.

28. Jim Hollyman, one of the Stockport ministers, provided me with excellent placement supervision.

Dallas, Texas (1974–75)

I was very fortunate to be awarded a WCC scholarship for one year of post-graduate study in the USA. When I applied for the award I decided that it was more important to have a year of study directed by a prominent theologian than to attend any particular institution. My burgeoning interest in process theology guided me to Schubert M. Ogden who was teaching at Perkins' School of Theology, a graduate school of Southern Methodist University in Dallas, Texas. It proved to be an exciting and memorable year for both of us.

I was enrolled on the Master of Sacred Theology program which most students completed in a calendar year, covering the requisite number of taught courses in the first two semesters and completing a dissertation in the third. My funding was based on two semesters residence, so financial necessity as well as a desire to see more of America before we returned home meant that I followed the example of the few who avoided allowing their time on the program to spill into a third semester. I agreed with Ogden that the majority of my time should involve reading primary texts rather than attending a lot of lectures, so other than taking the basic systematic theology course—thereby covering all the main Christian doctrines for the first time in a thorough way—the only lectures I attended were those of Albert Outler on "Wesley and the Evangelical Revival," to which I had been directed by my fellow students. This enabled me to read extensively, particularly the work of Charles Hartshorne, Rudolf Bultmann, Paul Tillich, John Calvin, and Friedrich Schleiermacher. It was liberating to be able to study theology from primary rather than secondary sources, and to engage with important texts in seminars and under the supervision of teachers who specialized in the thought of the theologians I had chosen to read. Gustavo Gutierrez's A Theology of Liberation had just been published in English and was the subject of much discussion. It seemed appropriate given my social and political commitments to write my dissertation on liberation theology, focusing on the theology of Juan Luis Segundo. A shortened version of this was subsequently published.[29]

After conducting the daily act of worship at Perkins one day I was taken to task very severely by some of the women students on account of my failure to employ inclusive language. It was my first serious encounter with the way in which feminism has challenged church thinking and practice. This was the beginning of some essential personal reconstruction. The experience led me to take very seriously the contribution of women theologians, some of whom, I discovered, shared my enthusiasm for process

---

29. See my "Juan Luis Segundo, "A Theology for Artisans of a New Humanity."

theology. I became aware of how contextual factors inevitably shape our theologies, and came to see that we need to do theology with an eye on the way its questions and conclusions are liable to be affected by gender, race, and social standing, and here I must acknowledge my debt to the work of Elisabeth Schüssler Fiorenza, Grace M. Jantzen, Sallie McFague (née Te Selle), Ruth Page, and Rosemary Radford Ruether.

Although the Bible plays a central part in my theology I have never had much time for theologies based wholly on biblical revelation. Doing theology from inside a narrow circle of faith has had no appeal. At its best, Barth's theology has always presented itself to me as a self-critical moment within liberal theology. Although a complete set of *Church Dogmatics* adorns my bookshelves and reveals evidence of having been read, my attention to Barth's work largely reflects my need to get a gist of what a member of the theological opposition is saying! When denouncing Barth's "new kind of fundamentalism" Reinhold Niebuhr argued that "we can escape relativity and uncertainty only by piling experience upon experience, checking hypothesis against hypothesis, correcting errors by considering new perspectives, not by the mere assertion of an absolute idea that is beyond experience."[30] Niebuhr had tried hard to debate with Barthians, but he gave up: "A positivism which stands above reason is not debatable so what's the use?"[31]

Under Ogden's challenging guidance my theology developed rapidly. Tillich provided me with a way of doing theology which pays attention not only to God's word addressed to us through the Christ event but also to the way God meets us through the world, human experience, and culture. Ogden had spent a great deal of his career developing the methodology for such a theology,[32] and I learned from him far more precisely what it means to do theology and how to be a theologian. Secondly, my reading of Hartshorne helped develop my appreciation of the way in which process philosophy can help us talk coherently and credibly about God. I discovered a conceptual underpinning which enables me to hold together what I have learned from science with my Christian faith.[33] Thirdly, I discovered that at Manchester I had been presented with too negative an interpretation of Rudolf Bultmann's theological program of demythologizing and existential reinterpretation. Rather than viewing this program as a means by which the Christian faith is trimmed down to what is believable today, and

---

30. Niebuhr quoted in Fox, *Reinhold Niebuhr*, 117.

31. Niebuhr in a letter to John Bennett, quoted in Fox, *Reinhold Niebuhr*, 123.

32. See Ogden's, *On Theology* and *Doing Theology Today*.

33. I have also been greatly helped by the writings of Arthur Peacocke and Ian G. Barbour.

therefore is guilty of ending up in doctrinal reductionism, I was guided to see it in a more positive light. Ogden reminds us that "the inner integrity" of Bultmann's theology lies in his early neo-orthodox "affirmation of the "infinite qualitative difference" between time and eternity."[34] Mythological formulations of the Christian faith, however, "completely obscure the fact that God's difference from the world is not merely "quantitative" but "qualitative."[35] Demythologizing is therefore called for when expressions of the Christian faith undermine the dialectical relation of God and the world. It follows that "the ultimate explanation of Bultmann's extensive use of existentialist philosophy is that it enables him to express more adequately than any other conceptuality he knows the underlying conception of God and man which he is primarily concerned to convey."[36] Removal of objectifying language about God thus sets theology free to formulate God-talk in a more appropriate way. I had been led to believe by some teachers in Manchester that the reason for Bultmann's demythologizing program is "the exigency of the present apologetic situation, in which Christians are required to witness to a "scientific" world," when actually "this exigency is not at all the *cause* of his proposal, but simply the *occasion*."[37] Fourthly, I discovered in Ogden' proposals for a *re-presentative* Christology a helpful way of understanding the relationship between Christians and other Faiths. Ogden is greatly indebted in this matter to F.D. Maurice who encourages us to recognize that "the responsibility of contemporary theology is to make clear that the hidden power, the inner meaning, the real substance, of *all* human happenings is the event of Christ."[38] The term "Christ" therefore is "the *eschatological* event, or *eternal* word of God's unconditioned love, which is the ground and end of all historical events whatever."[39] The Christ event is the decisive *re-presentation* in one historical event of the original possibility of our human existence before God. At the end of an exploration of the question, "Is there only one true religion or are there many?" Ogden claims therefore that "because of the utterly universal and all-embracing love of God decisively re-presented through Jesus Christ, there is a universal possibility of salvation for each and every human being and that, for the same reason, there is a corresponding possibility of as many true religions as there are religions so transformed by God's love as to be constituted by it and

34. Ogden, "Introduction," 15.

35. Ogden, "Introduction," 20.

36. Ogden, "Introduction," 21.

37. Ogden, "Introduction," 20.

38. Ogden, *Christ without Myth*, 182.

39. Ogden, *Christ without Myth*, 182.

representative of it."[40] Then, fifthly, the Dallas context highlighted the need to take seriously the thrust of liberation theology. A deeply divided city—both economically and racially—reminded me of my theological responsibility not only to answer questions of un-believers in an increasingly secular society but also those of the impoverished, marginalized, and dispossessed the world over. The liberation theologians may well be guilty sometimes of so stressing the *emancipatory* dimension of God's liberating work that they pay inadequate attention to God's *redemptive* activity, but they certainly provide a much-needed reminder that we can only participate in God's emancipatory work to the extent that we join in the Christlike struggle to hear the cry of the distressed and let the oppressed go free.[41]

While in Dallas we worshipped at First Community Church, whose Welsh minister, Bill Martin, had been informed by Charles Duthie of our arrival. Bill was an eloquent preacher and raconteur of gregarious disposition. He had been minister of Augustine-Bristo Congregational Church in Edinburgh when Duthie was Principal of the Scottish Congregational College. We enjoyed our regular Sunday routine of the early morning Communion Service, church breakfast, Sunday School class, and Service of the Word. The church was Congregational in polity and liberal in ethos. It was refreshing to be part of a Christian community in which many of the adults were actively exploring their faith. The ecclesiastical demographics of Dallas however are such that an "ecumenical" ministers' fraternal only attracted a small number from the very few liberal churches in the city, plus quite surprisingly some Jewish rabbis. We lived in Dallas knowing that to be a liberal Christian is to be "suspect" in the eyes of those caught up in the right-wing, narrow biblicism of the American South, but, nevertheless, we felt at home among an interesting mix of seminary and church friends. Pat enjoyed working at a local bank, amazing everyone in the car-dominated culture by walking to work—it helps when an umbrella is seldom required. Before returning to England we did our version of the Grand Tour, visiting some of the National Parks of the South West and then going up the entire West Coast, from San Diego to Vancouver, spending time in Los Angeles and San Francisco. Then we travelled through the Rocky Mountains, across Canada to Toronto, and then back into the USA to spend time in Washington and New York before flying back to England. We had been able to visit distant relations and make new friends in what was to be the first of several visits to North America to enjoy wonderful scenery and natural history.

---

40. Ogden, *Is There Only One True Religion ?* 104.

41. For the distinction between "emancipation" and "redemption" in the integral work of God's liberation see Ogden, *Faith and Freedom.*

PASTORAL MINISTRY: KETTERING (1976–81), STOCKTON-ON-TEES (1981–88), AND MONKSEATON (2009–14).

I enjoyed the unique mix of pastoral ministry: the conduct of worship, preaching, pastoral care, and carrying out a representative role in the community. My model of ministry has been greatly influenced by the principle laid out in Ephesians that those set apart for designated ministries within the church are called "to equip the saints for the work of ministry" (Eph. 4:12), so I have put a great deal of effort into lay education within the congregations I have served. That has taken the form of supporting and encouraging those who were teaching the young, or helping adults in their study of the Bible, as well as working with Church members on their faith development. I suspect that I often gained as much—if not even more—benefit when preparing for such educational settings as those who participated in them. Over the course of my ministry I covered in study groups all the major biblical books, avoiding repetition as much as possible. Along with the weekly writing of sermons this ensured that the Bible played a significant part in my ministry.

Edgar Jones saw more academic potential in me than I ever did in myself. It was through his encouragement that I convinced the URC authorities to construct my post-ordination training in a way which enabled me to engage in doctoral studies through the University of Manchester. My university fees were paid by the Coward Trust, which I have subsequently learned may mean that I benefited from profits accrued from the slave trade in two ways. John Handby Thompson has concluded that William Coward, whose wealth created the Coward Trust, was involved in this wicked practice, "but not as much as we might have surmised. There is a clear reference, however, to one Guinea, Jamaica, home trip in 1704 which clearly indicts him."[42] Then, secondly, Sir John Cass (1661–1718), an English merchant, Tory Member of Parliament, and benefactor of the college I attended in London was a prominent figure in the development of the slave trade. I hope that I may be proof that good sometimes emerges from wickedness. Progress on my PhD was slow, but I kept going though regular prompts from my supervisor and encouragement from John Slow, the Moderator of the URC East Midlands Synod in which I was serving. It was finally completed in 1984, seven years after I had embarked upon the project and well into my ministry at Stockton-on-Tees. The thesis was entitled "The Theology of Schubert M. Ogden: A Dialogue with His Critics." Maurice Wiles, the then

42. Thompson, "A History of the Coward Trust," 3.

Regius Professor of Divinity at the University of Oxford, was the External Examiner. One section of the thesis, dealing with Ogden's deployment of process philosophy in his doctrine of God, was subsequently published.[43]

The two major churches I served in my first two pastorates were as different as chalk from cheese. Toller, Kettering is set at the heart of a market town, tracing its Congregational history back to the Great Ejectment of 1662. The building was re-configured during my ministry to make it more useable for a lively congregation and the wider community. The congregation possessed commendable energy and initiative, with a willingness to attempt different approaches to worship. It is a close-knit, committed fellowship. St Andrew and St George, Stockton-on-Tees, on the other hand, belongs to the Presbyterian tradition. It was created by the amalgamation of the St Andrew and St George churches in 1934, at the suggestion of Presbytery when St George's was without a minister. The new church flourished, drawing into membership Scots who moved to Teesside to take up managerial and research positions at various expanding industrial companies, especially ICI. It thereby bucked post-war trends of numerical decline. The congregation was drawn from all over Teesside, many families moving from the communities in which they lived and were socially involved to attend Sunday worship in Stockton. But when de-industrialization became endemic to Teesside the congregation entered rapid decline: members left the area as a result of changing jobs; Scots ceased to come to work in an area which by the mid 1980s had a huge unemployment problem; and the acids of secularization had begun to eat away at the traditional pattern of Sunday life, with Sunday morning sports and shopping usurping any residual sense of obligation to attend church.

Looking back I feel that my move from Kettering to Stockton-on-Tees involved leaving a congregation eager to embrace the future for one that was very much hanging on to the past. Mission involves creating a cogent, credible, and communicable narrative which draws people into the Christian community: the old ways will not necessarily engage people of a different age. In common with many churches the members of St Andrew and St George had largely lost a *theological* sense of what it means to be a faithful church. This unfortunate trend is explored in Chapter 5. My time in Stockton was dominated by over-seeing a union of St Andrew and St George with two other Stockton-based URC congregations under the unimaginative name of Stockton URC. It was a painful process that sapped my energy and almost broke my spirit, but at one difficult stage I found some light relief in exploring the claim that A. E. Garvie, a notable Congregationalist theologian, stands among "panentheists of genius or

43. See Peel, "Is Schubert M. Ogden's "God" Christian?"

systematic ability" and "suggests that Christianity as such had no necessary ties with classical theism and no essential antagonism with panentheism."[44] Garvie was Principal of New College (1907–24), Hackney College (1922–24) and Hackney and New (1924–33).[45] Was it the case that via process theology my theology was running along similar lines to that of Garvie? It was, as I have shown in a published article.[46]

When I returned from twenty years working in theological education for my third spell of pastoral ministry in 2009 I found myself at St Andrew's, Monkseaton in another church belonging to the Presbyterian tradition. I am not the kind of person who rests content in repeating experiences. I enjoy rather more the stimulation provided by having to address new challenges and learn from fresh experiences. Just before I arrived, St Andrew's had completed an excellent building conversion, so I would not have to face a Kettering-type redevelopment project; and the closure of Trinity URC in Whitley Bay had boosted the size of the Monkseaton congregation, thereby ruling out the likelihood that I would need to be involved in uniting declining congregations as I had in Stockton. My focus was thus less managerial. I worked hard at conducting lively worship and constructing thoughtful sermons, alongside devoting a lot of time to pastoral work and enabling Bible study. Throughout my time at Monkseaton there was, however, an elephant in the room. The commendably large congregation tended to obscure the church's age profile. No congregation can survive indefinitely if the energy and enthusiasm of a largely early-retired leadership is not replaced by younger members. I found myself conducting far too many funeral services of once active members, but I did not see the arrival of many new members to replace them.

During my five years at Monkseaton I managed to continue a significant amount of reading and research. First, I completed my reading of Wolfhart Pannenberg's *Systematic Theology*, a project that had been constantly interrupted over several years. It provided an interesting Lutheran counterpoint to my more Reformed theological background. Its window on Luther's theology is very helpful. Secondly, over the years I had become very uneasy about some of the soteriological claims present in some Christian hymns, but what can we put in their place? I also had noted that there are many different ways of conceiving the work of Christ in the Christian tradition, including its early beginnings in the New Testament era. But which of the many atonement metaphors would I favour in *my* soteriology? When

44. Hartshorne and Reese, *Philosophers*, 153, 270.

45. For Garvie see Binfield and Taylor, *Who They Were*.

46. See Peel, "Alfred Ernest Garvie."

reviewing one of Alan Sell's books,[47] I was redirected back to Forsyth,[48] and then revisited Gunton[49] in search of an answer. It was not quick in appearing, although just as God's creative work need not be restricted to a particular moment in time I concluded that God's redeeming work also ought not to be regarded as constituted by the Christ event; it is rather re-presented by it in a decisive way. God's creative and redeeming activity is best seen as part of the endless outpouring of God's love. Thirdly, when the URC started to undertake a review of its system of Synod Moderators, I felt urged to contribute to it. I responded to two issues. First, given the unpopularity of the system in some quarters, I sensed a need to present an *apologia* for it *in principle*; while, in the light of the way I had seen the Moderatorial role develop *in practice*, I wanted secondly to challenge the way the Moderators were coming to resemble quasi-denominational chief executive officers. The result was *The Story of the Moderators*, a book which investigates the concept of translocal ministry within a Reformed ecclesiology. Fourthly, during 2012 I was invited to speak to several groups on the occasion of the 350th anniversary of the Great Ejectment. A paper given to the Cumbria Theological Society is representative of the thinking that my reflection on the events of 1662 generated. It is reproduced as Chapter 7.

THEOLOGICAL EDUCATION (1988–2009)

Our children, Andrew (b1977) and Heidi (b1980) were born in Kettering, received most of their early education in Stockton, but completed their secondary education in Manchester before going on to their university studies. Although it was sad to leave behind valued colleagues and friends on Teesside Manchester offered us wider horizons and fresh opportunities. I was appointed Tutor for Community-based Training at Northern College (United Reformed and Congregational), my Alma Mater when preparing for ordination. My role was to organize placement work and students' reflection upon it, coupled with developing a new course which fully integrated academic and placement learning, similar to that already run by the Northern Baptist College in the ecumenical Northern Federation for Training in Ministry of which we were a part. I valued the support and advice of a wide range of colleagues drawn from all denominations involved in the Federation. John Parry and John Sutcliffe were constant sources of support and encouragement. Various opportunities came my way. I was

47. See my review of *Theological Education of the Ministry*.
48. See Forsyth, *Work of Christ; Cruciality*; and *Justification*.
49. See Gunton, *Actuality of Atonement*.

invited to teach courses in the Department of Religions and Theology at the University of Manchester. My work became as exciting as it was demanding.

Although much of my reading in Manchester was of a utilitarian nature, the kind that is inevitably involved when teaching new courses, it helped plug some more gaps in my theological knowledge. I gained, for example, my first *primary* acquaintance with the work of Thomas Aquinas: I suspect that I am among many to have been influenced by process philosophy before fully getting to grips with the metaphysics it purportedly replaces. Several colleagues were interested in the theology of Jürgen Moltmann through the influence of Richard Bauckham, a leading interpreter of Moltmann who was then teaching at the University of Manchester.[50] I joined them reading the Moltmann *corpus* as it grew volume by volume. If Schleiermacher had already convinced me that Reformed theology need not be construed on hard Calvinist lines, Moltmann confirmed that there are indeed alternative, more liberal theological options available in the Reformed world. I have never been convinced about the credibility of the eschatological underpinning of Moltmann's theology but I warm to a lot of what he says about God's suffering in the world and his eschewal of anthropocentric portraits of God's creative activity. Alan Sell once opined that "It is as unsatisfactory to serve Christ's babes the dregs of the latest theological fashion as it is to force-feed them on the hard rusks of five-point Calvinism."[51] With Moltmann we had the height not the dregs of fashion.

I was encouraged to apply for the position of Principal at Northern College in succession to Jack McKelvey, largely on the back of a report about theological education which the College Governors had commissioned me to write following a research visit to the USA. I was flattered that people saw in me a role I had never coveted. My subsequent appointment was concurrent with further staff changes. The change-around allowed me to handover my placement supervisory work to a qualified practical theologian in order to take up the teaching of theology. I spent a lot of time during the Manchester years on addressing two important issues. The first concerned the nature of ministry required by the churches at the turn of the century. My reflections on this question led to the publication of *Ministry for Mission* and another published article.[52] Secondly, I was inevitably engaged with preparing students for *today's* Christian ministry. We had to take into account two new requirements: one relating to the training needs of the mature students who were then making up most of the ordinands; and the other financial due to the fall in fee-income

---

50. See Bauckham, *Theology of Jürgen Moltmann*.

51. Sell, *Testimony*, 11.

52. See "A Learned Ministry."

caused by lower student numbers. We had to answer questions such as: "What courses are appropriate for these new circumstances?" and "What can we afford?" It was clearly the case that only a minority of students were in a position of being able to receive the length and depth of ministerial education that were once normative. My conclusions about what is required in contemporary theological education are found in Chapter 8.

I enjoyed teaching at both the University and in the Federation, which later morphed into The Partnership for Theological Education, Manchester. My reading was influenced by the invitations I received to speak on particular subjects. I returned to P.T. Forsyth for example when I was asked to present a paper at a conference to commemorate the sesquicentenary of Forsyth's birth. It is reproduced in its published form in Chapter 3. Secondly, I convened a seminar studying the theology of Lesslie Newbigin, who on his return from distinguished service with the Church of South India made a significant theological impact on the British church scene during the 1980s when he championed "The Gospel and Our Culture" program.[53] My research for the seminar covered all Newbigin's books. I was astonished to discover that *Honest Religion for Secular Man*, which I appreciated reading when an undergraduate, is atypical: what preceded it was solidly Barthian and what followed advances a hard-nosed Christian exclusivism and displays a level of negativity towards the Enlightenment that I find unacceptable. In 1966 he wanted "to ask what must be the religion of a Christian who accepts the process of secularization and lives fully in the kind of world into which God has led us?"[54] Twenty years later he was finding little of positive worth in "the process of secularization," and claiming that today's world is more the work of the wicked witch called "Enlightenment" than of God. In a denomination which treated Newbigin like a saint I tried to point out what I saw as his theological shortcomings. In so doing I lost and gained friends in equal measure. I was invited to contribute to a *Festschrift* for Alan Sell, so I wrote an essay on Newbigin for it. It is reproduced here as Chapter 4. Then, thirdly, I was asked to write a book to serve URC theology in the way David Cornick's *Under God's Good Hand* had done so well for its history. Given the "ecumenical" nature of that theology my target was rather more mobile than the one well hit by Cornick. My strategy was to take Calvin and Schleiermacher as founders of different wings of Reformed theology. I then used their thought and that of others to illustrate the different ways members of each wing understand the major Christian doctrines. *Reforming Theology,*

---

53. See for example, Newbigin, *Other Side; Foolishness; Gospel;* and *Truth.*

54. Newbigin, *Honest Religion,* 10.

the resulting book, suffered from not having seen the hand of a copy editor, but it clearly reveals my own commitment to a liberal revisionist theology.

I look back on my time at Northern College with affection and satisfaction. The College produced some excellent ministers during this period. At Manchester I found a niche in teaching for which two pastorates had been the perfect preparation. It resulted through peer recommendation in my becoming a Fellow of the Higher Educational Academy. After ten years as Principal however the stresses and strains created by financial crises in the Partnership, difficult ecumenical relations, and falling student numbers caused by church decline almost obliterated the motivation which had driven me to leave pastoral charge—I was happier teaching theology than running institutions. I found myself led back to the North East.

At one time College Principals either retired or died in office; they did not have to think about what to do next in their ministries. Given the speed of institutional change however the modern tendency is for them to serve shorter periods than was once the case. I had been appointed Principal relatively young; hence the issue was acute, since I had eleven years to serve before retirement. I was convinced about the need for sound theology to be formed by, and an influential factor in, the church's mission. That suggested I return to more grass-roots work rather than seek further full-time involvement in a higher education setting. Secondly, moreover, I had acquired extensive theological gifts and acumen which if set to one side and not used in the church's service would suggest irresponsibility on my part. Taking the two factors into account led me to believe that I was now being called to a role nearer congregational life but with an explicit theological focus. Regrettably the URC possesses nothing akin to the Anglican "canon theologian." What transpired was that I found myself teaching half time for the North East Oecumenical Course (which had emerged from the former North East Ordination Course in an enlightened moment of ecumenical commitment) and working half time for the Northern Synod as its Development Officer.

We were pleased to return to the North East, living in the cathedral city of Durham with its distinguished University, and my having a role that theoretically would provide "the best of both worlds": grass-roots engagement and theological teaching, but things did not work out as planned. The next six years were very unsettling. First, I was off work for six months in 2004–5 being treated for bowel cancer. It took me an entire year to get back to full health. Secondly, I was elected to serve the URC as its Moderator of General Assembly 2005–6. The ensuing interruptions meant that I never got settled into either of my new roles. Then, thirdly, the URC decided in 2006 no longer to place ordinands on ecumenical courses, thereby somewhat compromising my position at NEOC. When it subsequently became clear that the Church of England also had no future use for NEOC, I resigned from NEOC to become the full-time Education and Training Officer for Northern Synod. It wasn't long though before a Synod Review ended my post along with others in a cost-cutting exercise. By August 2009 I had discovered the utter folly of expecting to have "the best of both worlds." My disappointment ought not to hide some very positive features of this vexed period. First, I was able to put solid work into key training areas in the churches: eldership, lay-preaching, presidency at the sacraments, ministers' in-service education, and general theological education. Secondly, I enjoyed the attractive NEOC culture, with its strong ecumenical commitments and structured liturgical discipline; I felt more at home in its worship than I often have done in URC congregations; and the quality of many of the theological discussions at NEOC was very high. Thirdly, I was able to gain further world church experience. In my Kettering days I had attended a European Area Council of WARC in Amsterdam. Almost thirty years later I was invited to join WARC's 50th Anniversary Celebrations in Singapore (2007). Shortly after that I served as a Theological Consultant to WARC's theological student program. This took me to Jerusalem, with all its religious history and divisions: it was another significant learning experience. Then, fourthly, my year as Moderator of the Assembly was one of the highlights of my ministerial life. A permanent reminder of the year is found in my *Encountering Church*, a collection of the sermons and addresses I delivered while in office.

ACTIVE RETIREMENT (2014 ONWARDS)

As I prepared for retirement two things were clear. First, I would not be faced with nothing to do. In an important sense retirement simply signaled my passage to *non-stipendiary* ministry. It also meant that I could bring my hinterland more into the foreground of my life: there would be more space for bird-watching, cricket, gardening, and music; perhaps even opportunities for overseas travel. Secondly, I wanted to retire from doing things which had often got in the way of my making a theological contribution to the church. I did not want to be burdened by bureaucracy—I have never been comfortable in a committee culture; nor did I want said of me what I have often heard said of aged preachers: "Oh! I do wish he'd given over when on top of his game!" And I certainly did not want to get in the way of a new generation. It followed that I had no sense of calling to a ministry of itinerant preaching; rather *active* retirement I believed should focus on theology.

During my ministry at Monkseaton I had become interested in the theology of Alan Sell, a URC colleague of an earlier generation, through reviewing several of his books.[55] The idea emerged to use some of the early months of retirement to engage with Alan's theology through writing a couple of articles. Shortly after Alan died in 2016 a modest writing project had become writing a full-length book. I enjoyed working through Sell's extensive literary output and the written responses to it. After the labour of two winters, *Crucicentric, Congregational, and Catholic* was duly published. The book engages with Sell's theology on the major doctrinal issues with the result that the book not only introduces Alan's theology to a wider public, but it also provides a window through which my own theological position can be glimpsed.

About the time the Sell project was coming to a close I received an invitation to join a group of writers drawn together by Clyde Binfield and Robert Pope to write a history of New College, London, where I had spent three happy years as a hostelman. Church history is not my field, but I had moonlighted into the discipline with *The Story of the Moderators*. My experience in theological education though perhaps qualified me to fulfill my designated brief: to trace New College's influence in the life of the churches it had served. Carrying out the necessary research at the Dr Williams's Library was very stimulating, another timely reminder though of how little of the history of Congregationalism I had at my finger-tips. New College's closure in 1977 was all of a piece with the general decline that has beset the mainline churches since the late 1880s. I found it interesting to read some of the extensive literature concerning the reasons for that decline, but the social historians and sociologists have not come to a common mind about it.[56] I suspect that several elements contribute to an adequate explanation, one of them being the failure of the churches to so narrate the Christian story that it grips people's attention, moves them at a deeply personal level, and motivates them towards God-centred and selfless lifestyles. At the heart of the matter is a theological failure to counter the acids of modernity. A theologian would say that though wouldn't he? The New College project is still on-going, having been stalled by, first, the temporary closure of the Dr Williams's Library, where the archives are lodged, and, secondly by the COVID-19 pandemic. Thankfully, other theological projects lay in the wings to occupy my mind, not least putting together this book.

55. See my reviews of *Nonconformist Theology; Theological Education of the Ministry;* and *Confessing the Faith.*

56. See the contributions to the debate by Callum G. Brown, Steve Bruce, Grace Davie, S.J.D. Green, Hugh McLeod, and David M. Thompson.

2

Can You Not Read "The Signs of the Times"?

A COMMON OBSERVATION MADE about theological colleges is that they very easily become divorced from reality.[1] It is said that they pursue agendas which are parasitic upon their own comfortable perceptions of what they are about, rather than ones rooted in the requirements of the churches. Some go on to claim that colleges maintain their hallowed traditions rather than model their *raison d'être* upon the needs of those placed in their charge for training "for the work of ministry" (Eph. 4: 12). It would seem therefore that the aims and objectives that colleges set and follow are not necessarily those that everyone in the churches believes they should be pursuing.

But equally churches also can become removed from reality. They often run with agendas that feed upon their comfortable perception of what it is to be a Christian fellowship. They also tend to maintain hallowed traditions and perennial practices rather than always model their existence upon the God-given requirements laid upon them to be in each time and place a sign, foretaste, and embodiment of God's rule over that time and place. So the agendas churches set are not necessarily the same as the agenda God has for them. Both theological colleges and churches therefore can abuse their vocation, which, among other things, includes the responsibility of equipping and enabling people to be Christians in contemporary society. Or, to put it

1. This essay develops a sermon delivered during the weekly Eucharist at Luther King House, Manchester on 13 July 1989.

in the broadest theological terms, both colleges and churches can become diverted from the task of ensuring that the ministry of the God revealed in Jesus is carried on in society as a function of the whole people of God.

Being a Christian today, in certain respects, will be no different to being a Christian in any age. In other respects it will be quite different. From biblical times to the present what Christians have said and done has been a response to the questions and needs of their age. We may believe that there is a common denominator running through the myriad witnesses down the centuries, but we would be misled if we ignored the plurality that in many ways reflects the way in which Christians have found themselves molding what they have said and done according to the shape of the context in which they found themselves. Being a Christian has always been a radical contextual undertaking, thus accounting for the way in which what being a Christian has meant and entailed has altered down the ages. There has been development and change in Christian belief and practice as Christians have responded to the unique problems and possibilities of each new era.

God calls Christians to relevant and realistic patterns of obedience and discipleship in each age. The only way we have of discovering what those patterns are is to stick to the task of finding out just what God is asking of us in our time. And, if we take the Bible seriously, what this is will not necessarily be the same as in the previous age. The God of the cosmic adventure is always on the move: "I am about to do a new thing; now it springs forth, do you not perceive it?" (Isa. 43: 19). Isaiah's witness is a model of the kind of divine activity displayed by the Bible from the story of the Exodus to the vision of the Eschaton. It would seem therefore that being a Christian in the contemporary world to a great extent turns on our obedience and discipleship being a faithful response to that which "even now . . . comes to light."

I take it that this is what the following story is all about:

> [Jesus] answered them, "When it is evening, you say, "It will be
> fair weather; for the sky is red." And in the morning, "It will be
> stormy today, for the sky is red and threatening." You know how
> to interpret the appearance of the sky, but you cannot interpret
> the signs of the times." (Matt 16: 2–3)

Some textual critics have now removed this story from the text of Matthew's Gospel and relegated it to a footnote. But it has some sort of parallel in Luke's Gospel, and in any case the footnotes of books are often as illuminating as the text![2] The obedience and discipleship of the Pharisees and Sadducees seem

---

2. See Luke 12: 54–56.

to have rested upon their making a faithful response to their interpretation of "the signs of the times." If they could be confident about the vagaries of the weather, surely they ought to have been able to discover what God was about from the historical happenings of their day in general and from the Christ-event in particular?

CONTEMPORARY CHALLENGES TO READING "THE SIGNS OF THE TIMES"

It all sounds so blissfully easy, but it isn't! In fact, it is so problematical that, not for the first time in reading the Gospels, one retrospectively feels a bit sorry for the Pharisees and Sadducees. Consider the implications of following a strategy of reading the signs of the times as a way of our discovering what is involved in being a contemporary Christian.

First, this strategy takes it for granted that there is a God, and that the Deity is involved in history as an objective reality with an ongoing purpose for the world discernible from contemporary events. Given the passage of intellectual thought over, say, the last two hundred years however such affirmations cannot be taken for granted. They have not only to be affirmed; they now have to be argued for in a public manner. The atheistic critique of reality may seem a minor irritation which can be dismissed with consummate ease inside a community well-stocked with ministers in the making; in reality however it has penetrated the intellectual mood of Western Europe more than most of us care to contemplate. Indeed, one of the most obvious signs of our times is the passing of people from practicing Christian belief to, if not usually atheism, certainly agnosticism, and often apathy concerning Christian claims and commitments. By my late teens, I had concluded that for the sake of intellectual integrity I had to make a conscious effort to reconcile the thought-world I had discovered through my scientific studies with the thought-world which underpins the God-talk, that is to say theology, of my Christian heritage. Some of my contemporaries seem to think that all such theological problems can be waved away by triumphalistic and emotional assertions. I see no reason however to support the anti-intellectual trend in the contemporary Church which ignores the modern intellectual mood of our society. I can understand why the Dean of Emmanuel College, Cambridge, urges people to take their leave of God and then invites them to view "God" as a word which refers to "a unifying symbol and eloquently personifies and represents to us everything that spirituality requires of us," rather than as a word which designates an objective reality, who in some sense stands over, above, and beyond the world.[3] I do not however have to accept Don Cupitt's view that God is "a humanly-needed way of speaking generated by the impact of the religious demand and ideal upon us" to recognize that "God" is a problematical concept in our society.[4] We only have to draw obvious conclusions from this century's Church statistics: there are many people today, not only Cambridge dons with a onetime allegiance to the Church of England, who do not accept the notion that the workings of God can be read off from the signs of the times. They join Laplace in saying: "I have no need of that hypothesis."

Even if we assume that the challenge of atheistic, or non-theistic, critiques of reality can be beaten off, we must ask secondly whether we can ever be in a position to read the signs of the times correctly. A few years ago, I found myself discussing a paper with two different groups of Christians in the same week. The unpublished paper concerned the Church's response to poverty. It made claims such as "the poor are punished in order to prevent others becoming poor" and that they are deliberately treated as "less eligible" in society. The paper concluded that the "structures and institutions of our society . . . are rigidly organized to favour the un-poor by denying access to the poor" and maintain a "bias towards the rich and more able members of the community." The first group with whom I discussed the paper lived on a large post-war housing estate which was experiencing acute unemployment, intolerable housing conditions, and great hardship. They immediately saw that the picture of society painted by the paper was true to their experience. The second group was a dedicated Church and Society Committee in a fairly well-heeled church. They reacted to the paper in a quite hostile manner, countering the conclusions and taking issue with the social and political analysis which supported them. Where the truth lay need not deter us. The point is simply this: when it comes to discerning the signs of the times, where one stands influences what one sees and whom one talks to often determines what one hears. There is not a neutral vantage point because we all view events from a perspective. One of the great theological prophets of the twentieth century reminds us that "There is no vantage point, individual or collective, in human history from which we could judge its movements with complete impartiality . . . so there are only vantage points of relative impartiality from which we view the present scene."[5] Reinhold Niebuhr's dose of realism and common sense needs prescribing to all cocksure Christians who, cavalierly looking out on the age in which they live, all too hastily come to absolutist convictions regarding

3. Cupitt, *Taking Leave of God*, 9.
4. Cupitt, *Taking Leave of God*, 133.
5. Niebuhr, *Discerning*, 15.

the ways of God. We so easily make God into a self-designated ally in our all too human enterprises and crusades. All our historical judgments reveal, as Niebuhr puts it, "a bewildering compound of unconscious ignorance and conscious rationalization of selfish interests."[6]

Given the problems of reading the signs of the times, people who think they possess complete certainty concerning the nature and task of being a contemporary Christian should be suspected of over-simplifying things. They also might be shown with hindsight to have been making meanings out of muddles in support of personal conjectures, vested interests, and self-esteem. But it is one thing to recognize the problems and something else to give up the challenge of reading the signs of the times simply because there are problems.

THE SIGNS OF OUR TIMES

We can press on with the task of reading the signs of the times knowing that tentative conclusions often are more holy than dogmatic assertions rigidly propounded as being the whole truth and nothing but the truth. All knowledge contains an interpretive element within it. We consequently only have "relatively adequate" judgments and conclusions available to us.[7] To some, this might seem nothing more than an attempt to make a virtue out of necessity. There is, though, a basic theological point at stake here: God is God and we are human. In the commendable interest of maintaining a working understanding of God's transcendence over us, ought we not to be rather more humble, and certainly more careful, about what we say about God in general and what God is up to in the world in particular? The final incomprehensibility of the divine Mystery would seem to demand this. Any judgments we make concerning the signs of the times will further need testing out with our sisters and brothers in the community of faith and beyond. We should expect the accurate ones to reflect what Christians have come to expect concerning God's work in the world, as the paradigm for that work has been revealed to us in the definitive story of God's work found in the Bible. Of course, God is always doing a new thing. Different divine activity at different times and places will however bear the same eternal qualities which mark divine activity always and everywhere: love rather than apathy, self-sacrifice rather than self-grandiosity, life-enhancement rather than life-denial, people being set free from themselves and for others rather than being constrained by themselves or by others. These are some of the marks of

---

6. Niebuhr, *Discerning*, 17.

7. For the term "relative adequacy" see Tracy, *Plurality*, 22–23.

God's kingdom. The task of reading the signs of the times consequently is far from being an exercise which is necessarily doomed to failure at the outset.

What then are the signs of the times which must instruct our contemporary obedience and discipleship? I mentioned earlier that we are living in a society whose members progressively this century have voted with their feet concerning institutional Christianity. Returning to Manchester after fourteen years I have noticed the demise which has afflicted many of the churches around here in that short time. I hear others in other denominations saying similar things. Nevertheless I do not feel that there is sufficient evidence to support Lesslie Newbigin's apocalyptic judgment that we are an out-and-out pagan society.[8] Recent events in Liverpool, as a city shared its grief in the wake of the Hillsborough football disaster, confirmed my pastoral experience. The Church's task is one of getting alongside people who have no time for the Church as they encounter its institutional form but who operate with a highly sophisticated residue of folk religion.[9] Nor have people universally given up on the spiritual dimensions of life. Many still claim to believe in God and most think Jesus is a key figure in world history, but they do not feel any need to make explicit commitments to organized Christian communities from which they feel alien.

A second sign of our times concerns the unwillingness, or failure, of many in the churches to see their understanding of, and participation in, society as just as much under God's gracious judgment as their individual thoughts and actions. Another way of putting this is to say that individualism is rife in our churches. During my last ministry, I repeatedly found myself caught in two worlds: the relatively comfortable world of those unaffected by Cleveland's recent de-industrialization with all its unemployment and misery, and the harsh world of those at the sharp end, the unemployed and poor, or to demythologize poverty and reinterpret it in Mrs. Thatcher's philosophy, the unequal! I did not think that I was pandering to some weak kind of Social Gospel when I could not help but see what was happening through the eyes of Israel's eighth century prophets: Amos with his plumb-line and his vision of the basket of fruit powerfully interpreted the scene theologically.[10] Nor could I ignore the preacher of what a friend calls the shortest sermon on record. The text was the opening sentences of Isaiah 61: "The Spirit of the Lord God is upon me because the Lord has anointed me to bring good news to the poor, to bind up the broken hearted." Jesus'

---

8. See Newbigin, *Other Side* and *Foolishness*.

9. On the role of folk religion in British society see Habgood, *Church and Nation*, 78–92.

10. Amos 7: 7–9 and 8: 1–3.

sermon consisted of one sentence: "Today, in your very hearing this text has come true" (Luke 4: 21). While not forgetting some notable exceptions, rank and file church members were not part of the pressure and activist groups that sprang up to do something about the effects of Cleveland's social and economic crisis. There was little evidence that the average churchgoer saw the church's role and duty to engage with such public issues or to stand with the victims in the name of the God of love and justice. The churches were very turned in on themselves, wearied by the task of simply keeping things going, and often giving the impression of protecting at all costs their safe environment of like minds in a hostile world. Amos' plumbline might come in handy to keep the church in good repair, but as a measure by which to judge justice in our society . . . ? And his basket of fruit would make an excellent raffle prize, but as a warning concerning what happens to communities which function upon the maxim that the only way to the promised secular Utopia is to make the rich richer and the poor poorer? Many Christian people seem to be as interested in such yardsticks for understanding society as they were in Amos' day, which as you know was not much.

ADDRESSING OUR TIMES

If my reading of the signs of the times is "relatively adequate," it would seem that first the vast majority of people in Britain are finding the church irrelevant and sometimes hypocritical, and secondly that many in the institutional churches do not have as a priority on their agenda the notion that being a Christian involves political commitments concerning our corporate lives. We are called, however, to minister to *these* churches in *this* kind of world. That might appear to be a bleak prospect. So it will be if we adopt either of the usual options paraded before us.

We can throw in the towel! Accepting the atheistic, or non-theistic, critiques of reality we can agree that the only meaning there is in life is that which we can rustle up by our mental ingenuity. We can give up on God and join the masses of the un-churched. Alternatively, we can ignore the signs of the times with a Canute-like tenacity, retreat ever further into yet more comfortable holy huddles, and shut out the world's hard realities. We can refuse to tackle any of the penetrating questions which modern thinking poses to our prevailing orthodoxy and orthopraxis by trying to shout ever more loudly our fundamental certainties, and by remaining faithful to our fixed practices. After all, we can say, the world is a totally sinful place: it is only going the way of all flesh, so why bother with it? Few, save some intellectuals among us, take the first alternative, but many Christians increasingly seem to be taking the second. Both responses to the signs of the times are defeatist in the extreme and highly unbiblical. We belong to a Faith delivered to us by faithful patriarchs and persecuted prophets, which has been made clear in Jesus and has as its central symbol an empty cross in the world's solid earth.

I believe that there is another way of responding to the signs of our time, a time which Adrian Hastings has described as "an age of apocalyptic, of doom watch, in which the tragedies of an anguished world have become just too many to cope with, yet in which there is the strongest feeling that there may be worse to come."[11] It starts with a clear affirmation that God exists as an objective reality. God is neither a figment of our fertile imaginations, nor a cipher by which we express our highest religious ideals and aspirations. Such widely different philosophers as Richard Swinburne[12] and Charles Hartshorne[13] agree that such a belief is rationally sustainable. Cupitt has certainly not had the last word.[14] It still can be argued that a theistic understanding of reality best fits the facts. The response continues with the observation that although people may have given up on God, God has not given up on people. The basis for this lies in the central Christian conviction that God comes to where people are in Jesus. In the Easter event, for example, we discover that even total dereliction and defeat carry within them God's promise of new possibilities. In spite of all the evidence to the contrary we can remain positive and hopeful. The whole of reality falls within God's grace and lies under God's judgment. When this perspective is worked out in the personal and corporate dimensions of everyday life's concrete conditions and events those who bear it can get alongside others to interpret their stories from the standpoint of Christ and so reveal both God's "Yes" and "No" to their lives. Undergirding this perspective is the assurance that sin and evil will not have the last word. There is a God who is forgiveness itself and those who trust their lives in God's hands will discover that God enables them to be set free from the guilt which otherwise stunts growth and creativity. This involves a serious exploration of what it means to say in our culture that God the Creator, Redeemer, and Sustainer exists as a loving power, presence, and purpose running through all things. What we know about God from the biblical witness then becomes the basis for prophetic protest against individuals and groups who bolster up the ninety-nine at

11. Hastings, *History*, 660.

12. See Swinburne, *Coherence of Theism*.

13. For Hartshorne see Bibliography.

14. See the criticism of Cupitt's position in Ward, *Holding Fast to God*.

the expense of the one, or favor the powerful and rich against the weak and poor. As this protest is fleshed out in concrete commitment the costly nature of this perspective becomes clear. The overall point is that there is an alternative response to the signs of our times which does not capitulate into any of the usual options. It is rooted in a living God who, as discovered in Jesus, is more than equal to all the negativity in our world.

In many ways the contemporary Church finds itself on the margins of twentieth-century life. Whether it has retreated to such a position voluntarily or been forced there by secular pressures can be a matter of conjecture. The important fact is that the Church now finds itself in a kind of exile. But, like Israel long ago, we can learn the lessons exile can teach us and once again become obedient to God and faithful in God's divine service. We are neither called to be people who have given up God in favor of the world, nor people who have given up the world in favor of God. Rather, we are called to be people who find God in the world through Christ and in the Spirit. Then, in response to the gracious God who meets us in the world, we are to offer the world back to God in thanksgiving through our labors at peace, love, and justice.

3

P.T. Forsyth on Ministry:
A Model for our Time?[1]

I SAT UNDER P.T. Forsyth for the best part of three academic years, his eyes peering down at me and his stern look suggesting disapproval of my undergraduate activities. The location was 527 Finchley Road, London, where I was an undergraduate reading chemistry, but, more to the point, where Forsyth arguably had been at the zenith of his ministry. Portraits often tell us as much about the painter as the subject, but the one which hung on the wall above the table where I dined during 1968–71 left me with the impression of Forsyth as a firm no-nonsense father-figure who had a clear idea about what constituted a proper undergraduate life. You learn a lot about my days in the hostel at New College by hearing me confess that the great principal-preacher of an earlier era did not get the dubious pleasure of having me as his number one fan. It came as no surprise much later to discover that at the heart of Forsyth's theology lay an unwavering awareness of the yawning chasm between the holiness of God and the sinfulness of human beings, and his firm conviction that at the center of human existence there lies a basic issue which can only be settled by "the grace of God in historic, moral, mystic action . . . upon racial guilt" in the Cross of Jesus Christ.[2] Somehow the painting of an unsmiling, somber, and threatening Forsyth matched the preacher who thundered that it will not do to believe

1. Originally published in Sell, *Theology for a New Millennium*, 171–208.
2. Forsyth, *Lectures*, 122.

39

that "All you need is love"[3] to address the waywardness of humanity—unless of course the love in question is the holy love of God revealed at Calvary.

I owe a lot to this period of my life. While in London I met my wife; midway through my chemistry studies I discerned a call to Christian ministry; and through the influence of Charles Duthie, the then Principal of New College, I started to read theology—when, of course, I should really have been honing up my knowledge on topics like thermodynamics, reaction kinetics and eutectics! The writings of Pierre Teilhard de Chardin started developing connections between my background in science and my Christian faith, while the sermons and essays of Paul Tillich gave me a basic approach to the theological task from which I have hardly ever wavered. But no one at New College suggested that I read Forsyth. This was an era when Forsyth's distinctive version of "the tradition of great theology,"[4] with Christ at the center, was the kind of orthodoxy which *avant-garde* liberal theology was hell-bent on overcoming.

During my preparation for ministry at Northern College, Manchester, the work of Forsyth was not mentioned in a single theological course I attended at the University. Tony Burnham, to his credit, in College courses extolled the virtues of Forsyth as a model for a young preacher to revere, but it seems odd that I was not required to read *Positive Preaching and the Modern Mind,* a reward that I was directed to by an American Methodist! No one in the student body at College was reading Forsyth but on reflection there was not much theology of any kind being read. Primary attention was being paid to changing society, or revamping crumbling Victorian church buildings, or, recently imported from the USA, non-directive counseling as a model for pastoral care. Working hard at developing a faith to live by and preach in ministry did not appear to be the all-consuming activity it perhaps should have been. A typical example of the way in which Forsyth's words come back to haunt us is found in this salutary observation:

> It has been the vice of our college system in past years that the men it sent out were often but autodidacts after all. They had to pick up or make their own theology. What they have done in the circumstances is wonderful. But what have the Churches not lost? And what a hunger exists for theology among preachers. They feel its need.[5]

---

3. The title of a Beatles' song which was popular with people of that era .

4. Cunliffe-Jones, "P.T. Forsyth," 354

5. Forsyth, *Revelation,* 109

During my preparation for ministry, therefore, it appeared that, while Forsyth may have been "A Nineteenth-Century Prophet,"[6] or in 1914 "A Theologian for the Hour,"[7] his contribution to contemporary theological thought was going to be minimal.

P.T. FORSYTH: THEOLOGIAN FOR THE 21ST CENTURY?

Now over a quarter of a century on and after being stimulated and challenged by Forsyth's thought, I suspect the same verdict will be announced on the impact his theology will likely have on the Church as the twenty-first century beckons. In several ways his theology seems dated or inadequate. Allow me to suggest six of them.

First, Forsyth offends those attitudes and speech which have been fundamentally influenced by the insights of feminism. The offence is more deep-seated than the fact that, along with all writers in the English language until quite recently, Forsyth does not use inclusive language. Nor can Forsyth be faulted for failing to see that God is beyond gender characterizations. He can assert, for example, that "God himself is more than a man" and that "The Divine is part womanly."[8] Forsyth will not accept that God can be imaged after the likes of either man or woman. "Against all forms of anthropocentrism, Forsyth's theology is contemptuous," asserts Colin Gunton, since "the deity in whom he believes is glorious in his transcendent self-sufficiency."[9] So what is the basis of objection? It is that Forsyth invariably associated "the heroic features of faith" stereotypically with male strength, power, and assertiveness and that what he considers distortions of true faith are linked by him to the "feminine."[10] Bewailing the lack of men in the Congregational Churches of 1917 he applauds those churches' women in a backhanded way:

> It is not so much that we have now more female Christianity, but that we have less male. The Christianity of the men has ebbed,

6. The title of a BBC broadcast by H.F. Lovell Cocks on 20 July 1948, the script of which is found in the Lovell Cocks papers at the Dr. Williams's Library, London.

7. Edwin H. Kellogg wrote an article entitled "A Theologian for the Hour: Peter Taylor Forsyth." [The information concerning the works referred to in n6 and n7 comes from the bibliography prepared by Leslie M. Curdy for Hart, *Justice*, 256–330].

8. Quoted by Binfield, "P.T. Forsyth as Congregational Minister," 172.

9. Gunton, "Real as Redemptive," 55.

10. Forsyth, *Rome*, 14.

and left the godliness of the women more conspicuous. It is realized much has always been due to them.[11]

Given what was happening in Western Europe at the time it was hardly
surprising that the churches were down in their male membership figures.
We have a right to ask what constitutes "female Christianity" and "the
Christianity of men"? Forsyth's answer is clear: the former is a religion of "the
heart" and "the temperament" with a preponderance towards sentimentality,
the latter "a faith for the mind, the conscience, and the will."[12] You will find
few better examples of sexual stereotyping in Christian theology. We now
realize that it reflects an impaired understanding of both people and the
makeup of Christian churches.

Secondly, Forsyth's theology does not have the benefit of recent work
in biblical studies. As a result his use of the Bible in framing his theology
appears to be at best overconfident and at worst naïve. He made the radical
observation for his time that the Bible is not the authoritative norm for all
Christian thought and practice; rather, he argued, the Bible is the authoritative
source of the norm. It is the Gospel which existed "before the Bible," and
"created the Bible," that is normative.[13] Years before neo-orthodoxy was to
take a similar line, Forsyth argued that Christianity is directly rooted in the
Word, or better the event to which an encounter with the Word gives rise—
"the personal cruciality of the cross";[14] and hence it is ultimately grounded
in the Bible insofar as the Bible is the *source* of the apostolic witness to
that Word. Of course, given his very unsystematic way of doing theology,
there are times when one can be led to think that he conceives the Bible's
authority for theology in quite a different way. For example, he describes
"the minister's charter" as "the New Testament . . . the precipitate of the
apostolic preaching at first hand," since the New Testament, is "the legatee"
of the "unique authority" of the apostles.[15] More usually however Forsyth
avoids making either the Bible or the New Testament authoritative in any
way other than as a source for a yet higher authority. Earlier in the same
book we find the following:

> We must go back to the Bible. The Christian back to the Bible;
> the scholar with all his splendid modern equipment back to the
> Bible . . . It is now back to that which makes the Bible the Bible.

11. Forsyth, *Lectures*, 19.

12. Forsyth, *Lectures*, 21.

13. Forsyth, *Positive Preaching*, 10.

14. Forsyth, *Revelation*, 104.

15. Forsyth, *Lectures*, 129.

> Back to that which is . . . within and beyond the Bible. Back to
> the Gospel of our moral redemption through faith in the pure
> grace and mercy of God in Christ crucified. That is the most
> certain thing in Christianity.[16]

The Bible therefore plays a fundamental role in Forsyth's theology, but
he could never be accused of bibliolatry; nevertheless, his confidence in
scholarship's ability to delineate a clear, unified, and authoritative account
of "the apostolic preaching" or "the Gospel of our moral redemption" today
looks decidedly utopian. As Ernst Käsemann has powerfully argued, the New
Testament displays "many different versions of the Christian proclamation,"
and one has to draw the obvious conclusion that both the Christian
Church in its polity and practice and also the very gospel itself were plural
phenomena in the early days of their existence.[17] And further problems for
Forsyth's way of using the Bible emerge when one takes into account the
way in which some exegetes today accept that the different standpoints of
readers invite multiple readings of the same texts. There is no easy route to
underpinning Christian thought and practice with biblical warrants when
the challenging conclusion is drawn that "all that can possibly be meant
by "biblical interpretation" is not any single way of interpreting the biblical
writings, but only a plurality of such ways, only some of which either are
or need to be orientated by the question or questions to which the biblical
writings themselves intend to give answer."[18] Some New Testament scholars
argue for a greater unity in the early Christian witness of faith recorded by
the New Testament, while others press the claim that the proper meaning
of a text is that intended by the original author. But this wide divergence
of opinion in the world of biblical studies only adds to the problem of
delivering positive outcomes from a "back to the Bible" strategy.

Thirdly, Forsyth's gift to illuminate and obscure in the self-same
paragraph is borne by a style of writing which delights in the contrast of
"either/or" rather than tenaciously exploring the subtleties of "both/and."
It might be argued that this is the legitimate exploitation of the preacher's
art, but it can lead people to conclude that Forsyth has not seen the
whole picture. Allow me to give an example of one such false antithesis.
At the very core of his theology rests his broad methodological decision
to advocate "revelation" over and against "reason." As we have seen, he
eschews anthropocentrism in Christianity and theology. His starting point
is the reconciliation of the human race with God, which is proclaimed in

16. Forsyth, *Lectures*, 69.

17. Käsemann, *Essays*, 95.

18. Ogden, *Doing Theology Today*, 44.

the Christian revelation: "The test and trial of all is the grace of God in Jesus Christ, and Him as crucified." And lest we have not got the message he immediately adds: "Everything is imperishable which is inseparable from that."[19] He was attacking a liberal approach to theological thinking which, while laudable in its apologetic attempt to speak to the age, had seriously reduced, he believed, the content of the gospel to what underpinned rather than challenged that age. That liberal approach began with the human mind rather than the "positive" theology which starts with the revealed Word:

> . . . by liberalism I mean the theology that begins with some rational canon of life or nature to which Christianity has to be cut down or enlarged (as the case may be); while by a modern positivity I mean a theology which begins with God's gift of a super-logical revelation in Christ's historic person and cross, whose object was not to adjust a contradiction but to resolve a crisis and save a situation of the human soul.[20]

But, we must ask, how can one grasp the "super-logical" revelation in a way which bypasses the cultural conditioning and relativity of all understanding? Every witness to Jesus has occurred in a particular context and has been interpreted through that particular context's cultural lens. There is, as David Pailin has pointed out, "a reciprocal relationship between revelatory insights and existing thought."[21] While Forsyth can readily accept that "the old faith" will need to be expressed in "a new theology" by each generation in the Church, he is quick to point out that this will involve "re-interpretation" rather than "revision."[22] He believes that while the form in which the gospel is expressed may alter its content is fixed. Where, however, is there a point in Christian history that provides us with a firm awareness of the gospel's content free of a contextually conditioned form? There is none, and the problem for Christian theologians from the first Easter onwards has been "how to distinguish between a proper apprehension of the reality of God revealed in Jesus as the Christ and an attractive, but basically fictitious, cultural invention."[23] Both in principle and in practice, reason *and* revelation are alike anthropocentrically conditioned. We cannot avoid starting with ourselves; all we can hope to do is to avoid the inevitable relativity of all thought slipping into a vicious relativism by attending to the checks and

19. Forsyth, *Positive Preaching*, 15.
20. Forsyth, *Positive Preaching*, 143.
21. Pailin, *Anthropological Character*, 136.
22. Forsyth, *Revelation*, 108.
23. Pailin, *Anthropological Character*, 138.

balances which emerge through the mutuality of inter-cultural enquiry, conversation, and debate.

Fourthly, one of the most challenging aspects of Forsyth's thinking is his belief that the Christian gospel is the sole means by which the world will be brought to its proper goal. He argues that

> what society radically needs is *salvation*; and it is salvation that the Church offers to all. The Church alone has this secret—the Church, the greatest product of man's past, and the only trustee of his future . . . the Church is the only society with a fulcrum outside the world; and therefore the only one that can move the world as a whole.[24]

Forsyth's exclusivist tones were matched by an unshakeable conviction that was evangelical in style and missionary in approach. His was the age in which large numbers of Christians began working "to evangelize the world in this generation,"[25] although he was not as confident as most of them were about the outcome. But it was also a time in which people's encounters with non-Christian faiths and ideologies largely lacked an awareness of the sincerity and insights of those who belonged to them. While there are still many who follow the exclusivist stance of insisting that there is no salvation outside the Christian confession of Christ as the Redeemer, others no longer can support such a contention. First hand encounter with non-Christians in our multi-cultural society has left them with a deep appreciation of religions other than Christianity. They find it difficult to believe that there is no salvific value in them. Rather than accept an *exclusivist* attitude of Christianity towards other religions, they want to be more affirming of those religions. This may involve people continuing to affirm that the Christ event *constitutes* the possibility of salvation, but making the added claim that the work of Christ can be seen "anonymously" in the other great world faiths;[26] or it can involve people arguing that the Christ event is *representative* rather than constitutive of the possibility of salvation;[27] or it might mean that people travel across the theological Rubicon to a *pluralist* view which sees all world faiths as different but in some degree legitimate means of offering salvation.[28] Whichever position such people adopt will be

24. Forsyth, *Lectures*, 4–5.

25. The title of a missionary program of the time.

26. See the work of Rahner in *Theological Investigations*, Vols. 5, 6, 14 and 16 for a sophisticated exposition of the "inclusivist" position.

27. For a sustained defence of "pluralistic inclusivism" (as distinguished from Rahner's "monistic inclusivism") see Ogden, *Is There Only One True Religion?*

28. See Hick and Knitter, *Myth of Christian Uniqueness.*

opposed to statements like this: "It is only by Christ's holy work, translated into the holy society of the Churches, that Society at large can be converted into the holy Kingdom of God."[29] This accounts for a further reason why many contemporary people will consider Forsyth's theology inadequate.

A fifth source of inadequacy in Forsyth's theology is highlighted by those who perceive its agenda to be parochial when set in a global context. The problem which is the starting point for his theology is human sin, and for Forsyth it is sin which causes the offense of which the human race is guilty before God. However, as Raymond Fung has observed, the primary problem which besets the inhabitants of the Two-Third's World is not that they are sinners but rather that they are repeatedly and systematically being sinned against by a global economic and political system which maintains them in grinding poverty and merciless dependency.[30] Their problems are not self-inflicted but imposed by others; they are political rather than personal, social and not simply individual. From the perspective of the underside of history therefore Forsyth's prescriptions for human ills will appear to be merely palliative; he will be dismissed as naïve, since few today can seriously subscribe to the view that the simple and straightforward way to establish justice and equality in society is to work on changing the lives of individuals. Yet this was Forsyth's strategy: "Set that right in every man by what sets right also the race, and right views and right relations will follow as night the day."[31] Robert Paul acknowledges that "Forsyth was perhaps too optimistic at this point."[32] It's always tempting in a Western sitting room to wax eloquently about the world becoming a better place, as more and more people turn from their personal sin through their encounter with the event which has seen "the destruction by God in Christ of sin's guilt and sin's distrust, and sin's blocking of the sky."[33] But, as Reinhold Niebuhr has taught us, sin is a most complex phenomenon, and it is found in its most virulent form in social, economic, and political manifestations which prove to be somewhat immune to the kind of individualist strategies typically advanced by Western theology.[34] Following Forsyth, Colin Gunton insists that "The Church's being, acts and words . . . fulfil its responsibility to society" when they are directed to the basis of "all human social life . . . in redemption."

29. Forsyth, "Holy Church," 33.

30. I owe my theological understanding of the Shakespearean distinction between being "a sinner" and being "sinned against" to Robert Fung's series of letters on evangelism published by the WCC.

31. Forsyth, *Positive Preaching*, 40.

32. Paul, "P.T. Forsyth," 51.

33. Forsyth, *Positive Preaching*, 40.

34. See Niebuhr, *Moral Man*.

This leads him to a clear conclusion: "The primary task is not to organize the world, but to be within it as a particular way of being human, a living reminder of the true basis and end of human life."[35] But, we may ask, is the basis of "all human life" found "in redemption" *alone*? Is there not a further dimension, one that flows out from Jesus' injunction that we love our neighbour as our self—as well as loving God with all our heart and mind? Isn't the theme of "emancipation" also to be brought into view if we are to give an adequate account of God's liberating work? If that liberating work involves the "emancipation" of people as well as their "redemption," then it is legitimate to argue that "the Christian community" is here to do something more than "remind the state that political and moral programmes are secondary to and dependent upon redemption." In obedience to the One whose liberating work encompasses *both* "redemption" *and* "emancipation," the Church also *ought* to be engaged in social and political activity to establish "political and moral programmes" that become the context in which "the creative transformation of relationships" does take place.[36]

The underlying criticism of Western theology's overt emphasis on a classical redemption-centred view of God's liberating work leads to our sixth and concluding reason for believing that Forsyth is likely to continue as a marginal figure in contemporary theological developments. Many see his work (like that of Barth *et al*) as a self-critical moment in the history of liberal theology rather than liberal theology's obituary.[37] Whatever may have been the mistakes of liberal theology, the argument runs, we must not attempt to go behind liberalism so much as go on from it. And nowhere ought this approach to be more in evidence than in consideration of the work of Christ. Paul Fiddes for example raises a perennial issue. "How can a particular event in the past have an effect upon our experience of salvation today?[38] And he concludes that Forsyth's theology does not provide a satisfactory answer to this question.[39] Trevor Hart, however, tries to show that Forsyth may in fact manage to hold together both objective and subjective dimensions of the saving work of Christ in his soteriology.

> Forsyth . . . because he sees atonement primarily not as a mat-
> ter of either the status or the experience of individual persons,
> but an adjustment of the cosmic order of things which thereby
> inevitably has universal implications . . . presents both aspects

35. Gunton, *Actuality*, 193

36. Gunton, *Actuality*, 193

37. See Ogden, "Truth, Truthfulness, and Secularity."

38. Fiddes, *Past Event* , ix.

39. See Fiddes, *Past Event*, 105–106.

under the one rubric of the self-realization of the Holy: first, in the order of reality, and secondarily, as that "reorganization of the universe" works itself out in actuality and history.[40]

Be that as it may, the liberal suspicion of Forsyth's emphasis on theology's heart residing in an objective atonement is not easily overcome. Pailin has argued that "the images of the divine and the divine-human relationship suggested by some models of the atonement . . . are so fundamentally misleading that they impede rather than enliven faith's self-understanding."[41] Like many others, he objects to accounts of the work of Christ which pre-suppose images of God that are "pre-Christian (or sub-Christian)," and which take their leave from some of the worst rather than best features of human beings—"hostility, anger, offence, injured dignity" rather than "sorrow, pity, loving concern and patient hope."[42] Instead, Pailin insists that "Christian believers and theologians should take radically seriously the insight into the divine nature presented by the life and death of Jesus, and not distort it by interpreting it in terms of sub-Christian views of God."[43] But that is precisely what Forsyth would have argued he has done, and, against Pailin's favoured idea of the Christian understanding of God as "a father who runs forward to welcome home a son who has come to his senses,"[44] he would no doubt assert his understanding of the Holy One who, when the law of the divine moral order is broken, expects restitution to meet the requirement of the divine life. As Hart puts it:

> God . . .could not waive his moral order, but must honour it, for the guilt of humanity is no mere matter of private and personal affront, but rather of a public justice, a public truth, in which God must safeguard not his own honour or his own feelings, but truth itself.[45]

However sophisticated the interplay between God's holiness and love may be in Forsyth's treatment of Christ's work, the priority which he places on the holiness of God is an understandable reaction to a liberalism which cuts down Christian love to the size of human kindness; but it does not do justice to the understanding of love rooted in what is involved in the laying down of one's life for one's friends. It is easy therefore to see why Pailin argues that

40. Hart, "Morality," 30.
41. Pailin, "Doctrine," 71.
42. Pailin, "Doctrine," 75.
43. Pailin, "Doctrine," 76–77.
44. Pailin, "Doctrine," 76.
45. Hart, "Morality," 27–28.

Forsyth is tied to a vision of God constructed after the manner of a cosmic moralist rather than his preferred Whiteheadian "brief Galilean vision" of God operating "in quietness . . . by love."[46] And Forsyth's theology is so "perilously like the old orthodoxy" against which liberal theology originally rose up that many contemporary people are "not going to be dragged from the sunlit air of simple faith in the love of God" to become committed to a view from which they had thought they had escaped.[47]

There are good reasons therefore to believe that Forsyth's theology is not going to be formative for shaping our theology at the dawn of the new millennium. This does not mean however that we do not have important things to learn from Forsyth. And it is in his writings on the nature and function of Christian ministry, I believe, that some of those insights occur.

A SACRAMENTAL VIEW OF CHRISTIAN MINISTRY

Forsyth's thinking on Christian ministry can be mapped out by considering his opposition to the sacerdotal and hierarchical understanding displayed in Roman Catholic and Anglican polity and practice, as well as his deep unease about the perception of Christian ministry which he found operative in the Congregational churches of his day. As is often the case we discover what a person is for by observing what that person is against.

Forsyth delineated two principal forms of Christianity. He saw them as being rooted in quite different understandings of God's grace. The Catholic form is essentially sacramental, while the Protestant form is evangelical.

> The Catholic and the Evangelical idea of faith are incompatible, because each claims to be absolute. The priest of the sacraments has no room for the minister of the Gospel; the ministry of the Word has no place for the vicarious priest.[48]

In the Catholic view grace, according to Forsyth, is the "infusion of the divine essence into our souls."[49] It is akin to "a sort of antiseptic influence made to pervade the spiritual system like new blood."[50] By contrast the Protestant view understands grace as "an act and way of God's treatment of us."[51] It involves God's merciful action upon the human will.

46. Pailin quoting Whitehead in "Doctrine," 77n7.
47. Cunliffe-Jones, "P.T. Forsyth," 353.
48. Forsyth, *Rome*, 140.
49. Forsyth, *Lectures*, 37.
50. Forsyth, *Rome*, 56.
51. Forsyth, *Rome*, 57.

> In a word, for Catholicism grace is magic, for Evangelicalism
> it is mercy. The grace of Evangelicalism is Christ, the Gospel,
> the Word. The faith that answers that is living faith in a living
> person directly in converse with the soul.[52]

For Forsyth therefore grace is not God's gift of a magical, subliminal power but the merciful activity of God operating on the will of sinful human beings. In the Catholic view the common access to grace is *via* participation in the sacraments; so, Forsyth argued, those authorized to administer the sacraments in effect become the means by which the people have access to grace. For Forsyth, an advocate of the evangelical understanding, grace is conveyed in the "hearing" of the gospel as the Word is preached and the Sacraments are administered. The believer therefore has access to God without needing recourse to a priest; so for an evangelical the church is "the priesthood of all believers." The result is that the sacerdotal emphasis in Christian ministry becomes greatly qualified.

> The true awareness of the Reformation was the rejection of
> priest and mass. And it was a rejection caused by the return to
> the Bible and the rediscovery of the Gospel. What dislodged the
> priest was the Gospel. It was the faith that made every Christian
> man his own priest in Jesus Christ.[53]

The "sacrificing priesthood" is replaced with the minister of the Word.[54]

Forsyth's objection to sacerdotal views of ministry was matched by his opposition to the monarchical episcopal system he saw in the Roman Catholic and Anglican Churches. He describes both episcopacy and the priesthood as "mere historic growths."[55] They are not of the *esse* of the Church. This does not mean however that Forsyth denied that there is a sacerdotal dimension to ministry, or that episcopacy is "a good polity among others."[56] He could say for example that he had "no objection to Episcopacy in itself" and confess that he could do his work "happily under a bishop, and feel honoured under the episcopate of many."[57] His argument was with a system which had linked together the priestly and administrative functions of leadership in an order of ministry that had become a constitutive dimension of the Church.

---

52. Forsyth, *Rome*, 57.

53. Forsyth, *Rome*, 59.

54. Forsyth, *Lectures*, 100.

55. Forsyth, *Rome*, 86.

56. Forsyth, *Rome*, 97.

57. Forsyth, *Lectures*, 42.

In the first century, Forsyth argues, the episcopate as we have come to know it was not a feature of ecclesiastical life. "Such an idea did not dominate the whole period of the undivided Church."[58] To insist upon episcopacy as a pre-condition for Christian unity therefore seemed to Forsyth tantamount to unchurching "all the Christian communities of the New Testament."[59] What ought to be the basis of unity is the gospel preserved in the apostolic preaching found in the New Testament and proclaimed faithfully by Christians today. The true apostolic succession is not found in an order of ministry.

> The Apostolic succession has no meaning except as the Evangel-ical succession. It does not mean, at the one extreme, a historic line of valid ordinations unbroken from the Apostles to the last curate. Nor, at the other end, does it mean merely cultivating the spirit of the Apostles, or their precepts for sanctification. But it is the succession of those who experience and preach the Apostolic Gospel of a regenerating redemption.[60]

Equally objectionable for Forsyth was the style of leadership that the bishops exercised. He could find no warrant for the monarchical approach which had emerged in the Patristic period.

> The original constitution of the Church, whatever it was, was not monarchical. It was corporative: until Cyprianism; and until the black years when first Constantine and then Charlemagne made it a State Church, and turned its officers into civil servants and its government to a bureaucracy.[61]

And, not surprisingly, Forsyth saw the dangers of an alliance between church and state which could lead to the Church's ministry coming under state control. He believed that the "spiritual necessity in the Reformation" would one day require the Disestablishment of the Church of England if the Reformation was ever to be considered complete: "The battle with the world for a free Gospel can only be won by a free Church; and a free Church is the inevitable effect of a free Gospel, of the freedom of the spiritual power."[62]

All this would have fallen upon welcome ears in Congregationalist circles, but an equal focus of Forsyth's attack was the ministerial practice of his denomination's churches. Here was one Congregationalist theologian

58. Forsyth, *Lectures*, 42.

59. Forsyth, *Lectures*, 42.

60. Forsyth, *Lectures*, 102.

61. Forsyth, *Lectures*, 72.

62. Forsyth, *Rome*, 23–24.

who recognized the way in which the doctrine of the priesthood of all believers had been so diluted that it had become synonymous with a view of ministry which does justice neither to church members nor ordained ministers. It was being used as a license to authorize anyone to do anything in the church—irrespective of ability and sometimes without due preparation. As a result, Forsyth pointed out how standards of leadership had declined. If it was true that "The Church will be what its ministry makes it" then it followed, for Forsyth, that churches needed a renewed vision about ministry if they were to regain their health and strength.[63] He is caustic about the way in which churches view their ministers.

> There are those who look on the minister simply as one of the members of the Church—the talking or the presiding member. They think anything else spoils him as a brother. They believe a Church could go on without a minister, only not so well, with less decency and order.[64]

While ministers must have colluded to some extent in this lowering of their stature, it is the church members whom Forsyth reminds about the task ministers are called to perform and of the esteem they should have in the church:

> . . . let the religious public at least have some consideration for the ministry, which it irritates and debases by trivial ethics, and the impatient demand for short sermons and long "socials." Let it respect the dignity of ministry. Let it cease to degrade the ministry into a competitor for public notice, a caterer for public comfort, and a mere waiter upon social convenience or religious decency. Let it make greater demands on the pulpit for power, and grasp, and range, and penetration, and reality. Let it encourage the ministry to do more justice to the mighty *matter* of the Bible and its brethren, and not only to its beauty, its charm, its sentiment, or its precepts. Let it come in aid to protect the pulpit from the curse of petty sentiment which grows upon the Church, which rolls up from the pew into the pulpit, and from the pulpit rolls down upon the pew in a warm and soaking mist.[65]

It was Forsyth's belief that the churches of his day were desperately in need of rediscovering their roots in the gospel. He called for "a reformation of faith, belief, and thought to make the Churches adequate to the nation, the

---

63. Forsyth, *Lectures,* 121.

64. Forsyth, *Lectures,* 123.

65. Forsyth, *Positive Preaching,* 100.

world, and the age, a bracing up and a coupling up of our Churches, and a renovated theology as the expression of the Church's rich and corporate life."[66] Ministers were to be a fundamental means by which that reformation came about. They are to take on a sacramental function at the heart of the church's life; they are called by God and set apart by the church to *convey*, and not merely declare, the grace of God.

> In the sacrament of the Word the ministers are themselves the living elements in Christ's hands—broken and poured out in soul, even unto death; so that they may not only witness to Christ, or symbolise Him, but by the sacrament of personality actually convey Him crucified and risen.[67]

Or in a more personal vein Forsyth can say this of his calling:

> How solemn our place is! It is a sacramental place. We have not simply to state our case, we have to convey our Christ and convey Him effectively. We are sacramental elements, broken often in the Lord's hands, as He dispenses His grace though us.[68]

A "higher" view of ministry is difficult to imagine.

In Forsyth's analysis of the work of ministers he turns our attention to four primary functions. First, ministers are preachers. In *Positive Preaching and the Modern Mind*, Forsyth presents a treatment of preaching which is full of tremendous insight as well as practical help. The book starts with the claim that "with its preaching Christianity stands or falls."[69] This in turn points to the crucial role of the preacher in the life of the churches. Preaching demands "complete immersion in the Bible," so it follows that "The ideal ministry is in real touch with the Bible."[70] Forsyth of course sees God's saving work in the Easter event as the kernel of the preached message: "This cross is the message that makes the preacher."[71] As well as being devoted to biblical reading and study, there is however also a need for "deliberate prayer," since without this ministers "easily become dilettanti not in theology only but in soul, religious amateurs instead of spiritual masters, mere seekers, and experimenters instead of experts of the Gospel and adepts of faith."[72] The minister's second function is pastoral work. This

66. Forsyth, *Lectures,* 104.

67. Forsyth, *Lectures,* 131.

68. Forsyth, *Revelation,* 121.

69. Forsyth, *Positive Preaching,* 1.

70. Forsyth, *Revelation,* 102, 13.

71. Forsyth, *Positive Preaching,* 49.

72. Forsyth, *Revelation,* 106.

is a continuation of the preaching function in that it is not merely a matter of the minister extending concern and kindliness to people; rather, it is the way the minister takes Christ to people "not for humane objects only, but for the sake of the Kingdom of God."[73] Ministers are sacramental in their pastoral endeavor as they become subjects of grace through which the gospel of grace works. The third function of the minister is more priestly than prophetic. The minister's conduct of public worship, and especially the leading of congregational prayer, is an important part of a minister's responsibilities. When carrying it out the minister is more sacerdotal than sacramental. This prompts Forsyth to make the following observations:

> As priest, the ministry offers to God the Church's soul, as proph-
> et it offers to it the salvation of God. In the minister's one per-
> son, the human spirit speaks to God, and the Holy Spirit speaks
> to men. No wonder he is often rent asunder.[74]

But, as our earlier discussion suggested, Forsyth argues that ultimately the minister "is sacramental . . . more than sacerdotal," since the minister

> is chiefly what he is for God. And for God he is agent of His
> Christ, the vehicle of His Word. And it is only God's Word to us
> that makes possible our Word to God.[75]

Fourthly, the minister has social and philanthropic functions in the wider community and society. Forsyth was so suspicious of any social gospel strategy that he tended to think that this function was already receiving enough attention by ministers at the time—or more truly far too much attention to the detriment of the other functions. The more ministers involve themselves in these matters, the less time there is for the preaching, teaching, and the liturgical side of ministry. Forsyth also makes the telling point that such a ministerial strategy "takes the work away from the laity."[76]

Forsyth therefore offers a theology of ministry in which the minister of Word and Sacraments is essential for the *bene esse* of the Church. There is a clear role for a body of people who are set apart in the church for purposes of leadership, particularly through the media of preaching and teaching. Such people are to be carefully selected for their office and rigorously prepared to undertake it. Forsyth's view of ministry was demanding. How else, he observed, can we get the heart back into the churches? "If the ministers do not rise to the level of ministry it is for the Church to see that they are better

73. Forsyth, *Lectures*, 135.
74. Forsyth, *Lectures*, 136.
75. Forsyth, *Lectures*, 136.
76. Forsyth, *Lectures*, 136.

selected and trained."[77] With its emphasis upon preaching and teaching one suspects that Forsyth's view of ministers imposed high theological demands upon them. It was certainly an educated ministry he was aiming to produce:

> . . . to be true at once to the Gospel and to the age the ministry must be an educated one. I mean as a whole. And by educated I do not mean learned, and I do mean more than merely trained . . . trained in the wisdom and knowledge which is the stored precipitate of past ages of earnest Christian experience.[78]

In modern terms we might say that Forsyth's minister is required to be a practical theologian who enables the whole Church to be aware and confident of the faith it holds. Speaking about preachers needing to be rooted and grounded in theology Forsyth remarks that

> it needs much skill in the treatment of truth to grasp with the right hand the marrow of the Gospel and manipulate with the other the civilization of the time, to stand with one foot on earth and the other in the infinite sea. Do not think this trained mind, this due knowledge, is a luxury of the literates. It is a necessity for the whole Church . . .[79]

While not part of an order, ministers are set apart among other things to maintain the order of the church. They are accountable to the demands which the gospel places upon them rather than the wishes of the congregation. Not out to impress people and have people take notice of them, ministers are pneumatics rather than charismatics. They convince by "the power of the word, the inner nature of the Gospel, the intelligent demonstration of the spirit.[80] Ministry "is not a matter of mental or miraculous gifts," as the out-and-out charismatic would have us believe; it is rather rooted in "the gifts of faith, hope and love in the Gospel."[81]

THE RELEVANCE OF FORSYTH'S MODEL OF MINISTRY FOR TODAY

It has been my experience in recent years that ordinands who have read Forsyth on ministry have found his model of ministry as relevant at the end

77. Forsyth, *Lectures*, 121.
78. Forsyth, *Revelation*, 109.
79. Forsyth, *Revelation*, 109.
80. Forsyth, *Revelation*, 112.
81. Forsyth, *Revelation*, 111.

of the century as it was at its start. This is partly because Forsyth's outline of the crisis facing the churches is more obviously real to us than it was in his day; in that sense, Forsyth was a prophet who largely went unheeded. What my students see very clearly is a contemporary church which has lost touch with its roots in the gospel, that does not possess a credible account of the gospel to share with others, and which has largely lost its confidence to be the church in today's society. They regard themselves as future ministers of the church charged with developing fresh patterns of leadership that will enable the churches to be reformed anew. And for a number of reasons the "model of ministry" provided by Forsyth resonates with their ideas and convictions about ministry.

First, Forsyth presents to us a "job" which is worth committing one's life to doing. Looked at realistically, the ministry of Word and Sacraments is awesome in its demands and almost impossible in its expectations. The temptation therefore is to cut it down to a series of tasks that are manageable and assessable by human criteria. So it is possible to draw up job descriptions and person specifications for the ideal minister, but in the process the cutting edge of the calling can become lost as patterns for ministry are made to fit congregational expectations rather than the demands of the gospel. The spiritual gets secularized and contact with the sacramental is lost. Forsyth's reminder that the minister is directly in the service of the gospel and only indirectly in the service of the church is salutary: "A man is an ideal minister not by his success with the public but by his stewardship of the word, by his adequacy and fidelity to Him that called him."[82] Far too much emphasis perhaps has been placed in recent years upon models of ministry which owe their content and shape to secular professions and their theories. So, for example, Christian patterns of leadership have been re-written in the light of management theory, pastoral care has been reconstructed in the light of non-directive counseling ideas, and mission has been re-shaped by insights from the social sciences. While secular disciplines have a great deal to teach us, there is the obvious danger that they become a powerful means by which the essentially sacramental nature of ministry is lost as ministry comes to resemble a series of activities which are formally little different to their secular counterparts. Forsyth's sacramental emphasis provides us with an outlook on ministry which sees it as a means of grace rather than a conglomeration of secular "works." And that is the kind of ministry to which many ordinands feel called—even if it is "awesome in its demands and almost impossible in its expectations" when judged by human criteria.

82. Forsyth, *Revelation*, 93.

Secondly, Forsyth presents us with a model of ministry against which we can assess contemporary ministerial practice. My observation of ministers at work suggests that there are models of ministry on display which come nowhere near the understanding set by Forsyth. Admittedly, ministers are forced into such styles of ministry due to the pressure of the circumstances in which they called to work. Those who serve in multi-church pastorates or some ecumenical contexts often have little time to do anything but manage decline. The practice of spreading ever fewer ministers over the churches was not devised out of a clear mission strategy; it has seemingly been adopted to prolong a chaplaincy model of ministry. Ministers themselves must share some of the blame for colluding in such developments. A close inspection of ministers at work suggests that some of the emphases on display, for example, are "management of an organization," "community work," "counseling," "social work," and "administration." It is frightening how many ministers have rationalized away as unimportant the emphasis upon the Word so typical of Forsyth's ideal minister. Let me firmly state that my argument has nothing at all against management, community work, counseling, social work, and administration; quite the reverse in so far as any local church will be enriched if it can pursue excellence in each field. What I'm concerned about is that ministers build up their congregations in the Christian faith so that such activities become the means rather than the end of discipleship. On their own they will never deliver what the church needs, although it can be freely admitted that management, community work, counseling, social work, and administration are what many ministers seem to focus their ministry on, wittingly or not. In 1899 Forsyth proclaimed, "What the Church needs as the condition of reformation is a regeneration of the idea of faith."[83] Why faith? Why not an emphasis on management, community work, counseling, social work, and administration? Forsyth's answer is clear:

> The mystery and the power of Christianity is faith—understood not merely as a religious sympathy or affection, but as direct, personal communion with Christ, based on forgiveness of sins direct from Him to the conscience . . . Believe in the Lord Jesus Christ, and thou shalt be saved—not in the Church, not in the sacraments, not in the priesthood.[84]

And might we not add, nor in ministry focused on management, community work, counseling, social work, and administration? Forsyth goes on to add: "All these have their great worth as exhibitions and energies of the Church,

---

83. Forsyth, *Rome,* 65.

84. Forsyth, *Rome,* 92–93.

not as conditions between Christ and the Lord," since "they are not objects of faith."[85] Today it can be argued that the church is in ever greater need of a reformation based on "a regeneration of the idea of faith." There is clear evidence that many church members lack a determination to think, feel, and do the things of God. This will only be cultivated in congregations that make worship central, take the Bible seriously, and gather in church meeting to discern the mind of Christ rather than decide on a show of hands what the members want to do. Forsyth's model of ministry is precisely what the church needs to enable those things to happen. The attraction of the New Age movement and events such as Hillsborough, Dunblane, and the death of Diana, Princess of Wales also suggest that there are large numbers of British people who have deep religious questions, profound voids at the heart of their lives, and an untapped spiritual dimension. Neither the church nor its ministry serves them well when the accent is placed on "religious sympathy or affection" rather than inviting "direct, personal communion with Christ." Churches delude themselves into thinking that they have totally attended to their task if they are well managed and well-versed in the arts of personal therapy and social involvement.

Thirdly, Forsyth's view of ministry is so designed that one of its primary aims is to set the church free for its own tasks of ministry and mission. The model is one of leadership by enablement. What a minister does in preaching, teaching or pastoral work is "to equip the saints for the work of ministry" (Eph. 4: 12). Forsyth argues that Christ ordained a ministry but that the church ordains ministers; and the latter is done to provide leadership for the former. He is adamant that the minister's task is to build up the church and make it effective for mission. Through preaching, prayer, teaching, and pastoral work the minister enables the churches to be the Church. Forsyth is clear that "it is the Church that is the great missionary to humanity, and not apostles, prophets, and agents here and there." So it follows that for a preacher "to act on the world he must, as a rule, do it through his Church."[86] Forsyth adds that

> the minister's first duty is to his Church. He must make it a Church that acts on the world—through him indeed, but also otherwise. He is to act at its head, and not in its stead.[87]

At this point, Forsyth's model of ministry helpfully steers a middle course between the Scylla of social gospel approaches and the Charybdis of

---

85. Forsyth, *Rome*, 93.

86. Forsyth, *Positive Preaching*, 52.

87. Forsyth, *Positive Preaching*, 53.

quietism. He is opposed equally to patterns of ministry that are so focused on social outreach that they underplay the role of building up the faith of the church members, and to those which focus upon building up faith at the expense of the church's activity in and on the world.

Given the importance that Forsyth attaches to the role of ministers in enabling the faith development of church members it is hardly surprising that, fourthly, he reminds us of the need in the church for ordained ministers who are rigorously prepared for their important task. This is an opportune reminder to Churches which due to declining memberships are facing a reduction in the numbers of available ministers as a result of either a recruitment shortage or financial necessity—or a combination of both. They are tempted to plug the gaps left by devising new patterns of ministry which require fewer qualifications, lower levels of preparation, and more modest responsibilities. In the clamor to have ecclesiastical leadership functions covered in the absence of stipendiary ministers, it is understandably tempting to rob the churches of some of their best lay-leaders, make them part-time, non-stipendiary ministers, and thus solve a deployment crisis in almost a financially neutral way. Where this has been done there is some evidence that it has been at the price of devaluing stipendiary ministry in people's perception and practice—as well as undermining the importance of lay ministry. Be that as it may, Forsyth's insistence that an educated ministry is essential for the well-being of the church cannot be underscored enough at a time when congregations are apt to hallow their buildings more than their ministers. In Forsyth's day it appears that people had more noble reasons to be cutting down on ministry.

> The condition of the ministry requires the attention of the Church quite as truly as the condition of the poor does. To provide a ministry equal to its own work is at least as much a concern of the Church as to provide work or play for the people. A Church that was keenly interested in technical or elementary education to the neglect of an education for its own ministry, elementary in the Bible and technical in theology, would be dying out as a Church.[88]

And, one is prompted to say, there is evidence of that happening. What Forsyth was pleading for was the provision at the heart of church life of leaders rooted in prayer, bible, and theology. Preparation for such a ministry in the nature of the case focuses upon the theological basis for the life and witness of the church. And today when the intellectual challenges to Christianity are even greater than in Forsyth's day, the need for theologically

88. Forsyth, *Revelation*, 96.

articulate ministers (to enable the church as a whole to become theologically credible) is ever greater. What important standards this man set:

> No man is entitled to discuss theology in public who has not studied theology. It is like any other weighty subject. Still more is this requisite if he sets to challenge and reform theology. He ought to be a trained theologian.[89]

There are few things more needed today than ministers who steeped in theology themselves can lead the churches to have a faith to share that arrests the hearts and minds of contemporary people.

Fifthly, Forsyth's insistence that success or failure in both the church and ministry should be set by standards that emanate from the gospel is salutary. The ethos of the Church Growth Movement in recent times has pandered to the worldly spirit of assessing value in quantitative rather than qualitative terms. The falsity is propagated that the faithfulness of the church and its obedience to Christ is measured by the numerical size of a congregation. Yet history shows that it has been when the church has been strongest in worldly terms that the seeds of its demise have been sown. The saplings of faithlessness and disobedience have sprouted forth heralded by the church's triumphal hymn of praise. Forsyth yet again has a word in season:

> There is hardly a Church that has not suffered from its success. And when I say suffered, I mean it has suffered in its power of witnessing the Gospel. It has gained comfort, affluence, and influence, but it has lost its prophetic soul, it has fallen from its apostolic insight and succession . . . Indeed, in organising themselves the Churches have often organised themselves into the world.[90]

Equal caution must be extended to judging the performance of a minister by similar criteria. This needs to be borne in mind now the church has moved into the era of ministerial appraisal. Forsyth warns against "producing a race of religious leaders with a general way and breezy charity, who would lead only as they spared and indulged their followers, and told them what fine fellows they were; whose speech was of rights far more than of duty; who would sacrifice society to their class or sect, and who were so full of the wrongs these endured that they had no word against the sins they cherish, or wrongs they inflict."[91] Such ministers may be popular, but they

---

89. Forsyth, *Positive Preaching*, 69.

90. Forsyth, *Lectures*, 65–66.

91. Forsyth, *Lectures*, 12.

are neither faithful nor obedient. Forsyth acknowledges that "If a rebuking and demanding Church must be an unpopular Church, then the Church must accept its unpopularity."[92] A corollary is that first rate ministers may receive bad reviews!

Finally, Forsyth's tremendous insight is again apparent when he tries to anchor the minister's life and work in prayer and spirituality. Ministers generally do not fail because of lack of training in professional skills. The causes of failure go much deeper since most of the acutest impediments in ministry cannot be overcome by the minister's own resources. Forsyth observed that the minister

> is a dealer in words; and it is very hard to keep them full of the Spirit, and yet to keep himself their master. He is a popular leader; and it is hard to lead the people without being led by the people to yield to them. The winning of souls, or the leading of souls, often costs the soul.[93]

Earlier he had argued that "the life which has religion for a profession is the most dangerous of all" since it is attractive of "so many temptations to unreality" particularly concerning "the deepening of the spiritual life."[94] And yet an ongoing "deepening of the spiritual life" is essential if ministry is to be successful, effective, faithful, and obedient. No one is going to be a sacrament through which God graciously meets people if they have lost touch with God in their own spiritual life.

> A preacher whose chief power is not in studious prayer, is, to that extent, a man who does not know his business. A stringent ethic would say he was in danger of becoming a quack. That of prayer *is* the minister's business.[95]

It is sad that until relatively recently very little was done in the preparation of ministers in the Free Church tradition to help them develop patterns of personal spiritual devotion which would sustain them in the demands of ministry. But it is the congregation which ultimately suffers when ministers find it impossible to say their prayers.

---

92. Forsyth, *Lectures*, 12.
93. Forsyth, *Positive Preaching*, 131.
94. Forsyth, *Positive Preaching*, 130.
95. Forsyth, *Positive Preaching*, 130.

CONCLUSION

While we have found that there are some rather obvious reasons why Forsyth's theology will not be conducive to the thinking of many today, his understanding of ministry is as appropriate a basic model now as it was at the turn of the twentieth century. But even at this point certain reservations begin to emerge when we remember that Forsyth's context was rather different to ours. Without in any way wanting to compromise my admiration for Forsyth's high view of ministry, I end by pointing out four areas which need to be addressed if Forsyth's insights are to benefit contemporary churches.

First, the church he saw emerging so clearly is now very much the church we see around us today. Almost a century of decline has beset the Free Churches since the prophetic voice of Forsyth asked the Congregational churches to engage in a root and branch self-examination. He was very confident that the right kind of ministers could turn around the situation, but many a faithful minister has not been able to neutralize the acids of twentieth-century secularism. The church's recent story is littered with faithful ministers who *have* been obedient: what resilience they have shown as their noble efforts have brought little reward! However prophetic Forsyth was, he could hardly have anticipated a society which can seem so apathetic. Cunliffe-Jones points to the need to attend to the apologetic dimension of Christian ministry rather more thoroughly than did Forsyth.

> However ultimate our Gospel, we have to let it make contact with a work-a-day world. The trouble is not that we are faced with a world so intransigently opposed to the Gospel that by no stretch of imagination can we suppose them to be reconciled. Rather are we dealing with a world whose habits have never been saturated in the Gospel.[96]

We have to work out anew in our time what it means to say: "The ultimate problem of human life has been met and mastered in Jesus Christ."[97] That will demand as much patient listening to the stories of contemporary people as preaching to them. The latter cannot be done adequately without the former having taken place.

Secondly, the nature of society has changed since Forsyth's day. Any worthy contemporary model of ministry will need to reflect that we live in a world that is multi-racial, a society in which equal opportunities are a basic right, a community which is ideologically suspicious of people in

---

96. Cunliffe-Jones, "P.T. Forsyth," 355.
97. Cunliffe-Jones, "P.T. Forsyth," 355.

authority, and a period when class and hierarchies are not so prominent. In Forsyth's day the Congregational minister walked down the High Street and his fellow citizens acknowledged an important figure; today most people do not know the URC minister in that kind of way. In an age when Christianity has to earn its place in society, the minister is likely to be by-passed rather than treated as someone to be revered.

Thirdly, styles of leadership differ from those in Forsyth's day. Any model of ministry which does not reflect contemporary norms of good leadership will be deemed inadequate. Just as the relationship between teacher and student, parent and child, employer and employee, has changed, so has that between minister and church member. Forsyth's model of ministry hardly does justice to the mutuality of relationship, the participatory endeavor, and collaborative spirit expected in modern forms of church leadership. It is significant for example that Forsyth hardly ever discusses the relationship between ministers and other church leaders, e.g. deacons and elders. His minister seems to work "on" the church in lonely isolation from the rest of the church members; the lay/ordained distinction is so clear at times it appears to be a complete separation.

Then, finally, we should recognize that far more is asked of today's ministers than in Forsyth's day. By and large, the absence of quality lay-leadership, a symptom of church decline, has added to the burden of ministry. In addition the churches have become increasingly bureaucratic as they have adopted more participatory structures and encouraged further lay-involvement. Ecumenical activity has added a further series of meetings to attend and activities to plan; the advent of the photocopier and information technology means that the quantity of administration asked of ministers has grown beyond imagination; and the requirements for churches to attend to issues of general health and safety and safe-guarding have imposed further responsibilities on ministers. It is sometimes difficult to envisage how the modern minister has time to tackle the essential work of ministry; often they don't, for that very reason.

It is to Forsyth that we can still turn for as challenging an account of that "essential work" as is available anywhere in theological writing, and until we re-invent ministry on the overall basis of his model, the churches will not have the leadership they need and deserve.

4

The Theological Legacy
of Lesslie Newbigin

LESSLIE NEWBIGIN WAS AN outstanding Christian: missionary, ecumenist, bishop, theologian, and pastor. None who knew him either closely or distantly can have failed "to recognize and respect the nobility of [his] character, the quality of his mind, and the depth of his devotion."[1] It is not surprising therefore that, following his death in 1998, there should be a bourgeoning literature about him. Geoffrey Wainwright has provided us with a fine biography which admirably fulfils its intention "to show Newbigin's theology as it emerged in the varied contexts of his life and work."[2] It also reflects the importance which he, George R. Hunsberger and others attribute to Newbigin's theology.[3] While Wainwright describes that theology as "an *authentic* representation of the scriptural Gospel and the *classic* Christian faith,"[4] Hunsberger opines that Newbigin bequeathed to the world church "a legacy of profound proportion."[5] Others have been less hagiographical and more critical in their appraisals of Newbigin's theology; some of the contributions to the "After Newbigin" international conference

1. Rodd, Review of *Lesslie Newbigin* .

2. Wainwright, *Lesslie Newbigin* , vii.

3. See Hunsberger, *Bearing the Witness*.

4. Wainwright, *Lesslie Newbigin*, viii. Italics mine.

5. Hunsberger, *Bearing the Witness*, ix.

in Birmingham during 1998 belong to that genre.[6] I will seek to honour the
Newbigin legacy by underscoring some important themes in his theology,
while also showing that his thinking was deficient at crucial points.

A BRIEF OUTLINE OF NEWBIGIN'S THEOLOGY

Newbigin was "a theologian by habit and a lifelong missionary by trade."[7]
His "trade" set down the parameters for his "habit" with the result that his
theology is both evangelical as well as orthodox. He attempted to present
an account of the Christian witness that does justice to the Christian story's
power to change the lives of individuals and societies. Newbigin's theology
was spoken from the church to the world: "Christian theology is a form
of rational discourse developed within the community which accepts the
primacy of this story and seeks actively to live in the world in accordance with
the story."[8] Unlike many evangelicals however Newbigin possessed a healthy
and forthright approach to social and political affairs. He recognized that the
church's vocation is to call and equip men and women to be signs and agents
of God's justice in all human affairs as well as to bring them into a personal
relationship with Jesus Christ: "An evangelism that invites men and women
to accept the name of Christ but fails to call them to this real encounter must
be rejected as false."[9] It was hardly surprising that one who sat under John
Maynard Keynes' feet at Cambridge (1930–31) later presented a powerful
critique of unbridled capitalism.[10] More than many, Newbigin was aware of
the need to do justice to both the vertical and horizontal dimensions of the
Christian gospel: "Evangelism which is politically and ideologically naive,
and social action which does not recognize the need for conversion from
false gods to the living God, both fall short of what is required."[11]

Others have already pointed out how remarkably consistent Newbigin's
theology was throughout his long career.[12] Only for the brief period
surrounding the publication of *Honest Religion for Secular Man* was there
any departure from the christocentric Trinitarianism for which he became
noted. His orthodoxy was underpinned by his grasp of what he called "the
central verities of the gospel" discernible from the canonical scriptures and

---

6. See Foust, *A Scandalous Prophet.*

7. Hunsberger, *Bearing the Witness,* 33.

8. Newbigin, *Gospel,* 152.

9. Newbigin, *Foolishness,* 133.

10. See Newbigin, *Foolishness,* 95–123 and Newbigin, *Gospel,* 198–210.

11. Newbigin, *Gospel,* 210.

12. See Wainwright, *Lesslie Newbigin,* 26 and Hunsberger, *Bearing the Witness,* 37.

the classical creeds.[13] Newbigin's theology therefore rests upon what amounts to a "canon within the canon" or something akin to the Irenaean "rule of faith"—a "story" which is read out of the Bible.[14] The Bible is authoritative for Newbigin because it is the source of *this* story. The story provides us with the "plausibility structure" (Kuhn) or "fiduciary framework" (Polanyi) upon which we can base our lives; it presents "a universal history" or "an outline of world history" for which the life, teaching, death, and resurrection of Jesus is the interpretive clue;[15] and it provides us with the unchanging heart of the Christian gospel. Familiar themes are covered by the story: creation, fall, election, redemption, and consummation. It concerns God's inexhaustible graciousness with men and women as well as human disobedience and intransigence. At its centre is "the absolute sovereignty of Jesus Christ"[16] and "the total fact of Jesus Christ."[17] This story is gospel: "the announcement that in the series of events that have their center in the life, ministry, death, and resurrection of Jesus Christ something has happened that alters the total human situation and must therefore call into question every human culture."[18] While Christianity may change through time, the gospel's substance remains unchanging. It is a dogma to be advanced and lived out.

Christian discipleship for Newbigin therefore is completely bound up with people "indwelling" this authoritative story.[19] Its starting point is "God's revelation of himself in Jesus Christ as this is testified in the Bible" rather than what contemporary culture might dictate.[20] With clear echoes of Karl Barth, Newbigin thus grounds his theology in a revelation which interprets the meaning, purpose, and destiny of life. Hence, "the gospel accepted in faith . . . enables us to experience all reality in a new way and to find that all reality does indeed reflect the glory of God."[21] This does not entail setting reason against revelation, but it does favor one "tradition of rational argument," namely, the gospel over and against the tradition of rational argument belonging to the contemporary secular spirit.[22]

---

13. Newbigin, *Gospel*, 139.

14. Newbigin, *Gospel*, 12.

15. See Newbigin, *Faith*, 46–53 and Newbigin, *Finality*, 65–87.

16. Newbigin, *Gospel*, 169.

17. See Newbigin, *Faith*, 57, 60 and Newbigin, *Foolishness*, 41. Newbigin also speaks of "a single happening . . . of decisive significance to all" (*Open Secret*, 57).

18. Newbigin, *Foolishness*, 3–4.

19. See Newbigin, *Gospel*, 97–99. See also Newbigin, *Truth*, 41–64 and Newbigin, *Proper Confidence*, 86–89.

20. Newbigin, *Honest Religion*, 42.

21. Newbigin, *Proper Confidence*, 96–97.

22. Newbigin, *Gospel*, 62.

Upon his return to England from India in 1974, Newbigin believed that he was encountering a terminally ill post-Christian culture: "Apart from those whose lives are shaped by the Christian hope founded on the resurrection of Jesus as the pledge of a new creation, there is little sign among the citizens of this country of the sort of confidence in the future which was certainly present in the earliest years of this century."[23] Later he was to lament: "In the closing decades of this century it is difficult to find Europeans who have any belief in a significant future which is worth working for and investing in."[24] Newbigin believed that he had encountered a society controlled by materialistic and utilitarian values, one that had lost a clear sense of purpose—a culture that "has proved bankrupt."[25] With the zeal of a latter-day Jeremiah he pointed to "a collapse of confidence in our culture" which reveals that we are facing nothing less than the death of "Western post-Enlightenment culture."[26] The philosophy of the Enlightenment has not proved capable of producing a worldview which holds culture together. All Newbigin experienced was shot through with fragmentation, with the twin evils of individualism and relativism rampant.

The plausibility structure of this ailing culture is "more than a body of ideas," Newbigin claims, since it is "a whole way of organizing human life that both rests on and in turn supports and validates the ideas" upon which Newtonian science came to be built, namely, nature understood in terms of the laws of cause and effect, with a utilitarian outlook squeezing out teleological concerns.[27] The power of reason in this philosophy can hardly be exaggerated: "No alleged divine revelation, no tradition however ancient, and no dogma however hallowed has the right to veto its exercise."[28] According to Newbigin, the resulting vision of the universe has no place for God. An atheistic outlook produces a pagan society which possesses a number of clearly discernible features due to its utilitarian emphasis. Newbigin points firstly to the way in which Western culture separates reality into "private" and "public" worlds, with religion belonging to the private domain and possessing no credibility when it enters the public realm in which Enlightenment pre-suppositions and thought hold sway. It follows secondly that religion trades in "values" while outside religion one enters the world of "facts": "The public world is a world of facts that are the same for everyone,

---

23. Newbigin, *Other Side*, l.

24. Newbigin, *Gospel*, 90.

25. Newbigin, *Gospel*, 191.

26. Newbigin, *Gospel*, 191.

27. Newbigin, *Foolishness,* 29.

28. Newbigin, *Foolishness*, 25.

whatever his values may be; the private world is a world of values where all are free to choose their own values and therefore to pursue such courses of action as will correspond with them."[29] The collective result of living on the basis of such dichotomies, Newbigin suggests, is that Western culture doesn't produce "enough nourishment for the human spirit" because it possesses no credible answers to the fundamentally important questions which are rooted in teleology and therefore cannot answer "the question, 'Why?'"[30]

Newbigin urges a return, first, to the vision of the Christian gospel provided by the Bible, and, secondly, to a religious outlook whose claims belong to the public domain. He calls us to live on the basis of God's self-revelation in Jesus, a story which not only brought the church into being but is to be shared with others. Western society needs converting—moving from living on the basis of a rationalistic frame of reference which has no place for the transcendent realm to living inside the Christian fiduciary framework. The Church has been given a tradition of understanding which once indwelt leads to life in all its fullness. While truth will therefore be discovered from inside the Church, it will only fully be known eschatologically when the promises contained within the normative story are made good. Christian truth cannot be demonstrated *a priori*. We are invited to place our faith in it, and then make it the foundation on which we understand and live out our lives. This act of faith however is not based simply upon personal opinion and, hence, merely subjective; rather, claims Newbigin, we make our act of faith with what Michael Polanyi calls "universal intent."[31] This carries with it the conviction that, "as the truth which is true for all," it must "be publicly affirmed, and opened to public interrogation and debate."[32]

With the grounds for evangelism thus established Newbigin invites us to live in Christian community confident that the Holy Spirit will give us a true understanding of history. That understanding, as we have seen, is rooted in a series of events concerning Jesus that make up the memory of which the church is the custodian. God has chosen and set apart the Church "to be the messengers of his truth and bearers of his love for all people."[33] To use Newbigin's typical expressions, she is called to be a "sign, instrument, and foretaste of God's purpose for all human culture"[34] and "a

29. Newbigin, *Foolishness*, 36.

30. Newbigin, *Gospel*, 213.

31. See Polanyi, *Personal Knowledge*. 308.

32. Newbigin, *Gospel*, 50.

33. Newbigin, *Gospel*, 85.

34. Newbigin, *Open Secret*, 163. See also Newbigin *Foolishness* , 124.

servant, witness, and sign of the kingdom,"[35] as well as "that community which bears the secret of the meaning of history through history."[36] But, as Newbigin never tires of making clear, this is an election to service rather than privileged status.[37] Christians are called to be "the bearers of the secret of his saving work for the sake of *all*."[38] No limits must be set to God's saving grace.

NEWBIGIN'S THEOLOGICAL LEGACY

Newbigin argues his position with remorseless vigor and absolute conviction. He writes with passion and lucidity. But what is the legacy of his theology? And where in the legacy is our contemporary theological understanding hindered rather than helped?

Ecclesiology

At a time when the Western mainstream churches are in numerical decline, and when many congregations lack vitality and a clear sense of their *raison d'être,* it is pertinent that we take to heart Newbigin's ecclesiology.

The Missionary Church

The following is a typical snapshot of Newbigin's ecclesial vision:

> The Church . . . has listened to the words 'Come unto me', but not listened to the words 'Go—and I am with you'. It has interpreted election as if it meant being chosen for special privilege in relation to God, instead of being chosen for special responsibility before God for other men. It has interpreted conversion as if it was simply a turning towards God for purposes of one's own private inner religious life, instead of seeing conversion as it is in the Bible, a turning towards God for the doing of his will in the secular world. It has understood itself more as an institution than as an exhibition. Its typical shape in the eyes of its own members as well as of those outside has been not a band of pilgrims who have heard the word 'Go', but a large and solid

35. Newbigin, *Foolishness*, 117.
36. Newbigin, *Gospel*, 77.
37. See Newbigin, *Gospel*, 80–88.
38. Newbigin, *Gospel*, 86. Italics mine.

building which, at its best, can only say 'Come', and at its worst says, all too clearly, 'Stay away'.[39]

Running throughout Newbigin's ecclesiology is the missionary context which provides the church with its proper shape. Like David Bosch, Newbigin knew that "Christianity is missionary by its very nature, or it denies its very *raison d'être*."[40] At a time when the word "mission" has been stolen by the secular world to enable organizations have a clear understanding of what they stand for, it is somewhat ironic that contemporary congregations by and large seem to have lost a clear sense of why they exist and what they are here to do. Instead of displaying evidence of being a sign and sacrament of God's love for the world they have come to resemble inward-looking, self-serving groups.

Part of Newbigin's legacy is that he has provided a mission statement for congregations who have lost their way and largely forgotten that they are chosen and sent to re-present God's way to people beyond their fellowships. So, in forthright fashion, Newbigin reminds us that "The church is a movement launched into the life of the world to bear in its own life God's gift of peace for the life of the world," and therefore that "It is sent . . . not only to proclaim the kingdom, but to bear in its own life the presence of the kingdom."[41] The primary task of the church is to engage in God's mission in, for, and with the world. This means that "the Church is not the source of the witness; rather, it is the locus of witness."[42] Newbigin was as dismissive of churches which totally involve themselves with this-worldly activities, as he was of those which exist solely for soul-saving. He believed that the church's essential activity centers upon channeling God's redeeming and emancipating love to individuals and society. The church therefore has been bequeathed an awesome task. What Jesus brought into the world was meant to continue through history in the shape of a community. The Church exists therefore to make history.[43]

Crucial to Newbigin's ecclesiology is the local congregation, the gathered out-cropping of the church in each place and time. When true to itself, the gathered church "derives its character not from its membership but from its Head, not from those who join it but from Him who calls it into being."[44] But since, like individuals, the church often falls short of its proper

39. Newbigin, *Honest Religion*, 101–102.
40. Bosch, *Transforming Mission*, 9.
41. Newbigin, *Open Secret*, 54.
42. Newbigin, *Gospel*, 120.
43. See Newbigin, *Gospel*, 131.
44. Newbigin, *Household*, 27–28.

calling, Newbigin accepts that "it is at once holy and sinful"[45] and, hence, *simul justus et peccator* (both justified and sinner).[46] He recognizes the divine vulnerability and risk involved in God choosing "a sinful community . . . a weak, divided, and unsuccessful community," to be the sign, embodiment, and foretaste of the Kingdom.[47] And the church clearly has no grounds for boasting, since repeatedly she has failed to live up to her calling; yet she retains that great calling and continues to have responsibilities through her often weak local gatherings.

Newbigin stressed the importance of the local gathered church at precisely the time when in Britain at least the congregation is under great threat. In the era of "believing without belonging,"[48] placing our faith and hope in local congregations might seem akin to Jeremiah's mid-summer missionary madness in buying the field at Anathoth (Jer.32), but it is difficult to envisage a future for Christianity without the "local . . . public and shared Christianity" which they represent.[49] In a way that Newbigin would have endorsed, Haddon Willmer has made an invigorating plea that the significance of the local congregation should not be underestimated. As he says, "In an increasingly punitively minded culture, divided between self-affirming people and those who are "taken out of society," congregations are places where we learn and witness to the saving and fragile way of being our true selves, in confessing sin and living by undeserved gift."[50] Nevertheless, congregations often are parochial places where the vitality of the world church hardly ever penetrates and a close group of like-minded people become isolated through their independency. It was to Newbigin's credit that he had the insight to recognize that a sound ecclesiology required not only a Protestant stress on the true church always being present in the local, covenanting community gathered around Word and Sacraments, but also the more Catholic emphases upon the church as a continuing historical institution. The idea that the church is a recurrently, repeated event constituted ever anew when local congregations assemble under Word and around the Table requires a further ecclesial vision which gives due attention to "the continuing life of the Church as one fellowship binding the generations together in Christ."[51] Newbigin's ecclesiology was

---

45. Newbigin, *Household,* 56.

46. Newbigin, *Household,* 29.

47. Newbigin, *Open Secret,* 59–60.

48. See Davie, *Religion in Britain.*

49. See Willmer, "Collapse of Congregations," 258–59.

50. Willmer, "Collapse of Congregations," 260.

51. Newbigin, *Household,* 50.

commendably balanced, spanning different traditions and emphases in ecumenically helpful ways.

The Ecumenical Church

Newbigin's ecumenical convictions were central to his theological vision and rooted in his belief that a divided church cannot heal a divided world. In *The Household of God* he laid out a principle which he followed throughout his life: "we cannot be [Christ's] ambassadors reconciling the world to God, if we have not ourselves been willing to be reconciled to one another."[52] Everything hinges of course on what we mean by "to be reconciled to one another." Newbigin was forthright and clear: it meant visible unity. A divided church is "a direct and public contradiction of the Gospel" and the substitution of "some partial and sectional message" for "the good news of the one final and sufficient atoning act wrought in Christ for the whole human race."[53]

The quest for church unity thus became a passion for Newbigin who argued that faithfulness to Christ required Christians to seek unity with each other. There can only ever be one body of Christians if the New Testament view of the Church as "the body of Christ" is taken with absolute seriousness. It is a matter of the greatest priority therefore that the Church recovers its "true nature and quality of . . . life as the visible fellowship of all who in every place call upon the name of the Lord Jesus."[54] Newbigin was as unhappy about divided denominations as he was about models of Church unity which remain content with the "reconciled diversity" strategy of federalism.[55] Nevertheless, he did not strive for any bland, monochrome uniformity. The following statement is typical of Newbigin's position:

> Properly speaking, the Church . . . should therefore have as much variety as the human race itself. Nothing human should be alien to it save sin. The very vastness of its diversity held together by the single fact of Christ's atonement for the whole human race should be the witness to the sufficiency of that atonement. It should confront man with no sectional or local society, no segregation of people having similar tastes and temperaments and traditions, but simply as the congregation of humanity

---

52. Newbigin, *Household*, 18.

53. Newbigin, *Household*, 149–50.

54. Newbigin, *Household*, 107.

55. See Newbigin, *Foolishness*, 144–46.

redeemed, as the family to which every man rightly belongs and from which only sin can sever him.[56]

As "a home for people of all nations and a sign of the unity of all" the church will only possess complete credibility when amidst a healthy diversity it speaks and acts in unison.[57] Newbigin knew that full well: "Splintered, confused, and compromised, the Church seldom sounds worth listening to."[58] His ecumenical commitment arose from his missionary mandate.

The Vocation of the Whole People of God

Finally, Newbigin very helpfully saw the church's role as equipping its members for their vocations in society (Eph. 4: 12). He affirmed the laity, maintaining that it is the job of ministers to enable and empower lay-people in their responsibilities in and for society. He never lost sight of the fact that the primary missionary location is daily life. The emphasis in his ecclesiology upon the gathered church is matched therefore by an equal stress upon the dispersed church. Believers must be prepared to live as a Christian counter-culture in the secular world, making what they stand for publicly heard and revealing a Christ-like disposition in their commitments and actions. This led Newbigin to a healthy view of lay-ministry, in general, and non-stipendiary ministry, in particular—"exercised by men who continued to fulfil their secular callings" not because there might be a shortage of paid ministers but "out of respect to the missionary character of the Church."[59] In a typically Reformed fashion, Newbigin consequently expected lay-people to have an uncommon degree of theological literacy[60] to equip them to fulfil their "subversive" role as Christ's "undercover agents" in society.[61] Meanwhile, Newbigin rightly bemoaned the way professional ministers are often prepared for their work, maintaining that it involves "far too much training for the pastoral care of existing congregations" and too little orientation "toward the missionary calling to claim the whole of public life for Christ and his kingdom."[62] It would be interesting to know whether the more recent contextual approaches to ministerial preparation have adequately addressed his concerns.

56. Newbigin, *Faith*, 82.

57. Newbigin, *Gospel*, 124.

58. Newbigin, *Truth*, 90.

59. Newbigin, *Honest Religion*, 114.

60. See Newbigin, *Foolishness*, 143.

61. Newbigin, *Truth*, 82–83.

62. Newbigin, *Gospel*, 231.

Missiology

A further aspect of Newbigin's theological legacy is found in his missiology. His proposals cut across approaches which appear modeled on commercial sales drives or military campaigns. In particular, he is sharply critical of the Pelagian tendency that regards conversion as a human achievement. A great deal of contemporary mission focuses so much on strategies, techniques, and head-counting that Newbigin fears it is not sufficiently directed by "the greatness and majesty and sufficiency of God."[63] Authentic mission arises out of a spontaneous response of joy and gratitude for what God has achieved in the Christ event. At its heart is "thanksgiving and praise,"[64] a natural outpouring "that cannot possibly be suppressed";[65] it is distorted when reduced to outreach activities aimed at prolonging the church's existence.[66] Not surprisingly, Newbigin provides us with a significant and perceptive critique of the Church Growth Movement.[67]

Central to Newbigin's missiology is the free and unpredictable activity of the Holy Spirit. It follows that the church must never suppose that it is the *agent* of mission. The church's responsibility is to tell the Christian story faithfully, forthrightly, and attractively; whether people respond is out of its hands. As Newbigin insists, "It is the Spirit who brings about conversion, the Spirit who equips those who are called with the gifts needed for all the varied forms of ministry, and the Spirit who guides the church into all the truth."[68] The individual who encounters the gospel must be allowed the opportunity to say, "No!" Coercion corrupts the message it seeks to propagate; human glory then usurps mission's proper goal: the glory of God.

Newbigin believes that mission is "the entire task for which the Church is sent into the world."[69] In so far as the Church has been chosen to live out as well as tell the Christian story, mission involves both performance and declaration. It is dialogical in nature, thus carrying with it the likelihood that the missionary church may learn things from the culture within which it operates. It is even possible that the missionary encounter will enable the church to get a firmer grasp of the gospel's richness. So Newbigin wisely challenges the arrogance and dogmatism of many missionary approaches

---

63. Newbigin, *Gospel,* 243.

64. Newbigin, *Gospel,* 127.

65. Newbigin, *Gospel,* 116.

66. See Newbigin, *Open Secret,* 66.

67. See Newbigin, *Open Secret,* 135–180.

68. Newbigin, *Open Secret,* 146.

69. Newbigin, *Gospel,* 121.

when he warns that "mission will not only be a matter of preaching and teaching but also of learning."[70] But however hard he tries to paper over the cracks opened up by some of the ruthless destruction of indigenous cultures by past missionary work, Newbigin on occasions still uses language which undermines the sensitive approach to mission he elsewhere advocates, e.g. "the invading culture"[71] as well as "assault" and "warfare."[72] "'Dialogue" or "conversation" is a more helpful model for understanding mission.

Newbigin is at his best though when he defines the Christian mission as "an acting out of a fundamental belief and, at the same time, a process in which this belief is being constantly reconsidered in the light of the experience of acting it out in every sector of human affairs and in dialogue with every other pattern of thought by which men and women seek to make sense of their lives."[73] But it is a moot point to what extent he is open in practice to genuine two-way conversion given the virtually non-negotiable understanding he has of Christian believing and his abhorrence of anything which even hints at syncretism. The sole reason why he seems to urge us to share the gospel in the language and idioms of our working context would appear to involve making its challenge to that context relevant. What he calls 'dialogue' often seems to be little more than monologue.

Newbigin's understanding of the church's mission contains three elements: bearing witness to Christ and possessing the Christ-like shape befitting the Christian counter-culture; corporate witness to society in service and evangelism; and the exercise by church members of their individual vocations in society. It is a holistic view which helpfully holds together not only the individual and corporate dimensions of the Christian task but also the so-called "horizontal" and "vertical" planes of Christian discipleship. The contemporary church would be wise to use it as the yardstick by which to judge its own endeavors.

Epistemology

If the social and political dimension of individualism is what Francis Maude has described as "weakest to the wall, law of the jungle, everyone for himself, no such thing as society,"[74] its religious aspect involves the assumption that all religions are similar, culture-bound means by which people deal with

70. Newbigin, *Gospel*, 118.

71. Newbigin, *Open Secret*, 166.

72. Newbigin, *Gospel*, 238.

73. Newbigin, *Open Secret*, 31.

74. *Daily Telegraph*, 8 October 2002.

their personal awareness of transcendence. As such, the various Faiths are equally valid, each putting forward claims granted truth status within their particular religious circle. But since religions deal solely with transcendence they should not be involved in public debates concerning the temporal affairs. The faith-claims of religion thus belong to the private rather than the public realm.

Newbigin's critique of the privatization of religion takes him back to Cartesian dualism and the bifurcation of reality into facts and values. While he hardly gives full credit for what this philosophical revolution bequeathed to the West, Newbigin correctly objects to religious claims being deposited in the private domain of values rather than the public arena of facts. Individualism's consignment of faith-claims and religious values to the private realm neither does justice to their metaphysical dimension nor to the way in which they claim universal intent.

> The church witnesses to that true end for which all creation and all human beings exist, the truth by which all alleged values are to be judged. And truth must be public truth, truth for all. A private truth for a limited circle of believers is no truth at all. Even the most devout faith will sooner or later falter and fail unless those who hold it are willing to bring it into public debate and to test it against experience in every area of life.[75]

In so far as Christianity makes universal claims in its proclamation of Jesus Christ as the Savior of the world, and views the life, witness, death, and resurrection of Jesus as having cosmic significance, Newbigin's opposition to Western society's demotion of religion to the world of opinion is valid and welcome.

It is very easy to see why Western society wishes to consign religions to the private domain when we consider the damage they have wrought in the public sphere. Polly Toynbee for example not only thinks that we are often the victims of "the over-valuation of religion," but she also maintains that "religion is not nice, it kills: it is toxic in the places where people really believe it."[76] Indeed, she passionately believes that "religion belongs to the personal, never in the public sphere" and, on the basis of a horrendous bill of indictment, presses us to confront religion—the very opposite of Newbigin's strategy of confronting Western culture with the Christian gospel. Faced with such a powerful argument, Newbigin's commitment to "going public" with Christianity will only be carried through credibly if we recognize the evils which have emanated from past missionary activity. While Newbigin

75. Newbigin, *Foolishness*, 117.

76. *Guardian*, 6 September 2002.

correctly reminds Christianity's critics that the Church is no different to individuals in being both justified as well as sinner this side of eternity, and is also right to point out that at its best the spread of Christianity brought with it recognizable benefits, we never really sense that he owned the less wholesome results of missionary endeavor and Christian activity. Three points emerge from this observation. First, Newbigin's argument concerning the public nature of the Christian gospel is in danger of becoming a fresh form of Christian imperialism. Secondly, in the midst of shocking historical evidence, all future Christian mission needs to start not only by recognizing its past errors and asking God's forgiveness for them but also with what Michael Taylor has called a "degree of astonishment that, if the gospel is as strong as a prophet like Newbigin suggests, after two thousand years of missionary endeavor, after Christendom, the Enlightenment, and modernity, it still leaves a divided, violent, and ambiguous world at much the same moral and spiritual level as it was."[77] If "by your fruits you will be known" is as reliable a criterion for Christian adequacy as the Bible makes out, it could be that the roots of the West's current disillusionment with mainline Christianity have less to do with the atheistic machinations of Descartes and Enlightenment thinking but rather more to do with the gap which has opened up between theory and practice in Christianity. We must do justice to the crucial sense in which going public with Christianity is not just a declaratory but also a performatory matter. Recognition of the requirement "to do the truth" is crucial in our society if those commentators are correct who tell us that contemporary people are not just looking for a rational case for believing so much as evidence that belief positively alters people's lives and leads to the world being a much better place. Thirdly, if our attempt to make the gospel public in our plural society is to gain a positive hearing, then it will necessitate what Lynne Price has called "a more reciprocal, dialogical relationship with the life of the world."[78] However much Newbigin claimed to be open to new truth and fresh insights,[79] his public utterances and many writings increasingly revealed an exceedingly dogmatic disposition. Indeed, he often showed precious little evidence of his position being open to modification in any way.

Newbigin adopts the Augustinian slogan "*credo ut intelligam*" (I believe in order to understand) and follows Polanyi's thesis that all knowledge is irreducibly personal, to argue that the starting point of all enquiry lies in affirmations which cannot be questioned but must be held in faith. All

---

77. Taylor, "Afterward," 242.

78. Price, "Churches and Postmodernity," 109.

79. See Newbigin, *Truth*, 34–35.

investigation has to start on the basis of things which have to be taken as read. It follows that our critical facilities are not primary. They only ever become active on the basis of what we hold on trust: "What is primary is the act of attending and receiving, and this is an action of faith."[80] As far as Newbigin is concerned therefore "the active principle in the advance of knowledge . . . is faith."[81] In the process of knowing validation only comes at the end, so Newbigin's position not only involves the claim that "our most fundamental beliefs cannot be demonstrated but are held by faith"[82] but also necessitates a direct recourse to a kind of eschatological verification when those beliefs are questioned. Validation, he tells us, can only ever arrive "as the outcome of this process of exploration."[83] Needless to say, Newbigin is confident that the Christian "fiduciary framework" which is the basis for the Christian pilgrimage will not be found wanting: "we expect to find, and we do find, that the initial faith is confirmed, strengthened, and enlarged as we go on through life."[84]

What is the content of the fiduciary framework which Newbigin invites us to take on trust? He is quite clear that it is not "a set of beliefs that arise, or could arise, from empirical observation of the whole human experience."[85] What has to be taken on faith is "the announcement of a name and a fact that offer the starting point for a new and life-long enterprise of understanding and coping with experience,"[86] nothing less than "the revelation of God in Jesus Christ.."[87] Christian theology can proceed rationally then only on the basis that this revelation is received in faith. It follows that "commitment to Jesus Christ" is Newbigin's "point of entry" into a theological investigation.[88]

Few would want to deny that all investigations proceed upon the basis of things taken for granted. It is rather difficult for example to conceive how science could operate without the prior assumption that the universe is both contingent and rational. However, Newbigin puts matters on a somewhat different plane when he argues that people should take as read the fiduciary framework of the church, making that the lens through which to observe and understand reality. This quickly becomes obvious when one compares

---

80. Newbigin, *Other Side*, 20.

81. Newbigin, *Honest Religion*, 84. See also Newbigin, *Gospel*, 243.

82. Newbigin, *Other Side*, 27

83. Newbigin, *Finality*, 63.

84. Newbigin, *Gospel*, 243.

85. Newbigin, *Foolishness*, 148

86. Newbigin, *Foolishness*, 148.

87. Newbigin, *Finality*, 22.

88. Newbigin, *Finality*, 21.

the content of what he regards as the given fiduciary framework with, say, the "faith" that is presupposed by all scientific endeavor. The following is a list of beliefs which Newbigin would have us accept on the basis of the testimony of others: (i) Jesus as the Word of God incarnate;[89] (ii) the bodily resurrection of Jesus from the tomb on the first Easter morning;[90] (iii) the Ascension;[91] (iv) the Second Coming;[92] (v) an objective atonement wrought in the Cross of Christ;[93] (vi) a consummation of history which reveals the proper meaning of salvation in history's goal[94] and will involve the Millennium;[95] and by no means least (vii) the doctrine of the Trinity.[96] In other words, Newbigin expects people to take as given or accept in faith just about the entire pattern of orthodox Christian believing. That particular expectation is of a different order, say, to the scientists' trust in the contingency and rationality of the universe. It involves accepting several doctrines which on reasonable grounds other Christians have questioned or even chosen to jettison. Newbigin's strategy thus turns out to be little less than putting his own chosen understanding of the content of Christian believing beyond debate. In spite of all his talk about processes of investigation or journeys of exploration his theology is rooted in take it or leave it dogmas.

The question thus arises concerning the grounds that people have for adopting the Christian fiduciary framework. Many of the beliefs Newbigin views as essential "givens" only ought to be accepted after reasonable consideration has been given to them. What has happened is that, conveniently for his theological methodology, Newbigin has turned Polanyi's understanding of faith (*viz* accepted understandings that constitute what he calls "tacit" knowing) into his particular biblical understanding of faith. As Thomas Foust has argued, faith thus becomes "a misnomer," since it means

---

89. See Newbigin, *Household*, 113; *Open Secret*, 17; and *Foolishness*, 90.

90. Time and again, Newbigin asserts belief in the empty tomb as the fulcrum of the Christian world-view. See Newbigin, *Household*, 114, 119, 136; *Faith*, 44, 56–61; *Gospel*, 11–12, 108; *Truth*, 10–11; and *Proper Confidence*, 77.

91. Newbigin, *Household*, 114.

92. Newbigin opines that no theology which is bound to the Scriptures and the Creeds can formally deny faith in Christ's coming again. See Newbigin, *Household*, 82, 126, 129–134; and *Gospel*, 102, 121.

93. See Newbigin, *Household*, 115–118, 150; *Faith*, 54, 70–71; *Open Secret*, 27, 56; and *Foolishness*, 123, 126.

94. See Newbigin, *Household* 137; *Finality*, 60–61; *Open Secret*, 118–119; and *Gospel*, 87, 101, 110.

95. See Newbigin, *Finality*, 86

96. See Newbigin, *Open Secret*, 28–30; *Foolishness*, 90; and *Truth*, 17.

different things for Polanyi and Newbigin.[97] Nor will it do for Newbigin to make out that Augustine is the out and out fideist he would like him to be. Foust continues:

> . . . not only is there difficulty between Polanyi's and Newbigin's concepts of faith, but Newbigin and Polanyi are also presenting an incomplete understanding of Augustine on this point. Augustine did not assert that there is no knowledge without faith. He held that a certain amount of rational evidence for Christ is necessary before one believes, but after one believes it, one can go on to find new reasons to believe. Augustine is a moderate fideist and not a fideist as Newbigin and Polanyi suggest.[98]

In short, Newbigin's view is based upon a significant misunderstanding of Augustine, an error shared by Michael Polanyi, the philosopher of science to whom Newbigin turns when advocating his brand of fideism. Reason has a more fundamental part to play in Christian theology than Newbigin ever allows. While, to some extent, all verification must look to the end of the adventure of knowledge, waiting the time when any falsification of our ideas and theories has finally emerged, it is important that our substantive ideas and theories are based upon more than blind faith at the outset of our explorations. Otherwise we provide folk with a license to believe anything, however fanciful it might be.

Newbigin's confidence in Christianity's fiduciary framework was ultimately unshakeable—even if in a plural world we might have expected Christian attitudes to involve what Price calls "faithful uncertainty"[99] or David Tracy describes as knowing with "relative adequacy."[100] Such intellectual hesitancy was dismissed by Newbigin since, for him, it represented the weakness of liberal theology: "The mind open at both ends admits everything but finally holds nothing."[101] But living in a dialogical engagement with fellow Christians and those of other Faiths or none does not necessitate total agnosticism. Contrary to Newbigin's fears, "a pluralist or relativist . . . can have firm convictions and commitment"; hence *everything* is never up for grabs.[102]

---

97. See Foust, "Lesslie Newbigin's Epistemology," 155.

98. See Foust, "Lesslie Newbigin's Epistemology," 156–157.

99. Price, "Churches and Postmodernity," 110.

100. Tracy, *Plurality*, 22.

101. Newbigin, "A Decent Debate about Doctrine," 12.

102. Taylor, "Postscript," 241.

Gospel and Culture

A fourth area in Newbigin's theological legacy concerns the impetus he provided for a radical discussion concerning the relationship between the Christian gospel and contemporary Western culture. Newbigin's analysis of Western culture is overly simplistic, arguably based rather more upon his prior theological predilection than a convincing understanding of the empirical realities on display. His depiction of the West, shaped as it has been by the Enlightenment and moving through its modernist to postmodernist phase, is nothing short of apocalyptic. He argues that there has been a "collapse of confidence in the great project of the Enlightenment."[103] As early as 1961 he was announcing the disintegration of Western culture,[104] a theme that became ever more pronounced in his later writings.[105] Newbigin believed that there are signs that Western culture is heading for "impending death";[106] he observed what he believed was "systematic scepticism";[107] and he concurred with a Chinese philosopher who could only find "bleak nihilism and hopelessness . . . reflected in the literature, art, and drama of our society."[108] Words like "relativism," "pluralism," "individualism," and "narcissism" were regularly used by Newbigin to describe Western culture's plight as he advanced a case for a Christian missionary encounter with the West. He believed that we have lost a sense of direction, a pattern of purposefulness which can only be provided by Christian eschatology. A utilitarian outlook has now largely robbed the West of any worthwhile teleological frame of reference,[109] and only hope generated by the fact that "the crucified Lord of history has risen from the dead and will come in glory" will restore confidence to our culture.[110] As he put in *The Household of God*:

> Hope in the Christian sense is no mere human longing for an uncertain future. It is rooted in the life of God himself and founded on His own promises. It is the echo in our hearts, given to us by the Spirit, of that mind which was in Jesus who for the joy that was set before Him endured the Cross, despising the

---

103. Newbigin, *Proper Confidence*, 33.

104. Newbigin, *Faith*, 15.

105. See Newbigin, *Proper Confidence*, 102.

106. Newbigin, *Proper Confidence*, 35.

107. Newbigin, *Gospel*, 28. See also Newbigin, *Proper Confidence*, 76.

108. Newbigin, *Proper Confidence*, 47.

109. Newbigin, *Foolishness*, 34–41.

110. Newbigin, *Gospel*, 101.

shame. It is an anchor of the soul, a hope sure and steadfast and
entering into that which is within the veil. The future is really
future, and we long for it.[111]

Given Newbigin's theological presuppositions, *whatever* world we might
happen to live in this side of eternity inevitably is bound to "lieth in the
evil one."[112]

The impression sometimes given is that Newbigin, a saintly and
theologically wise Bishop, returned to Britain upon his retirement, where,
reading "the signs of the times," he prophetically announced that Western
culture was terminally ill on the basis of what he saw, but that might
claim too much for the man's insight, while it hardly does justice to the
way Newbigin's theological standpoint led him to a pejorative view of
the empirical evidence. One of the major reasons why he came to such a
negative view about Western culture lies in the theology clearly displayed in
The Household of God (1953). This thinking provides him with the lens with
which to view the British scene. He adheres to the Augustinian—Calvinist—
Barthian wing of Reformed theology, thus holding a perception of salvation
rooted in the world's absolute need for an atoning act by which God can
forgive a fallen race. Great stress in this theological scheme is placed on
the total depravity of human beings, with a resulting skepticism about all
human worth and achievement becoming rather inevitable. "Hope," in this
outlook, is essentially otherworldly since nothing in this world is of *real*
worth. What, however, if we use as our lens another theological outlook,
one which has its origins in Irenaeus (and interestingly partly shaped the
theological outlook of John Oman, Newbigin's College Principal and one of
his theological teachers)? What if the human predicament is not so much
a fall from perfection to a state of alienation from God but alternatively is
conceived as being concerned with the ups and downs of immature people,
who born in "the image of God," are on a journey towards becoming in
"the likeness of God"? Salvation could then be envisaged as a gradual
transformation of life which can occur when people make an ongoing
response to God's graciousness towards them. Lest this alternative view is
seen to involve a doctrine of necessary and inevitable progress for individuals
and the human race, we ought to emphasize that on the earthly pilgrimage
we can progress to hell as much as to heaven. Affirming the possibilities of
being human and the value of the temporal order need not entail going soft
on sin. The point to be made is this: Newbigin's understanding of Western
culture is arguably largely dependent upon the theological framework he

111. Newbigin, *Household*, 122–123.

112. Newbigin, *Household*, 79.

brings with him. Adopt a different framework and one need not arrive at the unnecessarily pessimistic and apocalyptic assessment of modern culture for which Newbigin became somewhat notorious.

Newbigin's obituary note on Western culture seems somewhat premature, even after the world shaping implications of 9/11. Was he hankering after a by-gone age which was actually less wholesome than is usually painted? Perhaps unwittingly he never totally liberated himself from the Christendom mentality which fuelled so much missionary activity? We will perhaps never fully know why he presented such an unnuanced account of Western culture and left himself open to criticism by those who came to regard him as a backwoodsman intent on affirming a plausibility structure that had its less wholesome elements and turned out to be oppressive for millions. I read The *Other Side of 1984* in one sitting after visiting two church members in hospital. Both had one thing in common, namely, they were still alive due to the medical science made possible by the same Enlightenment so savagely under attack in what I was reading. In fairness to Newbigin, he was prepared to acknowledge our indebtedness to the fruits of the Enlightenment.[113] He gratuitously admits that the "'light' in the Enlightenment was real light"[114] as well as opines that "No one, surely, can fail to acknowledge with gratitude the achievements of this period of human history."[115] He also displays a willingness to acknowledge that God may actually be at work in "secularist and anti-religious movements."[116] But it is actually very difficult to believe all this when wading through his exceedingly anti-Enlightenment, anti-science, and anti-technology polemics. Whatever happened to the even-handedness which accepted that "The triumph of secularization is certainly not the triumph of the Kingdom of God; but neither is it simply the work of the devil"?[117] Only a very narrow and otherworldly eschatology can prompt the following claim: "Almost everything in the 'plausibility structure' which is the habitation of our society seems to contradict . . . Christian hope."[118] Perhaps the qualifier "almost" provides some room to contain the celebrations of my two church members concerning the success of their medical treatment? Be that as it may, Newbigin repeatedly failed to recognize fully that however much the Enlightenment (and, hence, science) is responsible for many of our

113. Newbigin, *Other Side*, 16.

114. Newbigin, *Foolishness*, 43.

115. Newbigin, *Gospel*, 223.

116. Newbigin, *Faith*, 46.

117. Newbigin, *Honest Religion*, 29.

118. Newbigin, *Gospel*, 232.

contemporary ills, we will most certainly need it to provide some of the resources to achieve their healing.

Contrary to Newbigin, the ethos ushered in by the Enlightenment still has a great deal of life in it. As Michael Goheen has suggested, its view of freedom is a gain that must not be lost—although it is not scriptural.[119] Far from being a "wicked witch" seeking to undermine Christianity an argument can be put forward to suggest the reverse. Andrew Walls for example maintains that "there was a Christian appropriation of the Enlightenment which was not all a betrayal of Christian faith."[120] The Enlightenment actually provided the "world" in which Western Christianity became culturally appropriated, thereby enabling Christianity to be credible in that world. While Newbigin untiringly insisted that theology must be appropriate to the biblical story, he was opposed to finding the kind of rapprochement with culture that often enables the gospel to be heard credibly. Rather ironically, it is only through the very process of syncretism he loathed that Christianity has repeatedly re-invented itself and thus remained alive.

CONCLUSION

The purpose of this essay has been to explore the theological legacy Lesslie Newbigin has bequeathed to us. Whichever way readers feel the balance of judgment needs to fall on Newbigin's theology, it is a sign of a thinker's greatness that they leave behind a significant debate about issues that were a lifetime concern. Whether we are one of Newbigin's doting disciples or a member of the extensive group of his critical interlocutors really does not ultimately matter. The *real* Newbigin legacy has been that he has made us all think theologically about confessing Christ in the modern world. For that we can be most thankful.

---

119. Goheen, "The Missional Calling of Believers in the World," 48.
120. Walls, "Enlightenment, Postmodernity and Mission," 150.

5

Whatever Happened To Theology?

THE BURDEN OF THIS chapter resides in my passionate belief that the church's nature and practice ought to be anchored in sound theology. After pointing out how central theology was to the emergence of early Christianity I offer a brief account of my understanding of theology's nature and task. The reason for writing the paper which now forms this chapter was a deep concern about the way URC congregations known to me seldom seem to engage in critical reflection on their life and witness, a surprising tendency when most of them are having to cope with exponential numerical decline. Surely in such grave circumstances we might expect more theological analysis of the church's position, problems, and possibilities? I offer some reasons for this sin of omission—but they are not unique to the URC. At a time of crisis in Western Christianity *all* the churches need to return to the theological drawing board.

THE CENTRALITY OF THEOLOGY IN THE EVOLUTION OF EARLY CHRISTIANITY.

When we read the New Testament we eavesdrop on some of the theological conversations in the early Christian congregations, and particularly we get an insight into the minds of some of the formative Christian pioneers. We discover the significance Jesus had for different Christian communities as they tell their story about Jesus in the gospel narratives, those "perspectival" discourses which seek "to articulate a living memory for the present and the future;"[1] we unearth examples of primitive Christian liturgies—baptismal creeds, communion prayers, and congregational hymns, early stages of the journey which led to the rich diversity of worship within Christianity; we encounter Christians grappling with what it means to be a distinctive community of people shaped by the Spirit of Jesus, when challenged by a prevailing culture in which there *were* divisions between Jew and Greek, slave and free, men and women (Gal.3: 28), and at a time when witnessing to God's reign over all things was dangerously subversive and contrary to Caesar's claim to rule over the lives of the Empire's many citizens. "Give to the emperor the things that are the emperor's, and to God the things that are God's," Jesus had said somewhat ironically, all his followers knowing full well that nothing ultimately belongs to Caesar, except Caesar's perverse plans and Draconian deeds (see Mark 12: 13–17 and parallels).

By doing theology the early churches grew more sophisticated in faith, developed their congregational life, and generated distinctive practices based on clear ethical principles. As we experience the theological process taking place we are reminded that we do most justice to the New Testament when we return to it ever anew to engage with what James Barr has referred to as "the classic sources for the expression of Jesus and of God."[2] Instead of getting caught up defending claims of biblical authority based upon notions of "inspiration" and "inerrancy," we can revere the Bible for more pragmatic reasons: it is our sole access to the foundational events of Christianity, and it sets those events in the context of the religious traditions out of which they arose. We hear from the New Testament the testimony of the early witnesses to Jesus. That testimony arose from theological reflection which drove them forward to fresh understandings of faith and practice. This testimony of course is not *archetypal* for us. It is far from ever being "an ideal form that establishes an unchanging timeless pattern . . . or principle"[3] but it does offer us a *prototype*, or given the diversity of the New Testament witness we are perhaps on safer ground to speak of *prototypes*—patterns and principles which are "critically open to the possibility of [their] own transformation."[4] Theology therefore is as much concerned with the living and hence developing history of the community called church as it is with discovering its continuing theological identity. It becomes the means

---

1. Fiorenza, *In Memory*, xxii.
2. Barr, *Bible in the Modern World*, 118.
3. Fiorenza, *In Memory*, 33.
4. Fiorenza, *In Memory*, 33.

by which the church reconfigures itself to meet the opportunities and challenges of different times and places.

In his very influential book, *The First Urban Christians,* Wayne Meeks notes that "Urban society in the early Roman Empire was scarcely less complicated than our own," and he suggests that "Its complexity . . . may well have been felt with special acuteness by people who were marginal or transient, either physically or socially or both."[5] The Apostle Paul and the other Christian pioneers clearly worked hard at creating "a new social reality" called the *ekklesia* which included those who were "marginal" and "transient."[6] They developed counter-cultural communities rooted in a belief system which outstripped its rivals in breadth and vision. The church did not drop ready-made from the sky; it was created through trial and error as the early Christians in obedience to God sought a praxis which was appropriate to their memory of Jesus and credible in their society.

Rodney Stark argues that "What Rome . . . achieved was political unity at the expense of cultural chaos."[7] Not surprisingly this state of affairs generated a culture of spiritual yearning, as men and women weighed down by life's uncertainties searched for meaning and hope in their lives. Christianity was one of several religious options to which they could turn.[8] Through the close but open networks created by extended families, trade encounters, and social contacts, Christianity spread as church members invited their relations, friends, neighbors, and business contacts to join the *ekklesia*.

Christianity was successful for a number of reasons, all of which would not have held firm without theological underpinning. First, its major doctrines enabled Christianity "to be among the most sweeping and successful revitalization movements in history."[9] Rather than being abstract ideas remote from worldly realities, Christian doctrines are rooted in real life, guiding personal ethics, and driving social action. Secondly, Christianity was encountered through the members of communities whose love of God was matched by their love of one another and those beyond the church. Jack T. Sanders notes that "Christians excelled at caring for their own."[10] They also would come close to the ill when others remained at a distance. As Stark puts it:

5. Meeks, *First Urban Christians,* 104.

6. Meeks, *First Urban Christians,* 104.

7. Stark, *Rise of Christianity,* 144.

8. See Sanders, *Charisma,* 120–1.

9. Stark, *Rise of Christianity,* 211.

10. Sanders, *Charisma,* 135.

... because Christians were expected to aid the less fortunate, many of them received such aid, and all could feel greater security against bad times. Because they were asked to nurse the sick and dying, many of them received such nursing. Because they were asked to love others, they in turn were loved. And if Christians were required to observe a far more restrictive moral code than that observed by pagans, Christians—especially women—enjoyed a far more secure family life.[11]

Christianity as a result generated a worldview which endowed human beings with dignity, respect, and worth. As Stark puts it, "Christianity brought a new conception of humanity to a world saturated with capricious cruelty and vicarious love of death."[12] A third reason for Christianity's success was that in a world surrounded by death it offered hope, Sanders reminds us that

there is no evidence in early Christian literature that the longings that led people to become Christians were prompted by urban misery; so we need to remind ourselves just what it was that Christianity did offer. It did not offer cleaner or safer streets, better sanitation, or freedom from earthquake, fire, famine, and pestilence. What it offered was eternal life.[13]

Early Christianity had a rugged eschatology to match its vision for humanity. Nevertheless, fourthly, the inclusive attitudes and generosity of spirit found within the early house churches became a means by which some of the most acute problems besetting contemporary urban communities could be resolved. Christianity provided norms and values for community which helped address many contemporary ills. What the early Christian pioneers put in place was not just a new urban religious movement but what Stark refers to as "a *new culture* capable of making life in Greco-Roman cities more tolerable."[14] Particularly significant in the "new culture" was its counter to prevailing patriarchy through the way in which women were given equal places in the membership and leadership of the church.[15] Christianity was attractive to women because within the church women enjoyed

11. Stark, *Rise of Christianity*, 188.

12. Stark, *Rise of Christianity*, 214.

13. Sanders, *Charisma*, 152.

14. Stark, *Rise of Christianity*, 162.

15. See Fiorenza, *In Memory of Her* for an account of the way in which women played important roles in the earliest Christian churches. And, as Stark says, "there is virtual consensus among historians of the early church as well as biblical scholars that women held positions of honour and authority within early Christianity" (*Rise of Christianity*, 109).

higher status than in the surrounding patriarchal culture. The church by condemning infanticide and coerced abortion overcame some of the means by which women were abused in a male dominated world. Christian women gained greater marital security and equality through church membership. In its earliest days of course "Christianity was primarily a household phenomenon, all churches being house churches; and there women had traditional leadership roles."[16] Finally, Christianity was successful due to "its cohesiveness expressed in its forming itself into a transnational civil society, and its constant adaptability."[17] Its ability to become "all things to all people" (1 Cor 9: 22) and thus generate the ecumenical and international fellowship which emerged between churches and across nations gave it relevance in different contexts and more than localized appeal.

It is inconceivable that the success of early Christianity would have taken place without a high level of serious thinking about what it means to confess Jesus as Lord and Savior, and a serious consideration of the place and purpose in society of the Body of Christ. The first Christians followed Jesus, and as they followed, through critical reflection, they learned how to be more faithful, discovering contextually what it meant to be the church, that community of men and women described so aptly by Rosemary Radford Reuther as "the avant-garde of liberated humanity."[18] Theology came naturally to them, for this was an era well before what I have called theology's "'clericalization', 'professionalization' and 'secularization.'"[19]

Gustavo Gutierrez reminds us at the start of his ground-breaking *A Theology of Liberation* that theology is "intrinsic to a life of faith seeking to be authentic and complete" and "essential to the common consideration of this faith in the ecclesial community."[20] Churches which pretend they can live without theology find themselves lurching between accommodating the gospel to the spirit of the age (reductionism) or a sectarian tendency which believes that the church should totally ignore the questions and trends of contemporary culture (irrelevance). The issue is not so much whether we have theology in the church—we have a lot of that: it is usually other people's rather than our own, the leftovers from times when we last had some really joined up theological thinking within the church. The real question is whether our Christian self-understanding and church life are underpinned by an *adequate* theology.

16. Sanders, *Charisma*, 154.

17. Sanders, *Charisma,*, 170.

18. Ruether, *Sexism*, 162.

19. See my *Reforming Theology*, 9–11.

20. Gutierrez, *Theology of Liberation*, 3.

During my year as Moderator of the General Assembly certain things became very clear.[21] First, amidst rampant numerical decline the shape and style of the future *ekklesia* will need to be rather different to what we have inherited from the Christendom world of Nonconformist chapel culture: temple-building needs to give way to the flexibility of tent-pitching, as we become the church at the heart of people's lives, commitments, and interests. Secondly, we have to come to grips with the spiritual yearnings abroad in contemporary society. People may be voting with their feet about mainstream churches, but belief in God still holds up despite the predictions of the atheistic apologists; meanwhile, increasing numbers of people are taking the spiritual dimension of life with great seriousness. Thirdly, the church's contemporary missionary task must now be largely taken up by addressing these two facts, and making positive connections between them, so that we move on from the situation in which we now find ourselves, that of being, in John Drane's words, "a secular Church in a spiritual society."[22] One aspect of the secular character of much of the contemporary church's life concerns the seeming reluctance of church members to attend to spirituality and share faith with others, but it also involves the deep reluctance of churches to reflect theologically on their life in the search for ever new patterns of obedience. For a long time a gap between church and academy has been noted. Alan Le Grys opines that "the gap is becoming wider as less interest is shown in scholarship by congregations made up of people who are suspicious, fearful or simply bored by the demands of academic research," with the outcome that "such congregations may become ill-informed, and have to rely on naive sound bites or dogmatic assertions based on a pre-critical use of the Bible."[23] It would not be going too far to say that there is a high degree of theological illiteracy abroad in the United Reformed Church, and other British mainstream churches for that matter.

To some extent this lecture is a development of a claim I made in one of my addresses as Moderator of General Assembly:

> Hitherto, I have often tended to say that we do not think enough about what we say and do, but in fairness that is not true. At every level of the church, there is a lot of thinking going on. Indeed, some might say that we spend so much time thinking that we never get round to doing much! But the kind of critical and constructive thinking I understand as theology has not been

21. See *Encountering Church* for addresses and sermons which illustrate some of the following observations.

22. Drane, *McDonaldizaton* , 54.

23. Le Grys, *Preaching,* viii.

central to many of our debates and discussions over the years. We have not been in the habit of assessing the adequacy of our life against the normative Jesus traditions in scripture, nor have we tested the credibility of our witness against contemporary canons of truth.[24]

Before providing evidence to support this claim, I need to outline in more detail my understanding of theology.

THEOLOGY: THE CRITICAL AND CONSTRUCTIVE SECOND STEP

Christian theology is the process and product of critical reflection on Christian praxis.[25] The content of what Christians say and do forms the data upon which theology reflects, so as the liberation theologians insist "Theology *follows*; it is the second step."[26] We interrogate Christian practice to judge its adequacy. That provides us with the critical dimension of theology. Then we take a second step in order to create new and evermore obedient and credible expressions of faithfulness and witness against the backcloth of the changing agendas of different times and contexts. There is some truth in the observation that Christian "answers" are largely parasitic on the world's changing "questions," even if we must show that Barth did not totally die in vain by holding fast to the equally important recognition that sometimes we only discover what the real questions are when the prevailing Zeitgeist within which we live has come under the scrutiny of the gospel. We engage in theology not simply to enjoy some of its glorious mental gymnastics—even though God does provide that pleasure for some of us, but to give us a more adequate Christian praxis.

At the heart of theology is a two way conversation between Christian praxis and worldly context. From one side comes the challenge to view human praxis according to Christian criteria, as they are normed for us by Jesus' liberating praxis to which the gospels bear the earliest witness; while from the other side comes the challenge to construct human praxis

24. Peel, *Encountering*, 99–100.

25. My understanding of the nature and task of Christian theology has been largely shaped by two strands of thinking. The first has its roots in Paul Tillich's "method of correlation" and belongs to my teacher Schubert Ogden (see Ogden, *On Theology* and *Doing Theology Today*); the second comes from the so-called liberation theologies (see Gutierrez, *Theology of Liberation* and Segundo, *Liberation of Theology*). For a sharp critique of the methodology of liberation theology see Ogden, *Faith and Freedom*.

26. Gutierrez, *Theology of Liberation*, 11. See also Segundo, *Liberation of Theology*, 7–38.

on the basis of what a particular culture considers truthful, enlivening, and hopeful. Theology which emerges from such a conversation will be adequate if it does justice to both sides of the interaction, thereby being not only *appropriate* to the normative Christian witness but also *credible* in the contemporary context. One way of understanding why there has been, is, and always will be theological differences in the church is to recognize the inevitable difficulty of knowing what weight to give to each side in the theological conversation. A robust doctrine of the universality of God should always remind the more earnest Christians among us however that God's presence and wisdom are not confined to the witnessing Christian community, even if many of us would want to join those Christians who see in the Christ-event God's decisive re-presentation of the praxis of love which has created the world, holds it in being, and draws all things together.

While the twin criteria of theological adequacy are always *appropriateness* and *credibility* they are radically situation dependent. Different ages gain fresh insights about Jesus; meanwhile the rich diversity of cultures within the human family sometimes makes it very difficult for us to decide what in fact a credible praxis is. Such realities remind us that theology will always be contextual and provisional, both within and across its cultural expressions. Particularly important to remember is the way in which what one age accepts as normative a later age may with hindsight come to regard as ideological. Sometimes theological development is not for the best—for example we will want today to hold in high esteem the inclusive patterns of church membership and leadership which clearly existed in the New Testament house-churches, rather than venerate the patriarchal and hierarchical policies of later periods which led to the marginalization of women and the tendency to clericalize the church. Some things our forebears believed were congruent with the Spirit of Jesus we now disown, and the changes of perspective and thought a future era or different culture throws up will often challenge received orthodoxies.

An essential part of theology's task therefore is to unmask the idols bequeathed to us and to sift out living tradition from dead traditionalism; thereby the church becomes truly *reformata et semper reformanda*—and sometimes at some personal cost to those who lead the theological analysis. We need reminding that those whose theologies advanced the normative praxis of God's liberating love and justice against the tyrannies of their age were often oppressed on account of their stance. Segundo reminds us that theology can be a very dangerous activity. In contrast to the safe ethos of the seminary and university faculty environment, theology "was not a 'liberal art' for men like the prophets and Jesus" who "died before their time because of their theologizing, because of their specific way of interpreting the word of God and its implications for the liberation of the oppressed."[27] Nor have theological practitioners always been safe from the church when their views and judgments clashed with the prevailing orthodoxy. What some Christians have done to fellow Christians they have disagreed with is unthinkable when measured against the praxis of Jesus.

This reminds us that theology can become controversial as well as costly, and it perhaps explains why some Christians do not want to get involved with it, an easy course of action for them to take in a postmodern age which tends to relativize truth and equate it with the private opinions of individuals. At the very least we are clearly reminded that theology, like every mode of human enquiry, is not elevated above human self-interests or the various political and ideological ways in which human beings assert power over others. The Christian church however is called to love God and neighbor, thus developing an utterly selfless praxis in an inclusive community which contains none of those contemporary divisions that are equivalent to the Jew-Greek, slave-free, men-women dichotomies of the Greco-Roman world. Given that particular high calling, it is essential for us to ask of any theology: "Who is this theology for?" "Who benefits from it?" "Does it serve the interests of the Gospel?" "Is it simply keeping the Church in its comfort zone?"

Theology is done in various contexts by individual Christians and within churches as well as in theological seminaries and university settings. There is an unfortunate tendency for suspicion and hostility to abound between the practitioners in the different contexts, but wherever Christian theology is done the same criteria of adequacy apply: Is it *credible* at the interface between church and world? Are we presenting the scandal of the gospel, or is it our woolly thinking and enshrined habits that are the scandal? Nor should we have arrived at the situation where there is a yawning intellectual chasm between church and academy, pulpit and pew. As David Tracy[28] suggests, the public discourse which is theology must stand up in the "three distinct and related social realities" in which theology is found: "the wider society, the academy and the church."[29] Where we do theology will sometimes provide influences so powerful that they will "effectively determine the theology," but nevertheless Tracy argues that there need not be an ultimate conflict between the theologies which arise out of the different contexts. We are to operate on the assumption that, "However personally committed to a single public (society, academy or church) a particular

27. Segundo, *Liberation of Theology*, 26.

28. Tracy's early work was heavily influenced by Ogden, an erstwhile colleague at the Divinity School of the University of Chicago. See his *Blessed Rage for Order*.

29. Tracy, *Analogical*, 5.

theologian may be, each strives, in principle and in fact, for a genuine publicness and thereby implicitly addresses all three publics."[30] While there need not be an ultimate conflict between the theology which arises out of, say, the church and a university or a pastoral setting and a political pressure group, it remains the case that gaps do open up between theologies coming from difficult settings. Integration must then be sought. The basis for such integration can only be that the theological practitioners involved should together address what Tracy calls "the paradigms for truth in the church tradition, the paradigms for rational enterprises in the academy, the models for rationality in . . . contemporary society,"[31] thereby seeking an account of Christian praxis which satisfies the requirements of each public.

THE DEMISE OF THEOLOGY

In presenting the evidence to support my contention that there is a desperate lack of theological thinking from top to bottom in the URC I will be referring to trends I have encountered within its life. I do not believe that these trends necessarily started with the URC, but it is my considered view that during the URC's life we have done little to counter them. Those of us whose roots lie in Congregationalism will know that P.T. Forsyth about 100 years ago was attacking Congregationalism for its lack of theological muscle, yet compared to the current scene, the churches of Forsyth's era were numerically thriving! Forsyth, nevertheless, was very clear about what was required:

> . . . we need a new deep, and piercing intelligence of the Gospel, and especially a new moral intelligence of it; not so much a new fervour, nor more of the Spirit (in the common use of the term), not of course less piety but more faith; less occupation with meetings, committees, schedules and conventional jingle from press or pulpit, and more immersion in a Bible brought up to date, more of the Word and its power, a new insight which is not a revival but a reformation. We need a reformation of faith, belief, and thought to make the Churches adequate to the nation, the world, and the age, a bracing up and a coupling up of our Churches, and a renovated theology as the expression of the Church's rich and corporate life.[32]

30. Tracy, *Analogical*, 5–6.

31. Tracy, *Analogical*, 29.

32. Forsyth, *Lectures*, 104.

Sometimes Forsyth reads like a prophet crying in the wilderness; at other times he seems to be speaking to our time. Let us face up to the depressing contemporary evidence in conversation with him.

First, locally, regionally, and nationally the church's agenda is not being driven by theological thinking. As an itinerant preacher for the past twenty or so years I have heard a lot of church notices and been presented with many church magazines. You find little mention in them of well-attended activities which enable folk to think about faith, to discover their Christian heritage, to be challenged regarding their vocations, or to review the church's mission. In conversation with our people one discovers a deep-seated biblical illiteracy and a naivety of theological outlook which makes it hardly surprising that they are not confident apologists for the gospel. Where serious study of the Bible and theological reflection take place it is a minority pursuit among a raft of activities which are designed for fellowship, recreation or entertainment. We are much more likely these days to put the church's future in the hands of accountants, statisticians, and management consultants than allow theology to take the lead. How else could we have arrived at a situation whereby the United Reformed Church has been dragged through three years of debate about structures and finance when we all know that the real problem will remain whatever the structures we have and well after the last bean has been counted? How long will we go on putting the cart before the horse? The problem is that most of us are no longer clear about what we believe; otherwise we would be excited about faith and want to share it with others. The issue we face is both spiritual and theological. As Forsyth concluded regarding the consequences of a lack of serious theological thinking in the Victorian churches:

> You cannot expect ill-fed people to devise much wisdom, or do much good. And many in our active churches are very hungry as to the soul. They are anaemic in the Spirit. They are fed upon sentiment and not on faith. They have hectic energy—and lean-ness of soul.[33]

We have lost a sense of mission and purpose proportionate to the absence of serious theological reflection on our Christian praxis. The result is that we end up running an institution having lost sight of what it is for.

Secondly, we have transformed the Church Meeting into a democratic business meeting. Some of my Anglican friends envy the democratic ways of the URC, thereby displaying complete ignorance about the basic principles of church government in the Reformed confessions. It is no fault of theirs that

---

33. Forsyth, *Positive Preaching*, 119.

they have observed our democratic ways, and if they want to follow them that is their decision, but let no one kid themselves that democracy is the Reformed model of government. We do not meet to take decisions on a show of hands, but to seek the will of God, to discern the mind of Christ, and to heed the prompting of the Spirit. It is not our wishes we need to fulfil when we meet, but the needs of those beyond the church whom God places before us to serve. The issue in Church Meeting is not one of running the church for our benefit, but the serious matter of constantly reshaping our worship and witness so that it connects with those outside the fellowship. Alan Sell argues that the Church Meeting is where "those who have sat under the preaching of the Word and received the bread and wine at the Last Supper gather to do their contextual theology in fellowship, and by the Spirit through the Word."[34] Sell may have a somewhat perfectionist view of the Church Meeting in Nonconformity, one which hardly fits even some of the outstanding examples of the "church-in-meeting," but he is correct to set theology at the heart of them. As our democratic ways have taken root, and our Church Meetings have become trivialized by being tagged on at the end of worship services, the place where Congregationalists at their best did theology has been vacated. Similar points can be made about those Elders' Meetings which increasingly come to resemble a committee that runs an organization called the church rather than the leadership team which has spiritual oversight of a missionary congregation. The fulcrum upon which Reformed ministry balances is removed when serious theological thinking does not take place in the Elders' Meeting when exercising oversight of the church. The result is a church without heart and purpose. Listen again to Forsyth:

> We . . . become the victims of an outward pride, of Church sta-
> tistics, of denominational egoisms and competitive numbers,
> of position instead of service, of a belief in machinery instead
> of faith. We trust devices more than majesties. We are more at
> home in discussing devices to increase membership than in ac-
> quiring the power from on high which makes a smaller Church
> a better Church.[35]

The logic of this world though does not allow one to believe that a smaller Church can be a better church. Only sustained theological analysis will establish that particular truth. Our deep fears about the Church's numerical decline are a further example of our being dominated by all kinds of thinking save the theology we need.

---

34. Sell, *Commemorations*, 353.
35. Forsyth, *Lectures*, 39.

Thirdly the centrality of preaching in the Reformed churches is an indication of not only why Reformed ministers have generally been expected to be theologically well-educated, but also of the fact that as the congregation listened to the preacher the people were engaging theologically in a process of Christian nurture. It follows that if the quality of preaching goes down, it is likely that the level of theological engagement in a Reformed congregation quickly follows. It is now a widespread view among those who believe they can remember hearing something different that the standard of preaching has indeed gone down in recent years. I repeatedly hear about committed people who are wondering where they can go to hear good preaching in the URC. Perhaps the beleaguered minister of the current multi-pastorate era, with all the attendant ecumenical responsibilities, and possibly a lack of quality lay-leadership, has not the time to put in the preparation which is needed to produce quality preaching. Or perhaps the modern minister of our IT multi-media age does not believe in the value of preaching at all? There may be some truth in the latter suspicion insofar as my research on the models of ministry ordinands most favor when entering their preparation for ministry does not suggest that they put "preacher" near the top of their preferred options: but whatever means other than preaching such ministers find to communicate the faith to others what Forsyth says about the preacher also applies to them:

> For the preacher it is most true that his theology is an essential, perhaps the essential, part of his religion. He may be quite unfit to lecture in theology as a science, but he is the less of a preacher, however fine a speaker, if he have not a theology at the root of his preaching and its sap circulating in it.[36]

Fourthly, theological discussions in the United Reformed Church seldom get beyond internal navel-gazing concerning ecclesiological issues. It was only to be expected that at one time during my life I would serve on the Doctrine, Prayer and Worship Committee. The experience was a huge disappointment and rather symptomatic of the malaise I am exploring in this lecture. My term of service occurred during a period when prominent members of the Committee were devoting themselves to the preparation of a new worship book, so liturgical considerations were paramount. Other than being asked to prepare responses to a couple of ecumenical documents, the only serious theological issue of note we considered in a five-year period was whether we should have an ordained diaconate. The notion that doctrine can be equated with ecclesiology is fanciful, while the

36. Forsyth, *Positive Preaching*, 137

theological conversation partners we most need to have are hardly ourselves and our ecumenical partners, if we are to define the *raison d'être* of the church missiologically. Where in our denominational life do we address together the great theological issues of this and every other age, concerned with the meaning, purpose, and destiny of life, as that is informed by the Christ event today in a world of hunger, violence, lostness, and yearning for something different? Having collapsed the ecumenical vision into a hapless series of church unity questions, it is hardly surprising that the most searching questions about the *oikoumené* (the whole inhabited earth) get eclipsed from our agenda. To borrow some words from John Hull, and to take them completely out of context, the narrowness and impoverished nature of our theology guarantees that while we may aspire to be "a mission-shaped church" we invariably end up with "a church-shaped mission."[37]

Fifthly, when we compare the College syllabus for preparing people for ministry at the point I first entered the Congregational College, Manchester with the one I helped shape when I was last at Northern College two things strike me. First, greater attention thankfully is now paid to personal and spiritual development issues and serious work is devoted to gaining and developing ministerial skills through placement work. Then, secondly, a concerted attempt has been made to cut through the notorious "theory-practice" dichotomy. As the applause rises to salute these achievements however we are tempted to overlook the inevitable and rather obvious fact that the change in the curriculum has carried a price. What has recently been added has meant that some things have had to be removed. Not only are most courses of preparation for ministry now much shorter than they were thirty years ago, an understandable eventuality given the increased age of most ordinands, but also some of what was once taught no longer is taught—and what has been dropped is further engagement with the traditional theological disciplines, thus generating a likely reduction in the church's theological knowledge base.

I have recently been working surrounded by two contrasting church cultures. One culture takes an increasingly minimalist attitude to ordination preparation for mature candidates, seemingly only concerned to get candidates into service and thus resolve an ever deepening deployment crisis. Two years part-time education (sorry the blessed word is "formation"!) is all that is required for those the Anglican bishops wish to fast-track. The other culture is moving to a situation where Roman Catholicism will have few full-time priests but will have mobilized lay-people to undertake

---

37. Hull, *Mission-Shaped Church*, 36. This little book is a stimulating and largely convincing critique of the Church of England report bearing the same name.

many of the duties once carried out by the ordained. It carries with it a clear commitment to prepare priests rigorously in separate periods over seven years in Durham, Rome, and Latin America, with an emphasis on scripture and doctrine, as well as numerous placement requirements at home and overseas. Seven years seems a long time of preparation, until one remembers that such a period was normative for younger candidates entering the Congregational College Manchester thirty years ago. Having a theological knowledge base within the ministry exercised by the ordained is a clear Roman priority.

It remains to be seen whether the URC can sustain its tradition of "learned ministry" against pressures from those who now see ministers in overtly functionalist terms, within churches which clamor for having ordained ministers, and given the anti-intellectual thread which seems to run through parts of the URC. I remember well a provincial meeting in the North Western Synod when the minister of the host church confessed to not having read a theological book since he left college. He drew laughter from those present, and even the Moderator was observed to smile. What ought to have happened was that the minister concerned should have been challenged for bringing Christian ministry into disrepute.

Sixthly, the Reformed tradition has traditionally viewed its ministers as the focus for theological work within the church. Some of those ministers (as well as some lay-people) have found a calling within theological colleges. As time has gone on the pressures placed upon such theological educators has become such that their contribution to theological scholarship and research has become rather minimalist when compared with their counterparts in earlier generations. Our colleges are now largely known (and it has to be said appreciated) because they educate our future ministers, not because they are hot-beds of theological thinking. In the new URC pattern of "Resource Centres for Learning," and within the developing ecumenical world of "Regional Training Partnerships," there seems every likelihood that more will be demanded from less, with the result that our theological educators will have their crucial role of being a focus for theological exploration within the church further curtailed. It was a repeated mantra of mine when I was on the staff of a theological college that I read and wrote more whilst in pastoral ministry than when working in theological education. I also remain profoundly puzzled about our regional priorities when our synods can create jobs for office managers, Moderator's PAs, accountants, property experts, children's workers, youth leaders, and training officers, but not a single one of them has yet seen the need for a theologian—not to do the thinking for the church, but to challenge and empower churches actually to think theologically.

CONCLUSION

We need to work thoughtfully at being a faithful and obedient church. Such a church will be undergirded by a mission imperative grounded in an adequate theology, a Christian self-understanding which possesses a grasp of truth, exudes authenticity, conveys core Christian values, and professes a Word for the age in which we live. The painful evidence indicates that many of our congregations fall short of that ideal. What keeps me hopeful is that I know of congregations which are theologically alert to their missionary calling. They are of various theological persuasions, maintain different liturgical traditions, and are found in a variety of contexts, urban as well as rural, inner city and also suburban. A mark of these congregations is the way they are trying to be faithful to their Christian heritage in a post-Christendom setting. They have recognized that the society of the postmodern paradigm requires fresh ways of being church, and invariably they chart their missionary course through serious theological study rooted in a renewed engagement with the classic texts of Christianity.[38] They stand out like beacons of light amidst a church culture that is irrelevant to most of our society.

The question is: "How do we create more churches like them?" Or to put it better, "How do we enable God to raise up such congregations?" I offer five interlocking principles for consideration:

Firstly, we must set theology at the heart of congregational life, enabling and empowering church members to think about the deep issues of faith. As Forsyth noted, this is no easy task given our all too human nature:

> A Church is made by what it believes . . . We must go back to the first deep, distinctive, and exclusive principles of our faith, which horses and carts will not drag people to face. Men will just be what their living faith and deep belief make them. But, when we press these principles, these powers, these realities, we are charged with being academic and with offering professional theology when what is needed is practical direction. But has the Church really come to treat the moral soul's whole reliance upon Christ's judging and saving death as a piece of professional theology?[39]

---

38. For the idea that church history is marked by a series of paradigms (e.g. Early Christian Apocalyptic, Early Church Hellenistic, Mediaeval Roman Catholic, Reformed Protestant, Enlightenment Modern, Contemporary Ecumenical, Postmodern) see Hans Küng, *Christianity*.

39. Forsyth, *Lectures*, 20.

It remains a mystery why the people I meet in pubs or on trains or at cricket grounds are more interested in talking about belief than most of our church members. Vibrant churches of course continue their theological explorations as they set their vision on the church's future and develop their congregational life. What this all boils down to is the need for serious thinking about why we are Christian and what we are called to be and do with other Christians in the Body of Christ.

Secondly, we must recognize that one of the principal duties of ministers of Word and Sacraments is to be a focus for theological thinking in the church. Whether from pulpit or in pastoral work or amidst the "church-in-meeting," ministers should be able to generate and resource those theological conversations which seek faithfulness and obedience. They will not have all the answers, though through their ongoing prayerful study they ought to be able to point folk in the right direction; nor will they possess all the really important questions, but they should be expected to have discovered some of them.

Thirdly, we ought to select candidates for ministry who have the will and aptitude needed for the theological task. This is not actually a matter of intellect or academic qualifications, but rather one of ministers possessing a belief in the central core tasks of the Reformed minister of Word and Sacraments. It is not always the best minds who make the church's most able theological practitioners, but it will be no good generating this emphasis in ministry unless our ministers and churches recognize that ministers need freeing up for the theological task. As I am fond of saying: "Ministers are not here to do the church's work; but they are here to make the church work." Central to that task is the role of theological animation within and beyond the congregation.

Fourthly, candidates need preparing adequately for their theological role. This involves colleges and courses standing firm against the tendencies of church leaders and many in the church to take a functionalist view of ministry, one that is task driven rather than sacramentally shaped. Quite often the church gets the ministers it wants, rather than those it desperately needs. We have transformed some excellent lay-leaders into very ordinary ministers, without realizing the negative impact such strategies can have on the church's lay theological leadership; we need to ask in what ways have those of us involved in theological education colluded in and with these attitudes, whereby we have welcomed the candidates we have so desperately needed to keep our institutions alive and our jobs safe? Can it truly be said that we have adequately modeled the ministry of "theological practitioners" in the maelstrom of our colleges and courses?

Fifthly, the church might be led to value its theological educators more if we returned to a Reformed practice, no longer alive in the United Reformed Church, but still in existence in other parts of the Reformed family, of recognizing theological educators as possessing a distinct office of ministry, those whom Calvin called "teachers."[40] The way our universities have developed in recent years means that save in those few places with church-related, endowed professorial chairs, the churches cannot any longer rely on secular educational support for their theological learning and research. Not only do we need to generate our own scholarship much more, but we also will be short-sighted if we do not protect the designated teaching posts we have. In the light of the church's current uphill struggle to reconfigure faithfully and obediently a case can actually be made for increasing such posts. Far from being a time to close colleges, it is actually a time when we need to expand our theological provision. A prudent organization wishing to climb out of decline does not slash its research and development base.

40. Calvin, *Institutes*, 4.3.4.

6

Sola Scriptura: the Achilles Heel of the Reformed Tradition?

THE BIBLE HAS PLAYED a central role in the life of the Reformed churches, but there is a considerable amount of evidence to suggest it no longer holds the authority it once did. In the first part of this chapter I will explore some of the reasons why this is the case, before moving in the second part to discuss ways in which the Bible still possesses lasting value and deep significance for Christian faith and contemporary churches.

THE AUTHORITY OF THE BIBLE

In the late 1960s I became aware of embarking upon an intellectual project aimed at integrating into a unified account the learning I was gaining at the interfaces of my life. I was living in an era when the very task I was embarking upon was the essential theological program of some of the most influential Christian thinkers: one thinks of Paul Tillich's commitment to doing theology on "the boundary" by correlating what we know from common experience and reason with the Christian witness of faith;[1] and Rudolf Bultmann's insistence

---

1. The phrase "on the boundary" summarizes Tillich's theological methodology. It recalls the theologian's need to have one foot in the world and the other in the inherited Christian tradition, but it also reminds us of the way in which God is encountered in the deep mysteries of life beyond our normal comfort zones. It became the title of an autobiographical sketch published posthumously in 1966, which earlier had appeared

that sound Christian understanding is only gained by a critical examination of the faith claims handed down to us, in which all the objectifying language of myth is removed ("demythologizing"), followed by the constructive task of restating the basic claim of God upon people's lives in ways which impact upon contemporary people ("existentialist reinterpretation").[2] In other words, I was not lacking encouragement when embarking upon this theological journey.[3] There was plenty of gentle encouragement not to restrict my search for and encounter with God to the religious world. God is alive in the world, not confined to the church. But I need to say more about the "world" and "church" in which I was discovering myself.

I have never known a time when my awe and wonder concerning the natural world has not led on to a fundamental belief that at the very heart of reality lies a creative, sustaining, and renewing power that I have learned to call God. Today, as I look at birds through my telescope I renew a life-time of being held captivated by a natural world through which God has placed a claim upon my life: the theological word to describe this is "revelation." Needless to say, I have always found alluring those arguments which start with the order and beauty of the natural world and end up by concluding

---

in *The Interpretation of History*. For an account of Tillich's "method of correlation" see his *Systematic Theology* I, 67–73. For some examples of it at work see the collection of essays edited by Kimball entitled *Theology of Culture*. In the "Foreword" to this collection Tillich describes "most of [his] writings" as an attempt at trying "to define the way in which Christianity is related to secular culture" (*Theology of Culture*, v).

2. Not only does Bultmann's reception in the English speaking world suffer from an overemphasis upon the critical phase of his theological program ("demythologizing") at the expense of due recognition of its constructive phase ("existentialist reinterpretation"), but also the first English translations of his seminal writings were so lacking that the technical terms on which his thinking is dependent hardly represent Bultmann's intentions. It is not surprising that Bultmann felt largely misunderstood in the British theological world. So care is needed when attending both to primary and secondary literature concerning Bultmann. Reliable starting points are *New Testament and Mythology and Other Basic Writings* and *Existence and Faith: Shorter Writings of Rudolf Bultmann*. However much we may be critical of an existentialist interpretation of the Christian witness of faith on the grounds of its lacking the essential social and political dimensions of the movement which owes its existence to Jesus it is disingenuous to critique Bultmann's work as wholly reductionist when in fact it is rooted in constructive—and even quite evangelical—intentions.

3. The first draft of this lecture was written on 14 March 2012, the day of the funeral of Donald H. Hilton. Donald was one my early mentors. His early encouragement was vital in my personal and theological development. But I had already decided to avoid jumping into Barthian circles well before he passionately invited the United Reformed Church to adopt "an elliptical faith" in his 1993 address as Moderator of the General Assembly. Donald shared the conviction that there are two criteria of theological adequacy: one grounded in common experience and reason, the other in the Christ event—each in turn taking us to the twin centres of the ellipse.

that there must be a first cause which gives rise to that order and beauty, namely, God. Given all the dysteleological factors in the created order, and however much I may be persuaded to believe through encounters with the natural world that the world is God's creation, I have never been rationally convinced that the existence of God can be proved fully and finally in this way. I have never been satisfied therefore with what Bob Ekblad calls "Gore-Tex theology" because, as he says:

> Identifying a beautiful and comforting God in creation is easy when you are hiking in the forest for pleasure with all the right gear, food, water filter, and first-aid kit. God in creation looks far less attractive and positive when you are slogging barefoot up a muddy hill under the scorching tropical sun, with a five-gallon plastic canister full of contaminated water or a heavy load of firewood.[4]

What is certain however is that I was driven into scientific study through what I call "revelation." Even though I was never to become a professional scientist I retain a healthy respect for evidence led learning.

There have been many times in my Christian ministry when I have yearned to be with people who take greater care when evaluating the credibility of what they are saying, just as I have received powerful reminders of what I left behind when I headed off for ordination. One recent such occasion was the 2012 Richard Dimbleby Lecture delivered by Sir Paul Nurse, the then President of the Royal Society. Nurse talked about "the ability to prove that something is not true" being at the heart of science.[5] That methodology, he claimed, distinguishes it "from beliefs based on religion and ideology, which place much more emphasis on faith, tradition, and opinion."[6] I noted with interest that Nurse fell well short of claiming with the evangelical atheists in the scientific community that religious truths fall *totally* outside the canons of rationality. He then went on to remind us that science does not always operate in the realm of certainties, even though "we tend to think all science is equally secure, as if it is written in stone."[7] The role of consensus within the scientific community often plays a greater part in scientific advancement than the existence of knock-down certainties. His conclusion had me cheering:

---

4. Ekblad, *Reading the Bible*, 143
5. Nurse, *New Enlightenment*, 5.
6. Nurse, *New Enlightenment*, 5–6.
7. Nurse, *New Enlightenment*, 6.

I am passionate about science because it has shaped the world and made it a better place, and I want to see science placed more centre stage in our culture and economy. Our present economic troubles have promoted a debate about the future of our economy, and that future must include a major role for science. We need a new Enlightenment, an Enlightenment for the 21st century, and Britain is the place to do it with its history of freedom, rationality, and scientific achievement. We need more science in Government, the boardroom, and public services . . .[8]

And, I found myself shouting, the church! I have lived rather too long in an environment whose thinking has been dominated by those who belittle the achievements of the Enlightenment, or who dismiss rival theological views as rationalist, simply because their holders decline to take endless speculative propositions as givens before they jump into the circle of faith. There is something revealing as well as pathetic about the somewhat idle thought that the likes of Lesslie Newbigin or Colin Gunton were framing their polemics against the wicked witch called "Enlightenment" at the same time as they availed themselves of modern medicine, flew around the world to theological conferences in jet planes, or used computers to produce their writings.[9]

The language of "the circle of faith" takes me to my second world, the one I was plunged into at birth. I am a "first-born" Christian. I have never known a time when I was not an active, assenting, participant of a gathered community of God's saints, the movement which seeks to follow in the steps of Jesus Christ. This does not mean that I have not had doubts or difficulties about the faith tradition in which I have grown up. In fact, quite the reverse is the case, with the result that my theological development has been marked by key alterations of perception at different moments on my personal journey concerning what faithful and authentic Christian faith entails. However, it does mean that I have never had sufficient grounds to reject the witness I have received that in the life, ministry, and death of Jesus we are presented with a definitive picture of God's gracious nature along with a claim upon our lives to express gratitude to God through our worship of God and service of all those God places before us as calls upon our lives. This takes me once again into the realm of revelation. I have been *drawn* into a commitment through a story which I inherited by being born and raised in a Christian community. This story, told by early Christians about what they understood as God's action for the world in Jesus the Christ, has

8. Nurse, *New Enlightenment*, 17.

9. On the theology of Newbigin see Chapter 4. What I say there about Newbigin's critique of Enlightenment culture applies also to similar opinions in Gunton's theology.

been received by me as a *re-presentation* of what I have been persuaded about through my experience within the world and reflection upon it.[10]

The Jesus story from the world of faith brings into focus the reality of God which I glimpse fleetingly through simply being human. It makes fully explicit what was erstwhile implicit. Above all else, it becomes an interpretive key which opens the door to the God who is not simply God, but is God *for us*. Jesus has not brought me in touch with a God who has somehow had a change of mind and heart about the world; rather he comes before me as the re-presentation of the one and only God: the God of Abraham, Sarah, Moses, and the prophets. In redemption I am repeatedly being brought back into a positive relationship with my creator. Both "creation" and "redemption" then are words used to describe different moments in the universal and gracious activity of God.

Central to my engagement with science and faith is the belief that both can provide positive outcomes for persons and communities. Neither can rest at the level of theory; both need fleshing out in ways which lead to the enhancement of life. Science is not neutral: its results can annihilate the planet or enhance culture and civilization; nor is faith neutral: as history shows it can lead to war, bigotry, and abuse, or, as Jesus sought to open up for us, "life" in all its abundance (John 10: 10). Neither can ever remain an end in itself since the following question always invites an answer: "Who is this science or faith for?" Both realms have a habit of becoming self-serving, so part of my intellectual journey has involved developing clear political commitments which maximize the well-being of others and the less fortunate in particular. Commitments to economic justice and fairness in the global economy, environmental responsibility, racial, gender, and sexual equality, and world peace subsequently have followed from both sides of what some regard as an impossible divide.

During a large part of human history science and religion were united under the name of "theology." At other points in history they co-existed together, science being regarded as revealing the laws which govern the universe, thus showing how God's activity takes place. Undoubtedly, this was the theological ethos in which the majority of Christian intellectuals understood the implications of Newton and Einstein. But there have been other occasions when Christians have so enthroned their beliefs that whenever science has thrown up alternative ways of understanding, persecution of scientists has resulted. It took the Roman Catholic Church

10. The term "re-presentation" is central to the theological methodology of the thinker who more than any other has shaped my approach to theology. See Ogden, *On Theology* and *Doing Theology Today*. Ogden's indebtedness to the theological programs of Paul Tillich and Rudolf Bultmann will be obvious to careful readers.

until 1992 to recognize its mistaken attitude to Galileo who had advanced the Copernican over the Ptolemaic theory concerning the earth orbiting the sun. The name of Galileo remains connected with Christian opposition to scientific discoveries that eventually end up being embraced by later generations of Christians.

While we can understand why the evangelical atheists in the modern scientific community are resolutely opposed to religion we should not excuse them for their habit of misrepresenting the religion they wish to oppose.[11] Against the venom flowing from the pen of the likes of Richard Dawkins for example those Christians whose grasp of science does not give them access to what can become a very complex debate can take heart from the existence of equally eminent biologists who do not conclude that Darwinian views undermine their faith in God.[12] The manner, style, and content of a great deal of the science/religion debate leaves much to be desired. Feeling a sense of loyalty to both camps I often want to say "a plague on both your houses," after the manner of Terry Eagleton who says:

> Religion has wrought untold misery in human affairs. For the most part, it has been a squalid tale of bigotry, superstition, wishful thinking, and oppressive ideology. I therefore have a good deal of sympathy with its rationalist and humanist critics. But it is also the case . . . that most such critics buy their rejection of religion on the cheap. When it comes to the New Testament, at least, what they usually write off is a worthless caricature of the real thing, rooted in a degree of ignorance and prejudice to match religion's own. It is as though one were to dismiss feminism on the basis of Clint Eastwood's opinions of it.[13]

The two realms I have tried over the years to inhabit with integrity and passion have both thrown up spokespersons that are an embarrassment, not least when the Bible comes into discussion.

Part of the problem concerns differing attitudes to tradition: Is the past determinative for the future or is it the springboard for novelty and newness? Generally speaking I have found a tension at this point in my quest for a theological synthesis between faith and reason, religion and science, church and society. Scientists revere the past because they know that they have to learn what it teaches them. The scientific consensus agrees what are the established building blocks upon which all scientific thinking points in the pursuit of learning new things. Some of the "new things" will become the

11. See Eagleton, *Reason*.

12. See Spencer and Alexander, *Rescuing Darwin*.

13. Eagleton, *Reason*, xi.

presuppositions on which future enquiry is based, having replaced former ones now deemed inadequate. So science displays a decidedly forward-facing momentum. Religious believers and thinkers conversely give the repeated impression that the purpose of the past is not to learn from it so much as live in it. Apologists for the Reformation for example are fond of saying that the Reformers were not trying to inaugurate a new church but to return to a classic way of being the church found somewhere way back in early Christian history. Tell that to those who found themselves severed from what had helped sustain them religiously for centuries: everything during Cromwell's era must have seemed pretty new, even if everything was under-scored by Scriptural warrant. Rome and Geneva by and large were up to the usual institutional tricks, authorizing what they decided to do on the basis of some recognized authority located in the past, namely, in the first instance the accumulative wisdom of the Magisterium down the ages and in the other by reference to an authoritative book, the Bible. Magisterium or Bible, the authority was deemed privileged, non-negotiable, and beyond criticism.

Although we know with hindsight that Roman Catholic thinking has *developed* over the centuries, thereby historically undermining its often perceived backward looking approach to the acquisition of truth, the Reformed world cannot evade a similar conclusion. Clear scriptural teaching wholeheartedly accepted in earlier generations is today passed over in an embarrassed silence by those who apply their commonsense. We do not believe that the sun revolves around the earth; we do not believe that mental illness is caused by demon possession; we cannot accept that our station in life reflects our standing with God; we do not expect the world to end by divine intervention but at a time in the distant future through intolerable heat or cold; and we do not believe in a cultural honor system in which to maintain divine approval we have always to perform good works to those immediately above us on the ladder: slave to mistress, mistress to husband, husband to the political ruler, and head of state to God. Although we still find some who for reasons best known to them wish to defy the current consensus of opinion, the simple fact of the matter is that unlike some of our forebears the vast majority of us simply do not accept biblical assumptions and teachings on a wide range of issues. And one reason why we can live with this, as well as deflect some of the guilt showered upon us by the fundamentalists for our supposed departure from what they regard as clear and unequivocally binding teaching, is based upon the observation that inside the Bible itself we witness clear evidence of the principle of "setting to one side" and "moving on" when it comes to claims and practices that are found wanting. The obvious example is the early church's complete dismantling of what I referred to earlier as the first century honor system.

No statement could possibly have been more counter-cultural in the first century Mediterranean world than Paul's watchword concerning the make-up of the church: "There is no longer Jew or Greek, there is no longer slave or free, there is no longer male and female; for all of you are one in Christ Jesus" (Gal.3: 28).

Paul's *leitmotiv* contradicts the clear Scriptural view on the God-given make up of society inherited by the early Christians. Its implications for inclusivity in societies around the world remind us of Christianity's political challenge to all who still seek to rationalize away their racism, or enslavement of others, or sexism, on the basis of biblical texts which pre-date the peoples' movement called "church." Any understanding of biblical authority which eschews *in principle* what I have called "setting to one side" and "moving on" denies practices which can be traced from within the Bible's pages. No amount of special pleading by biblicists is going to alter a wide consensus of opinion concerning a vacuous view of Scripture nowhere owned by the biblical writers themselves, namely that often termed "inerrancy."

Another major plank on which the biblicists' case stands is the claim that the Bible, and hence all the diverse literature which makes it up, was and hence is inspired by God. The Reformation battle cry of "*sola scriptura*" rests on the claim that the Bible is the Word of God. This claim was the basis for the Reformers saying that the Bible is truly authoritative when compared with the supposedly merely human conclusions of the members of the Roman Catholic Magisterium down the centuries. But over two hundred years of biblical scholarship has now left us with a scholarly consensus which agrees that there is no *prima facie* evidence that the writers of the biblical literature were any more or any less human than the members of the Magisterium. What is the New Testament if not the *primary* traditions of Christianity? In what formal way does the New Testament differ from subsequent Christian writings? Why cannot more recent Christian writings be regarded as inspired as those in the biblical canon? The entire idea that the biblical canon has a unique claim to be divinely inspired involves what Paul Capetz calls "prior theological commitment to a notion of biblical authority that stands in significant tension with, if not outright contradiction to, a consistently historical interpretation of the Bible as a human document subject to all the possibilities of ideological distortion we detect in other ancient texts."[14] I fail to see how in the church the Bible is *formally* different in status to say that of *The Wisden Cricketers' Almanac* in cricketing circles and of course this year's errors in *Wisden* will be corrected in the next year's edition! Nevertheless, I am inspired by reading the Bible in a *materially* different way from how a

14. Capetz "Theology," 469.

cricket tragic like me becomes inspired *by Wisden*. This helps point to the way in which a reconstructed view of biblical authority might be developed, one based on how the Bible *functions* in the Christian faith community. At the end of the day, I have not found *Wisden* placing before me a story about God's graciousness towards us and the call to respond out of gratitude in love not only to God but also our neighbors.

The Reformed world's commitment to biblical authority preceded the advent of the historical critical method and all the subsequent diverse approaches to reading the Bible. One of its earlier and most influential advocates was John Calvin, an innovative exegete who suggests at times that he possessed a very enlightened view of biblical authority.[15] He believed that, while everyone in principle is able to grasp knowledge of God from the natural world, in practice because of our sinfulness we are like blind people groping in the dark. We are responsible for our failure to know God, so we are without excuse; but God graciously has provided us with the Bible to direct us to a clear knowledge of our Creator and Redeemer. In the Bible, Calvin maintains, God addresses us through a medium we understand, and through words, pictures, images, and stories the living word of God is heard by us. The Bible functions then as spectacles which enable us to bring our otherwise confused knowledge of God into clear focus.[16]

Significantly, Calvin does not hold a totally negative attitude towards our natural ability to know God: we may possess "weak vision"; but we are not totally blind.[17] He trenchantly objected to the contemporary Roman Catholic view which maintained that it was the church's responsibility to decide what weight is to be afforded to the Bible. Rather, he ruled conversely that the church is to be grounded upon Scripture. The faithful do not believe that the word of Scripture becomes for them the Word of God via the authoritative teaching of the church, nor on the basis of their own reason, but through what Calvin calls "the secret testimony of the Spirit."[18] This represents a sacramental view of scripture in which the Bible becomes a means of encountering the redeeming and liberating Word of God. The biblical words are of ultimate significance, but only because *through* them we encounter Jesus Christ.

Calvin believed that the Scriptures contain all that is required for Christian belief and practice. His doctrine of 'the sufficiency of Scripture' is remarkably extensive. Sometimes he seems to suggest that we are prohibited

15. See Calvin, *Institutes* , 1, 6 and 1, 7.

16. Calvin, *Institutes*, 1, 6, 1.

17. Calvin, *Institutes*, 1, 6, 1.

18. Calvin, *Institutes*, 1, 7, 4.

from looking outside Scripture for guidance, thereby insisting that the Bible contains all that we need. With breath-taking ease he also can claim that the Bible is not distorted by anything earthly, that its parts harmonize together perfectly, and that its authority has been confirmed repeatedly. Any distinction that he seems on other occasions to draw between the Word of God and the words of Scripture is completely collapsed when for example he talks of God having "his Word set down and sealed in writing" and of the Old Testament being "composed under the Holy Spirit's dictation."[19] Are we to regard Calvin therefore as the innovative exegete who possessed an enlightened view of the authority of the Bible, one who in a nuanced kind of way was a herald of more modern ways of reading Scripture? Or is he to be used as the champion of those views of biblical authority which claim that Bible is the inspired and inerrant Word of God?

While what we know today as "fundamentalism" was originally the creation of one particular strand of Calvinism, other committed Calvinists move in a direction more able to accommodate historical criticism. Charles Cranfield, for example, reminds us that "the Bible does not make claims for *itself*" since it is always referring "to an authority other than itself."[20] It is Jesus Christ that is the norm that is never normed: "The Bible is not the Word of God independently of HIM, but only in relation to HIM, as testimony to HIM."[21] Secondly, Cranfield recognizes the very human character of the biblical writings. He tells us that "Calvin too, though it is true that he frequently speaks of the Holy Spirit's 'dictating', makes it clear that he regards the Scriptures as fully human documents as well as recognizing in them the Word of God, and he freely admits the presence of inaccuracies."[22] So, contrary to the biblicists, Cranfield uses Calvin as his support for a view of biblical inspiration which is "not the secular marvel of a mechanically infallible book, but the divine miracle of God's free grace which condescends to use frail and sinful men and their stumbling witness as the vehicle of His own Word."[23] But when pressed on the issue of why the Bible is authoritative, Cranfield answers in a way reminiscent of Karl Barth:

> That it has divine authority, that it is God's own Word, this I cannot prove. I simply confess it. I confess it, because I am forced to do so, forced by the Bible itself. It has imposed its authority upon my mind and conscience by virtue of its contents, and I

19. Calvin, *Institutes*, 4, 8, 6.
20. Cranfield, *Bible*, 4.
21. Cranfield, *Bible*, 4.
22. Cranfield, *Bible*, 7.
23. Cranfield, *Bible*, 7.

know that now I cannot refuse to acknowledge its authority as the authority of God's own Word without trampling on what personal moral and intellectual integrity I possess.[24]

One can go along with this answer until the point that what is regarded as authoritative becomes, say, some incredible cosmological assertion or an unverifiable historical statement or an unacceptable ethical judgment. Christians, when at their best, hear God's word truly speaking to them through the Bible's texts, just as they may well hear that selfsame Word through the preaching of the church, but the sad fact is that the Bible, as well as preaching, has a track record of becoming the vehicle for the delivery of absolutely toxic messages. Not only can we sympathize with those who bewilderingly conclude that anything can be proved by the Bible, but there seems no limit to the human atrocities that have been given biblical authorization by Christians. Unless real discernment is exercised on the biblical texts we are at the mercy of beliefs, attitudes, and practices of an all too human nature being credited with divinely appointed status, when actually they are completely the product of our ignorance, insecurities, and lack of charity.

Reformed Christians have inherited a situation which lures them into believing that they can ride two horses. First, we have our commitment to the Bible. *The Westminster Confession* speaks of the Bible's ability to deliver "the infallible truth, and divine authority" when its words are opened up for us as the Word of God through "the inward work of the Holy Spirit."[25] This directs us to the heritage of the affirmation in *The Basis of Union of The United Reformed Church* that "the Word of God in the Old and New Testaments, discerned under the guidance of the Holy Spirit" is "the supreme authority for the faith and conduct of all God's people."[26] But, secondly, we have the commitment to take due account of the findings and approaches of biblical scholarship. This means that it is rather unlikely that most contemporary Reformed Christians would join the Westminster Assembly of Divines in claiming that "all things necessary for [God's] glory, man's salvation, faith, and life, is either expressly set down in Scripture, or by good and necessary consequence may be deduced from Scripture: unto which nothing at any time is to be added, whether by new revelations of the Spirit, or traditions

---

24. Cranfield, *Bible*, 3.

25. Thompson, *Stating The Gospel*, 13.

26. Thompson, *Stating The Gospel*, 251. The text of *The Basis of Union* is updated in successive editions of *The Manual* published by the URC at intervals to take account of Assembly decisions.

of men."[27] God did not stop addressing us when the ink dried on the New Testament pages. The Westminster divines claim too much for the biblical writers and too little for subsequent Christians on the matter of inspiration. Far more likely now are we to warm to the following statement agreed by the Congregational Church in England and Wales in 1967:

> The Bible must be read with fully critical attention if the Church is to discern the truth which is binding and not be in bondage to what is not binding; for the Bible is not free from human error and confusion and contradictions. It is a trustworthy means of grace, not in the sense that it is impervious to criticism but in the sense that through its records we are able to know God reliably and trust him confidently.[28]

Paul Capetz argues that "premodern persons cannot be held accountable to the requirements of historical-critical exegesis since they had no access to a mode of interpretation that had to await modernity for its emergence."[29] We cannot with integrity believe therefore that we can retain pre-critical approaches to biblical authority *as well as* take due note of the last two hundred years of biblical scholarship. What we now see happening so often is confused Reformed Christians feeling that they have to jump horses: from the fit young steed called "modern scholarship" (on whom prudent bookmakers have long since ceased taking bets) to an old worn-out nag called "biblical authority," as soon as scholarship or society comes up with conclusions that threaten their assumptions and certainties. The bottom line is this: "In showing the Bible to be fully explicable as a human product of the history of religion, historical criticism has made it very difficult for post-Enlightenment persons to continue to regard the Bible as the repository or criterion of all religious and moral truth."[30] To think otherwise is to flog a dead horse!

The burden is now laid upon me to show how the Bible possesses a lasting value and deep significance for individual Christians and the Christian movement, without our in any way having to give assent to redundant doctrines of biblical authority. Before I attend to that task a story will help reveal a crucial issue. A university colleague had just returned from sabbatical. He had been doing some research on the Pauline epistles, part of which had involved him reading up on all the interpretations which had been offered on a particularly controversial text. With wide-eyed enthusiasm

27. Thompson, *Stating The Gospel*, 13–14.

28. Thompson , *Stating The Gospel,* 227.

29. Capetz, "Theology," 481.

30. Capetz, "Theology," 487.

he announced his belief that he was certain now what Paul had meant when writing the text. Without thinking about the significance of my reply, I said: "OK, so now we know what Paul was meaning, do you think he was right?" It was if I had pricked a bubble! It was not that my friend believed that Paul speaks for God on matters religious and spiritual—though I have come across many in my time that do assume such a thing; rather, it concerned the fact that for him as a biblical scholar it was not self-evident when working with the biblical text that there is also a *theological* task to be done, one centered upon posing and answering two questions: "How is the claim made by the text to be understood today?" and "Is it true?" While we need historians so that the dead can be heard it is among the living that the final decisions have to be taken concerning the adequacy of Christian beliefs and practice.[31]

FINDING THE WATER IN THE WELL

At the ecumenical church I attended in Manchester for over fifteen years the Sunday service began as the Bible was paraded into the sanctuary followed by the worship leaders. The decision to do this had been the result of a great deal of heated debate, and I learned on the grapevine that the Anglicans and Methodists had largely gone along with it on the grounds that since it was a standard URC practice it had better be adopted in the interests of becoming an inclusive Christian community. Setting to one side whether or not such reasoning represents an approach to theology which gives ecumenism a bad name—after all not all "standard" practices are likely to be compossible and the time comes when decisions have to be made concerning the merits of competing practices—what was particularly noticeable to us as newcomers was the determined sit-down protest against what the Church Council had decided.

The small few who remained seated when the Bible was brought in turned out to be a radical group whose backgrounds lay in the Baptist and Congregational traditions. They were not prepared to risk collapsing the distinction between "the Word of God" and "the words of a book." They did not want to give an impression to the outside world that Christians are "people of the book" rather than part of the movement called "church," seeking to follow in the footsteps of Jesus. The underlying context for the protest lay in the rise of what is commonly called "fundamentalism," all the opposition in conservative theological circles to critical theology and biblical criticism, and the tendency in many church circles to turn a blind eye to

---

31. As Capetz says, "the chief task of a historian is to ensure that the dead get to have a say in our contemporary conversations" ("Theology," 484).

biblical scholarship and the mainstream secular consensus whenever either or both contradict an inherited view on an ethical issue. The Reformed need reminding sometimes that the classic symbol of Christianity is the cross and not a book.

Following a "paper Pope" all too easily converts an authoritative *source* into an authoritarian *norm*. While we must resist the idea that the Bible and God's Word should be viewed in separation, it is the hallmark of any adequate Christian theology that it always is aware of the distinction between them, not least because, as Robert Carroll has said, "at the centre of critical theology and the critical study of the Bible is a most welcome emancipatory movement away from post-Reformation tendencies to idolize the Word . . . and its concomitant tyranny over religious communities."[32] Hence we should proceed on the basis that critical scholarship is a central tool in opening up the Bible today in ways which are both honest and empowering. After all, "The critical reading of the Bible has exposed its errors and mistakes, its contradictions and contrarieties, its xenophobic values and its many advocacies of violence, intolerance and hatred of others."[33] Without it the Bible becomes toxic: an idol in our midst which diverts us from being addressed by God's Word for us today as we cling to conclusions, ideas, and practices which require at least correction if not even replacement.

The Christians who have most impressed me have been those who have shown evidence of practicing what they have preached. The apostle Paul reminded us of what I call the first law of human nature when he said that whenever he wanted "to do what is good," evil lay "close at hand" (Rom 7: 21). It always seems that what the Christian tradition has called "sin" gets in the way of achieving in practice what we want to do. Sometimes, the gap is slight; at other times, it threatens our very integrity. To a certain degree we all get lured away from our goals or find what we are engaged in twisted and warped. Matters are even worse when it comes to group activity. Here what I call the second law of human nature kicks in: good people when working collaboratively often end up behaving badly. Reinhold Niebuhr taught us to make "a sharp distinction . . . between the moral and social behavior of individuals and of social groups, national, racial and economic" because "In every human group there is less reason to guide and to check impulse, less capacity for self-transcendence, less ability to comprehend the needs of others and therefore more unrestrained egoism than the individuals, who compose the group, reveal in their personal relationships."[34] This largely

32. Carroll, *Wolf,* 22.
33. Carroll, *Wolf,* 24.
34. Niebuhr, *Moral Man,* xi-xii.

explains why we end up making so many bad decisions in the councils of the church.

Given the two laws of human nature it will be clear that I do not possess any idealistic expectation when it comes to our individual and collective capacity to practice what we preach.[35] Nevertheless, the unimpressive individuals and groups are those that do not come within hailing distance of matching their words with their deeds. This now is the case with the Reformed in the West when it comes to the Bible. Slowly but surely a basic fault line has opened up between what Reformed Christians collectively say about biblical authority and how the Bible actually functions in their lives. It is not really a matter of devoted Bible readers somehow being led astray in their reading of Scripture, but rather the issue of an almost wholesale disregard of the Bible in their everyday lives. We have known for some time that the Bible is the world's great unread best-seller; we all know that only a small percentage of Reformed church members ever take part in Bible study groups in their churches—but given the nature of some such groups they may be forgiven that; and it is quite clear from my pastoral ministry that the vast majority of faithful church attendees conduct their complex lives without much reference to the Bible. This evidence leads to the conclusion that whatever the Reformed world has historically asserted about the place of the Bible among Christians individually and collectively, contemporary members of the Reformed churches in the West display a practical attitude to the status of the Bible rather similar in principle to the way many Western Roman Catholics treat their Church's teaching on birth control. Once people accept a responsibility to think for themselves and make their own decisions, the authority of others (whether the writers of religious books, the councils of the church, or church leaders) is questioned, particularly when what they are advocating is no longer credible or empowering. For the Reformed there is the added embarrassment that our claims of biblical authority come via conciliar decision-making processes. We all too easily look down our noses at the authoritarian leadership exercised by church

---

35. For this reason I gave a mixed reaction to the early treatises of so-called "libera-tion theology." While warming to an emphasis upon the social and political dimen-sions of the Christian Gospel, I could not treat the stress upon "orthopraxis" (often in negative opposition to "orthodoxy") as anything but suffering from utopian tendencies. While I accept the wisdom of the dictum "to know the truth is to do the truth" in its aspirational dimension I do not regard myself or anyone else as being in a position to possess *full* knowledge or have the ability to put it into practice *perfectly*. It is not only fundamentalists who have the tendency to claim as absolutes what can only ever be provisionalities. The Synoptic Gospels even go so far as recording Jesus as saying to an interlocutor: "Why do you call me good? No one is good but God alone" (Mark 10 18; see also Matt 19: 17 and Luke 18: 19).

leaders in episcopally ordered churches without fully recognizing our potentiality for waywardness when it comes to following the lead offered by church councils.

Before we can hope to re-acquaint people with the Bible, so that the Scriptures once again become central to their Christian discipleship, we must recognize the reasons which lie behind the current lack of engagement with the Scriptures among Reformed Christians. To put it in a way which reflects my title, we need to concern ourselves with why it is that so many of our Church Members never visit the well in search of the water. Four reasons are worthy of consideration. If a creative relationship with the Bible is to be fostered among Christians a "felt need" for the Bible will need to be generated, and that will only be achieved when the barriers to biblical engagement are addressed, always allowing for the possibility that what actually puts some people off Scripture is its challenging content. It could be that institutional Christianity has found a way for people to remain committed to the church without fully accepting the gospel as presented in Scripture in its manifold expressions.

The first inhibitor to a serious engagement with the Bible has been alluded to earlier. We live in a society in which human autonomy is precious. This means that people will only doff their caps to authority if and when those in authority are making sense and doing what is expected of them. When church leaders or councils advocate ways of thinking and behavior on purely biblical grounds, they often assume that human reason and experience play no part in theological judgments and Christian decision making. A theological assertion cannot be declared credible simply because it is shown to be biblical. Even those who tend to think this way undermine their position in practice when upon inspection it is clear that they believe, say, and do things which run contrary to biblical teaching. And when they emphasize the need to be biblical, without also equally emphasizing how Christians need to apply their minds and analyze their experience, they run the risk of being dismissed as "Bible bashers." We need to remember that one of the major barriers to people's engagement with the Bible is the example of past and present Christian use of the Bible.

Secondly, contemporary Christians belong to a culture which venerates "heritage" but has lost touch with the way "tradition" is a living voice of continuity in the passage from the old to the new. Heritage is a major industry capitalizing upon our fascination with the past. The Beamish Museum is close to where I live. It attracts millions of visitors who out of a mixture of intense interest coupled with mild amusement get a very good picture of past life in a Durham pit village. They visit the sweetshop, chemists, and doctors; they go down the mine; and they enter the church.

They experience a past from which we have moved on. One of the guides at this excellent tourist attraction ended up as one of my students. She spoke tellingly about overhearing conversations in the well preserved Methodist church at Beamish which assumed that what being church is all about is as redundant today as nineteenth-century medical practices. Along with the church, the Bible is viewed today as part of our "heritage"—something which belongs to our past.

This attitude was very much in evidence when the UK celebrated the four-hundredth anniversary of the completion of the 1611 King James Bible. Persons of prominence and stature were found in print and on air waxing eloquently about the role the Authorized Version played in the formation of English identity.[36] Michael Gove, the then Education Secretary, sent a copy of the King James Bible to every state school student "to help every pupil access Britain's cultural heritage."[37] What justified such an expense at a time of great austerity is a moot point when most school cupboards are not bereft of such Bibles, but Gove gave an indication of his reasons when he said:

> It's a thing of beauty, and it's also an incredibly important historical artefact. It has helped shape and define the English language and is one of the keystones of our shared culture. And it is a work that has had international significance.[38]

Revealingly, what he did not say is that the 1611 Version (i) is almost incomprehensible to many contemporary readers; (ii) contains so many inaccuracies in translation that no reputable biblical scholar would recommend it for use; or (iii) and more importantly that it might through the work of the Holy Spirit become the vehicle through which God's living voice is heard today bringing a word of judgment and grace upon *today's* world. The notion that the Bible is the source of a norm according to which individual and corporate life is to be critiqued is largely lost on our church members, not just high-ranking politicians.

Thirdly, mention of the incomprehensibility of the 1611 Bible reminds us that the Bible in any translation is difficult to understand. When it is also accepted that according to some hermeneutical theories all texts are capable

---

36. The very fact that one set of human beings (whether church, state, or in this case both) could attempt to *authorize* a version of the Bible is just one example of the many ways that over the years we have tried to enforce *our* reading of Scripture over those of others. Some of those who most revere the Bible are those most resistant to the idea that *somehow* they stand under the authority of God's Word as discerned from Scripture—rather than they over it!

37. *Guardian,* 26 November 2011.

38. *Guardian,* 26 November 2011.

of spawning multitudes of readings it quickly becomes clear that reading Scripture is not a straight-forward matter. It is a rather more difficult and complex business than the church has been prone at times to admit. I recall learning at school that one of the primary benefits of the Reformation was its making the Bible available to everyone, only later to discover that due to illiteracy almost being normative for people of that age most people actually only received their biblical teaching second hand from the ordained. Nor was I told how the new emphasis upon a book threatened the non-cerebral style of being religious which had sustained generations of Christians in their faith. The problem does not simply center upon an emphasis on biblical authority tending towards an overtly intellectualized pattern of believing; it also concerns admitting that even for those not lacking intellectual gifts the Bible remains a very difficult book to understand. The need for contextual awareness places great demands on the reader unless we are happy to settle for readings which risk twisting the text into whatever shape we might happen to like it. The books of Scripture are often acutely difficult to understand, but when they are interpreted in quite different ways by reputable scholars we can forgive the rank and file churchgoer for leaving the Bible on the shelf unread. Those who talk about "the *plain* meaning of Scripture" must be working with a different Bible to the one I sweat and toil over!

These three inhibitors to committed Bible reading place the reasons for the eclipse of the Bible in factors beyond the reader's powers. We must also face however the possibility that people do not engage with the Bible because its message is too uncomfortable and inherently challenging. As soon as Christians have the temerity to use the teaching of Jesus as the criterion for political policy or everyday events they are likely to be pilloried. This is particularly true if you are a bishop of the Church of England. And the fact that politicians are always taking bishops to task for their utterances on social and political issues causes me to think that there might at least be one thing in favor of episcopal governance—I await the remaining virtues which would finally convince me of taking leave of a more conciliar system!

In an article in *The Observer*, Victoria Cohen presented herself as a rather unlikely advocate of biblical Christianity when commenting upon a furor caused in some quarters by the House of Lords' bishops blocking proposed legislation on welfare benefits. She countered the right-wing press by reminding them that the bishops were only fulfilling "their job to do what the Bible tells them to do, i.e. look out for the needy, like the innocent children on whose behalf they raised the amendment, who might otherwise get lost." I recall that the URC was once described by Kenneth Slack as a church of *Daily Telegraph* readers being ministered to by readers of *The Guardian*.[39] Might it not be the case that one of the reasons why some do not engage wholeheartedly with Scripture is that they, like the right-wing press, do not like what they read? For Westerners the Bible makes very uncomfortable reading. As Cohen rightly points out it is very unfair on the Bishops to attack them for what they are saying when they are the messengers of a higher authority. The problem for the right-wing press

> is that the New Testament, if read as an economic tract, is in-nately rather socialist. It's all sharey-sharey. Jesus wanted every-one to get a bit of bread and fish. He was all about the divvying up and the helping one's neighbour. So, if Christianity is going to make itself heard on tax-and-spend policies, it has *got* to lean towards spreading the spoils around. There's not much the bish-ops can do about that. Their hands are tied. The gospels say what they say.[40]

In other words, when we put the teaching of Jesus alongside some of the working presuppositions of global capitalism from which Westerners all duly benefit (and often at the expense of others) we face an acute challenge similar to that posed to Israel by the eighth-century prophets. It is quite natural for people to want to avoid disorienting challenges to their ways of living, so can we be really surprised if they do not engage with Scripture?

When Western Christians engage with the Bible they almost inevitably tend to read from the perspective of a theology which often owes as much, if not even more, to Western presuppositions than it does to the biblical message itself. The various theologies of liberation have taught us to be alert to the ways in which our biblical reading is used to support religious thought and practice which fits our cultural assumptions and even favors our position in the world. When we receive the results of biblical scholarship from Latin America, Africa, or Asia we find ourselves reading Scripture through fresh eyes, while from within the West itself feminist readings of the Bible have pointed out and then challenged the masculine hegemony which historically shaped the Bible and subsequently has largely controlled the church's thought and practice. As the inherited presuppositions with which Westerners tend to approach the biblical text are challenged, the Bible starts to offer a powerful critique of Western culture and the religious institutions within it. It also points to the possibility of a more hopeful future than

---

39. This is a significant observation deserving of analysis and thereby consideration of its implications. I would add *Daily Mail* and *Daily Express* to the members' category and *I* to that of the ministers in the light of my more recent observations.

40. *Observer*, 29 January 2012.

what Walter Brueggemann calls "the dominant" community and culture.[41] As such it takes the stature of subversive literature: it challenges those in authority; it upsets the status quo; and it provides hope for those who are on the underside of history.

Brueggemann traces a strand within the Bible which begins with Moses, is kept alive by the witness of the prophets against the "royal consciousness" of those in power from Solomon onwards, and comes to its fulfillment in the life, witness, and death of Jesus.[42] It promotes and champions an alternative way of living to that evident in Egypt under the Pharaoh, in Israel under the Temple tradition, and in the contemporary West. The Exodus and the Crucifixion are all of a piece in that they lead to what Brueggemann calls "the formation of a countercommunity with a counterconsciousness."[43] Moses shattered "the religion of static triumphalism" with its "politics of oppression and exploitation" and its guarding of the position and interests of a favored few.[44] God was re-discovered as a God of gracious freedom who acts in favor of the downtrodden and marginalized. The "god" who orderly kept the *status quo* in place was shown to be an idol. Whether railing against the social and economic injustices of their day, or speaking tenderly to a nation bereft of hope in exile, the prophets kept alive the Mosaic tradition against the tendency in Israel for "the sovereignty of God" to become "fully subordinated to the purpose of the king."[45] Brueggemann argues that, from Solomon onwards:

> Royal reality rode roughshod over Moses' vision. The gift of freedom was taken over by the yearning for order. The human agenda of justice was utilized for security. The god of freedom and justice was co-opted for an eternal now. And in place of passion come satiation.[46]

Jesus follows the prophetic tradition in re-presenting the Mosaic vision of God as One who is attentive to the cries of the marginalized. The divine caring, weeping, grieving, and rejoicing cannot be overcome by either religion or state; it comes to a focus in Jesus. Brueggemann says: "Jesus is engaged not in social control but in dismantling the power of death, and he does so by submitting himself to the pain and grief present

---

41. Brueggemann, *Prophetic Imagination*, xvi–xvii.

42. Brueggemann, *Prophetic Imagination*, xi.

43. Brueggemann, *Prophetic Imagination*, 21.

44. Brueggemann, *Prophetic Imagination*, 6.

45. Brueggemann, *Prophetic Imagination*, 28.

46. Brueggemann, *Prophetic Imagination*, 35.

in the situation, the very pain and grief that the dominant society must deny."[47] The Crucifixion of Jesus brings an end to an old order which brings death in its wake. It reveals "God's odd freedom, his strange justice, and his peculiar power."[48] And, as the Cross becomes viewed from the perspective of Easter Sunday, the early Christians were amazed that God is able to bring life to even the darkest places. "That amazement gave energy, the only kind of energy that gives newness."[49] It created a counter-cultural community called "the church" which when true to its calling possesses "evangelical will for public engagement" against all current manifestations of the "royal consciousness" and on behalf of all its victims.[50] Energized by its memories, hopes, and suffering it is able to make a difference in the world.

Brueggemann is quite clear that American culture, churches, and Christians are caught up in everything which the prophetic strand within the biblical narrative sought to replace: "the hegemonic power of the 'royal consciousness' is all but totalizing among us."[51] As in the rest of the Western world the ethos of consumerism reigns. Brueggemann tells us that "Our consciousness has been claimed by false fields of perception and idolatrous systems of language and rhetoric."[52] We have lost our roots in a faith tradition and with that the memories which generate genuine hope. As a result, the counter-cultural community called church will appear in our society as "a curiosity and a threat," since it has "energizing memories and . . . radical hopes."[53] That it often does not live up to its calling as the guardian of "the prophetic imagination" means that the central witness of the Bible speaks against it every bit as much as challenging the current manifestations of "the royal consciousness" with which it gets compromised. It follows that the Bible does not trade in neutralities. The water at the bottom of the well is refreshing for some, but less palatable for others—particularly those who have a love affair with an idolatrous culture from which they continue to benefit. It is those who have felt-needs which the Bible directly addresses who are the ones that discover a real love-affair with Scripture. They thereby start adopting an approach to living and style of being church which is generous to the lost and hopeless. Brueggemann's work points to the requirement to generate a felt need to belong to a counter-cultural group which promotes

47. Brueggemann, *Prophetic Imagination* , 92.

48. Brueggemann, *Prophetic Imagination* , 99.

49. Brueggemann, *Prophetic Imagination* , 102.

50. Brueggemann, *Prophetic Imagination* , xvii.

51. Brueggemann, *Prophetic Imagination* , xi.

52. Brueggemann, *Prophetic Imagination,* 1.

53. Brueggemann, *Prophetic Imagination,* 1.

"the prophetic imagination." This will only become possible when people hear the critique of the present from the Bible's prophetic strand.

The message Brueggemann paints on a broad social and political canvas also applies to individuals standing in their sinfulness before the holiness of God. In *Reading the Bible with the Damned*, Bob Ekblad draws upon his experience of conducting Bible studies with those incarcerated for having committed horrendous crimes. It helped him "rediscover the Bible as a place where good news abounds."[54] When insiders in the church read the Bible with outsiders, Ekblad argues, our traditional readings are challenged. We begin to see with fresh eyes what hitherto was hidden from us. Conversely when the outsiders are those society is punishing, we quickly realize that they come to their biblical reading with a particular theological perspective that makes them particularly resistant to hearing good news from Scripture. This realization causes Ekblad to conclude that our reading of the Bible ought to be liberated from "the dominant theological paradigm, which assumes that blessing in this world is a reward for good behavior and exclusion a punishment for bad."[55] Also among the theological presuppositions "the damned" bring with them are "debilitating images of God and self."[56] God is conceived as a distant, celestial sovereign who predetermines everything, "a monster God whose demands are endless and desire for compliance insatiable."[57] Not only does this God have eyes permanently scanned upon all who might be acting wrongly, but this God is also regarded as being with those who enforce the law, the powerful, and the privileged. God therefore becomes a legalistic judge best kept at a distance if trouble is to be avoided. Bound up with this view of God is a resulting self-image dented by endless failures, lack of affirmation, and deep lack of self-esteem. Ekblad argues that the Bible opens up for such people when they find its central thread showing how God "unexpectedly sides with the powerless and condemns the powers to destruction."[58] Far from what they had been given to believe God is "a liberal, generous, good God who desires that humans enjoy life."[59] Then they can go on to realize they are not destined to become victims of fate. Rather they gain confidence and hope from realizing that God wills their spiritual healing from the sickness that hitherto has largely governed their actions. "Viewing sin as spiritual malady

54. Ekblad, *Reading the Bible*, ix.

55. Ekblad, *Reading the Bible*, 76.

56. Ekblad, *Reading the Bible*, 25.

57. Ekblad, *Reading the Bible*, 28.

58. Ekblad, *Reading the Bible*, 115.

59. Ekblad, *Reading the Bible*, 31.

and God as therapist or physician," Ekblad has found, helps those weighed down by guilt accrued from much wrong doing to find "a new perspective on the Bible and salvation."[60]

Ekblad shows how it is only through challenging the theology people bring with them to their Bible reading that the Bible is able to be "good news" for them. Central to the task of biblical facilitation is "Identifying and countering evidence that appears to reinforce the dominant theology in the biblical stories if the Bible is to be salvaged as the medium of an empowering word."[61] The Bible can be made to authorize different theologies. This then leaves the issue concerning which theology is the most adequate. Part of the answer to that question, Ekblad believes, involves us asking another question: "Whose side are we on?" Are we on the side of the state, the law, or the economic system? Or do we stand with the weak and vulnerable who are often at the mercy of the powerful? Ekblad argues that, given Jesus was the living embodiment of who God is and what God is like, our Lord's life and witness provide clear evidence about where Christians should stand and on whose behalf they should work. As Jesus remarked: "Those who are well have no need of a physician, but those who are sick; I have come to call not the righteous but sinners" (Mark 2: 17 and parallels). Once those weighed down with their past deeds "hear good news from a good God, they can hear themselves as addressed by God, forgiven for real guilt, released from false guilt, called to higher levels of freedom and responsibility."[62] Jesus opens up a view of salvation which centers upon "the liberation, healing, and total transformation and empowerment of the least."[63] Through careful facilitation those who initially come to Scripture believing it to be a place where they will be reminded of their inadequacies, prompted to feel guilt, and receive yet more punishment therefore can be led into the arms of "a gracious presence, who accompanies them in spite of their crimes and brokenness."[64] It is when people start to glimpse God's vulnerable love that hard hearts are melted, changes of character take place, and new lives are born. In a world which so often makes people feel everything is against them—including God—it is "good news" indeed to know that God is always for sinners.

Finally, to bring what I have been saying to a conclusion, let me state five principles involved in ensuring that the Bible can be a loving text.

60. Ekblad, *Reading the Bible*, 55.

61. Ekblad, *Reading the Bible*, 100.

62. Ekblad, *Reading the Bible*, 8.

63. Ekblad, *Reading the Bible*, 126.

64. Ekblad, *Reading the Bible*, 168.

Firstly, we must accept that the Bible is a human text. Whatever theories of biblical inspiration we put forward have to undergird what biblical scholarship has made blindingly obvious. This means that we may find sound reasons to bypass certain biblical teachings when the common consensus convinces us that strategy is appropriate. This holds even when we recognize that opinion sometimes is divided. We then have to decide which way to turn, perhaps remembering that passionate minorities have a history of being wrong as well as right. Another way to make this point is to say that the criteria for theological adequacy are two-fold: one takes us back to the biblical witness; the other directs us to common experience and reason. Both have to be satisfied, so in one sense the twin theological criteria are situation invariant. But since "the Lord has yet more light and truth to break forth from His word"[65] and human reason and experience are always evolving it also follows that in another sense the twin criteria are decidedly situation variant.

Secondly, however problematical the Bible may be for us and while acknowledging the many atrocities which have been done in its name, as well as all the backward thinking it has generated, we can be thankful that the Bible has inspired some of the noblest adventures of the human spirit. It has been the driving force of some of the better moments in world history, not just some of the worst. It invites us to come to an even-handed appreciation of it.

Thirdly, a creative approach to the Bible involves a two-way conversation in which we attempt a double-rapprochement: from the side of Scripture to the contemporary context, and from the side of the contemporary context to Scripture. Each side has questions to ask of the other; while each may have purported answers to questions posed by the other. This involves bringing together quite different thought worlds, recognizing that *they* certainly thought and did things differently back *then*, but also acknowledging that human nature has not changed all that much over the years. Dennis Nineham suggests that "the way to use the Bible is to discover what it was the biblical writers were responding to and then to respond ourselves in a way which, while being entirely appropriate to our own cultural situation, reproduces the biblical response *as far as possible*."[66] Not only may this involve a necessity to reinterpret the biblical witness, but there also will be the need to move beyond it in some instances. Our overall approach however needs to be more relaxed than the way many Christians have approached Scripture. As John Barton has said: "The authority of the Bible

---

65. From George Rawson's hymn, based on the parting words of Pastor John Robinson to the Pilgrim Fathers, 1620, found in *Congregational Praise*, no. 230.

66. Nineham, *Use and Abuse*, 135–36. Italics mine.

for faith is . . . not to be conceived of after the model of a code or textbook to which we can appeal to guarantee the truth of our beliefs, but after the analogy of a trusted friend, on whose impressions and interpretations of an important event or experience we place reliance."[67]

Fourthly, one of the reasons why we engage in a conversation with the biblical text is because we want to be put in touch with Jesus, "the pioneer and perfecter of our faith" (Heb. 12: 2). This means that the New Testament is crucial for both Christian discipleship and theology. But unless we are to succumb to Marcionite tendencies we must also acknowledge the essential role of the Hebrew Scriptures. They provide us with the background upon which Jesus' life and work is to be understood and also the early part of the biblical story to which, according to the early Christians, Jesus was the climax. We are never free from the fact that we are always taken inside the biblical story by the Christian church: "Not only is the canon of Scripture itself the product of the church's experience and decisions, but all the individual writings of the New Testament as well are expressions of the church's ongoing interpretation of the original apostolic witness."[68]

Fifthly, the Bible is the authoritative source for what is normative within Christianity. It has provided the church with its paradigmatic story. A complex web of events reported in the Bible has become strung together as a story which has taken on soteriological significance for Christian people. The authoritative nature of the Bible for theology therefore resides in its providing a story from which theologians can do their work imaginatively and with reference to which their formulations can be assessed. The story starts with Abraham. It moves out via Moses and the prophets towards Nazareth, with a pilgrim people for whom God's presence and promise was *implicitly* known in their wanderings and then came to be recognized *explicitly* in Jesus Christ. In Christ's name, the church took the story from Jerusalem to the whole of Judea and Samaria and to the ends of the earth (Acts 1: 8). By telling the story in the form in which it is discovered in the Bible the church has displayed the significance the Bible has for it and produced a criterion against which theological statements and the Christian life must be assessed for their adequacy with scripture. Barr reminds us that: "Whatever the nature of the real events, it seems to be on *the telling of the story in this form* that the effective status of the Bible depends."[69]

When I talk about "the paradigmatic story" being the ultimate criterion by which theological statements and the Christian life must

---

67. Barton, *People of the Book?* 45.

68. Ogden, *On Theology*, 58.

69. Barr, *Bible in the Modern World*, 83–84.

be shown to be appropriate I am suggesting that the Bible possesses an authoritative function because it contains a story which discloses the identity of God outside and inside God's self-revelation in Jesus. According to Barr, "It furnishes us with the *classic* literary expression of the people of God's experience in their contact with God."[70] It is a story rather than a record and its purpose is to awaken faith, aid understanding, and grant hope. When we seek the authority of scripture we do not confront a fixed quantum of truth, locked inside a privileged portion of the Bible, which we only have to understand hermeneutically and then make our thinking and deeds accord with it. Rather we encounter a paradigmatic story—what James Barr calls variously "a kind of literary myth of Christianity,"[71] "the basic foundation myth of Christianity,"[72] or a "canonical story"[73]—which provides paradigms concerning the God-world, God-person, and person-person relationships from which Christian thought and practice can be constructed imaginatively and according to which they are to be assessed for their scriptural adequacy.

70. Barr, *Explorations*, 122.
71. Barr, *Bible in the Modern World*, 58.
72. Barr, *Bible in the Modern World*, 137.
73. Barr, *Explorations*, 126.

7

Some Unfinished Business from the Great Ejectment of 1662[1]

WHEN THE MAJORITY OF people look back on 2012 they will recall the celebrations to mark the sixty years of Queen Elizabeth II's reign on the throne and the holding of the Olympic and Paralympic Games in London. It will probably escape them that 2012 also commemorated the three hundred and fiftieth anniversary of an event in English and Welsh life that in no small measure started to fashion the religious plurality we enjoy today.

The Act of Uniformity of 1662 achieved the opposite of its intentions. Instead of creating a uniform church over which the Crown was the Supreme Governor, the Great Ejectment which the Act caused proved once and for all that religious uniformity cannot be achieved by parliamentary legislation. Not only does 1662 mark the birth of a Nonconformist tradition which in Victorian times had become numerically equal to that of the Church of England, but it also reminds us of the persistence of a way of being church which originally was championed by Puritans who, in opposition to the 1559 Elizabethan Settlement, "established" their Separatist churches outside the jurisdiction of the Church of England. And, as Alan Sell notes, "the Separatists would have endorsed the line of the hymn had they known it: 'The Church's *one* foundation is Jesus Christ her Lord', from

---

1. A paper delivered to the Cumbria Theological Society on 6 September 2012. It emerged out of various talks and sermons delivered around the North East of England during 2012.

which sentiment they drew the negative inference that there is no biblical justification for supposing that the church can properly have a monarch as its temporal head."[2] The events of 1662 guaranteed that there never would be a monopoly of religion on these shores.

While to a large extent many of the issues for Christianity which resulted from the Great Ejectment have been resolved, and newer and more pressing ones have arrived with the emergence of a multi-faith Britain, there is still some merit in reminding ourselves of the causes and implications of the Great Ejectment. It also remains of value to re-examine what might be termed the "unfinished business," even hoping that by so doing reconciliation between churches can be further advanced.

This chapter begins with a brief historical overview which traces the causes of the Great Ejectment and then outlines its implications for those Christians who became known as Nonconformists. I will then present a survey of the theological disagreements undergirding the momentous events which followed St Bartholomew's Day 1662. Some of those disagreements have long since been settled, but others remain a thorn in the flesh for even the most committed ecumenical Nonconformist. Finally, I will advocate a well-known model of translocal ministry which has a notable ecumenical pedigree. The concept of "bishop-in-council" addresses questions and concerns both within Anglicanism and my own Reformed tradition regarding adequate translocal ministry. It could lead to a reconciled approach to the vexed issue of episcopacy if both traditions were prepared to own up to the inadequacies of what they have at present and be open to receiving fresh ways of working from their ecumenical partners.

THE GREAT EJECTMENT: CAUSES AND IMPLICATIONS

The worlds of religion and politics interacted in such complex ways during the sixteenth and seventeenth centuries that this period of history is not only interesting because very colorful, but also susceptible to superficial understanding through a temptation to read it largely from one particular standpoint. But whether in any re-run we would aspire to be Puritan or Laudian, Roundhead or Cavalier, Establishment Anglican or Dissenting Nonconformist, we would be wise to accept that the ongoing internecine conflict during this period hardly brings much credit on the community called "church." We find in this period of English history material for a blood-thirsty episode in that documentary series now emerging in my mind, entitled "Christians behaving badly." However much we are proud of

2. Sell, "Doctrinal and Ecumenical Significance," 232.

our 1662 forebears the story we should remember is rather less one-sided than those we find in some of the locally produced histories of congregations founded in 1662.

To keep things within bounds, let me begin with Elizabeth I's attempt to unify England under the auspices of an Established pattern of Christianity. She attempted to forge a so-called "Anglican Settlement" which sought to hold together Roman Catholic and Reformed theologies and polities. But, as I once heard an Anglican bishop remark about more recent turbulent times within Anglicanism, the great problem is that the "Anglican Settlement" is far from settled. Elizabeth was a pragmatist who tried to marry together Roman emphasis upon tradition and reason with the Reformed stress upon scripture when deciding what is authoritative for Christian thought and practice. It was not lost on Nonconformists that Elizabeth's "Settlement" always intended to keep church and state under monarchical rule, thereby never fully meeting the basic ecclesiological problem as many of them perceived it.

The Puritan wing of the church had already experienced patterns of worship which they believed to be more in accordance with those practiced by the New Testament churches than the ones contained in a prayer book with a Roman Catholic emphasis. They had little time for what was proposed by the 1559 Act of Uniformity, the third of three sixteenth century Acts of Uniformity, all of which attempted to enforce use of a *Book of Common Prayer* in the churches. Some of those Puritans duly formed Separatist churches. Most of them expected to return to the Church of England once it was thoroughly reformed, an eventuality which they considered inevitable such was their theological confidence in what they believed about the nature of the "true" church. That said, the very existence of Separatist churches reminds us that it is historically inaccurate to regard St Bartholomew's Day 1662 as the birthday of Independent churches. It was also the case that very few of those who were ejected in 1662 were Independents. By and large, the Independents had left the national church before that date, or been ejected following the Act for Restoring Ministers (1660). Many of the early Separatists were so severely persecuted that they fled to safety in Holland. It was from the communities they founded in towns like Amsterdam and Leyden that some of the Pilgrim Fathers were drawn who set sail for America in 1620.

As church history shows the organic unity of the Christian church remains elusive. It seems to come under the category of what Reinhold Niebuhr calls an "impossible possibility," an idea to be striven for but one which will never be achieved.[3] Perhaps Elizabeth I now looks down on the

3. "Without the ultrarational hopes and passions of religion no society will ever

United Reformed Church's attempt to break the ecumenical logjam with a sense of pity borne out of the experience of disappointment! But, given what she had inherited, she had the sense to see that trying to bring together the different religious factions was a precondition for there being peace and stability. Monarchs who immediately followed her, however, were not so politically astute. When Charles I failed to call Parliament for an entire eleven years, it was hardly surprising that there was universal outrage among Parliamentarians. He eventually called Parliament in 1640 only to get financial backing for his dubious policy in Scotland. Those Parliamentarians who didn't think that the 1559 Act of Uniformity had gone far enough in the direction of Rome asserted themselves and unity disappeared as the Puritan wing within Parliament in response pressed the case for further Reformation. A Civil War was the result. Cromwell was victorious and the Commonwealth period was born.

My education prior to the age of eleven was in Church of England schools. I recall learning about the Civil War through a kind of pantomime drama in which the audience was encouraged to hiss and boo whenever a Roundhead was centre stage; the "goodies" were Charles I and his gaudily dressed Cavaliers. I was too young to recognize the explicit attack on my Christian heritage. On the way to the Commonwealth period Charles I and William Laud, his Archbishop of Canterbury, were executed; many clergy were ejected, ostensibly on the grounds that they were ineffective and, often, absent from their parishes, but never because they were not Puritan enough; and the rank and file Christian was in danger of having the Christian tradition they had inherited and become accustomed to taken away from them. Those of us who want to stand on some high moral ground about the virtues of the Nonconformist stance in 1662 need to remember all this. During this historical period no branch of the church comes out smelling of roses.

When the monarchy was restored in 1660, Charles II's promise of freedom in religion was not matched by Parliamentary will. A hard line approach to all those who had supported the Commonwealth ensued. I will illustrate this by an extract from an account of the history of Toller Congregational, now United Reformed Church, in Kettering.

> In May 1662 a letter was delivered to [John Maidwell] at Ket-
> tering Rectory and as he read it he knew that the final challenge

---

have the courage to conquer despair and attempt the impossible; for the vision of a just society is an impossible one, which can be approximated only by those who do not regard it as impossible. The truest visions of religion are illusions, which may be *partially* realised by being resolutely believed." (Niebuhr, *Moral Man*, 81). Italics mine.

had come. He was faced with a stark issue—his home, living and security depended upon the sacrifice of his most deeply held beliefs. The letter told him the requirements of the new Act of Uniformity. It demanded that every man who ministered in the Church should declare "his unfeigned assent [and consent] to all and everything prescribed in and by the book entitled 'the Book of Common Prayer and Administration of the Sacraments and other Rites and Ceremonies of the Church according to the use of the Church of England'; together with the Psalter or Psalms of David printed as they are to be said or sung in churches; and the Form or Manner of Making, Ordaining and Consecrating Bishops, Priests and Deacons."

There was something cynical about the choice of date on which this Act was to be enforced—August 24th 1662. That day, St Bartholomew's, was already Black Bartholomew's Day to the men who recalled the massacre of the Hugenots (sic) 90 years before. Its choice meant too that those who refused to conform would suffer the maximum financial hurt, for the funds by which they lived became due in September.

. . . John Maidwell was under no illusion. To refuse to conform was to be thrown out of his living, to lose his home and to become a veritable outcast in his own land. Yet the alternative was to take a course that his conscience cried out to be utterly wrong and an outrage against so much that he believed. Poverty and persecution were the price of nonconformity; let us never forget it.[4]

That is a powerful story. It was replicated in over two thousand other rectories and vicarages. About one fifth of all the clergy were involved. It revealed an amazing nerve at a time when, as Doreen Rosman points out, "It was as abnormal . . . to dissociate from the national church, to which everyone belonged, as it is today to opt out of the school system and educate children at home."[5]

We can hardly over-stress the strength of conviction and depth of courage of those who made their sacrificial response to the 1662 Act of Uniformity. But, in the interest of historical accuracy, we ought also to acknowledge that among the majority of clergy who signed up to the 1662 Act were those Puritans who believed they should remain as a reforming presence within the State church. Also some of the Nonconformists, especially those who favoured a Presbyterian pattern of church government,

4. Goodman, *Great Meeting*, 6–7.

5. Rosman, *Evolution*, 67.

were never against the Establishment of religion in the way that some of those who later become referred to as Congregationalists most certainly were. What was an issue for them all, however, was how the church should be governed. And among Nonconformists as well as Conformists there were those whose opposition to the ministry of bishops was based mainly on the fact that the bishops were appointed by the Crown rather than upon an outright denial of the appropriateness in certain circumstances of personal *episcope* in church governance.

SOME THEOLOGICAL ISSUES OF THE GREAT EJECTMENT

In the aftermath of The Great Ejectment the early Nonconformists suffered intense persecution as Crown and State turned the screws ever tighter in their attempt to achieve uniformity in religion. Prior to the Ejectment Separatist Puritans had been denied access to any municipal office. The Corporation Act (1661) required that no one held such positions unless they had taken Holy Communion according to the rites of the Church of England, abjured the Solemn League and Covenant (1643) (which stated the intention of the English and the Scots to advance the Reformed faith), and accepted that it was unlawful to take up arms against the Crown for whatever reason. Then, after the events of St Bartholomew's Day 1662, further legislation hit Nonconformists very hard. The Conventicle Act (1664) made it an offence for more than five persons, in addition to the members of the household in which Christian worship was being conducted, to worship in ways not prescribed by the *Book of Common Prayer*. Fines and imprisonment faced offenders, who on a third conviction were transported. The Five Mile Act (1665) prohibited a Nonconformist minister from coming within five miles of a town or place where they had formerly ministered, unless they happened to be passing through on a journey. Meanwhile, the Test Act (1673) was specifically aimed at Roman Catholics, but it had knock-on effects for Nonconformists. No one could work for the Government who had not taken an oath rejecting the doctrine of transubstantiation and received Holy Communion according to the rites of the Established Church. And, as Albert Peel says, "the sufferings of the Nonconformists under these repressive methods defy description."[6] Between five and eight thousand of them died in jail during the reign of Charles II as a result of refusing to conform to the dictates of "an immoral King and intolerant Bishops."[7]

6. Albert Peel, *Brief History*, 59.

7. Albert Peel, *Brief History*, 59

Viewed through the lenses of our more ecumenical times the degree of religious intolerance during the seventeenth century beggars belief. There is no space here to outline fully the chain of events which led to Nonconformists being awarded religious freedom; but it was the determined witness of Dissenters and Nonconformists which forced an unwilling establishment to give limited toleration in 1689 and subsequently over the following century and a half to remove the other legal restrictions which had been imposed upon them. Nor, perhaps more interestingly, can I do justice to the positive outcomes arising from the position in which Nonconformists found themselves. Denial of access to English universities generated the need to create their own educational establishments. The Dissenting Academies were to play a significant role in the development of English and Welsh public education. Meanwhile, befitting churches which gave a high priority in Christian ministry to biblical interpretation, Nonconformist ordinands were set high academic standards to become learned ministers who could teach their particular outcropping of "the gathered saints" a biblically-grounded faith. All of which reminds us that sometimes good things can arise amidst periods of tyranny.

Mention of the centrality of the Bible for Nonconformists takes us to the first of the several issues upon which they battled with the Established Church. The Puritan cry of *sola scriptura* had gone out a long time ago, sounding the objection to setting the standards within the church concerning faith and order issues in "tradition" rather than the Bible. It put down a marker concerning Christian foundations "Reformed style." The Basis of Union of the United Reformed Church, for example, "acknowledges the Word of God in the Old and New Testaments, discerned under the guidance of the Holy Spirit, as the supreme authority for the faith and conduct of all God's people" (para.12).[8] While the phrase "discerned under the guidance of the Holy Spirit" should protect a church against adopting a narrow biblicism based on too easily equating God's word to us with the words written in ancient manuscripts, the statement also reminds us of an era when authority in the church resided in all too human traditions emanating from the Crown, aided and abetted by the Episcopate. Not only has that era long gone, but the ancient "scripture verses tradition" debate has been somewhat nullified by the conclusions of biblical scholarship stemming from a renewed awareness of the contextuality of the biblical books and the inherent traditions of Scripture. The old Protestant high-ground gets flattened out when we recognize that the New Testament records the primary

8. Found in the URC *Manual.*

traditions of the church concerning Jesus.[9] Meanwhile, the illogicality of claiming divine inspiration for the biblical books but ruling it out for any writings outside the scriptural canon perhaps is evidence of a pneumatology still held captive to the first century. What we find today is not so much an *inter*-church debate about the role the Bible plays in authorizing what we believe and practice, but *intra*-church disagreements which result in us finding allies in other denominations sometimes in equal proportion to those we cannot agree with in our own.

A second issue undergirding the bitter conflict surrounding the 1662 Act of Uniformity was Establishment. There is a world of difference in saying that the monarch is "the Supreme Governor of the Church" and that s/he is its "ruler and head"; but it became a merely verbal distinction in the centuries during which Protestant Dissent emerged and the birth of Nonconformity took place. Those who had been led to discover a way of being church in which those gathered in the name of Christ believed they had been given by God everything necessary for being the one holy, catholic, and apostolic church, took exception to being required to conduct worship according to the Book of Common Prayer, or to set aside their ministries because they had not been ordained by a bishop standing in a supposed historic succession. What crowned the entire miserable business was that the imposition upon their religious freedom was driven by the Crown. We may note Sell once more:

> Our Dissenting forebears did not suffer and die for the sake of having deacons rather than elders, believer baptism rather than paedobaptism, or even Calvinism rather than Arminianism. They suffered and died in the interest of God's right to call whom he will into the church by the Spirit, and for the sole Lordship of Christ within it.[10]

Thankfully, the kind of State interference in religion which precipitated the Great Ejectment is a thing of the past. What we hear today is an heir to the

9. See Chapter 6.

10. Sell, "Doctrinal and Ecumenical Significance," 249. In his Chairman's address to the Congregational Union of England and Wales, 14 May 1962, on the occasion of the tercentenary of the Great Ejectment, John Huxtable noted how it hurt "[the Dissenters'] consciences to see the Church wrongly allied to the secular power." While Huxtable, a great Congregational ecumenist, accepted that those who "paid the price of following conscience" were "right," and asserted that "we are proud to stand in their succession," his address went on to issue a clarion call to church unity: "Whatever justification there was for division in the past, and there was much, does not permit us to evade the challenge of God's will to unity: indeed denominational pride may become a grievous stumbling-block to the fulfilment of Christ's purpose for his people" (Huxtable, *Tradition*, 17, 18–19).

throne wondering aloud about the appropriateness of his one day becoming in a multi-faith realm, "Defender of *the* Faith," and a leading Government official telling the media that his Government does not "do religion."

We have come a long way since 1662. Given that it is a Presbyterian church which is "established" in Scotland we are reminded that among those ejected in 1662 it was mainly those who became Congregationalists (rather than Presbyterians) who were opposed to Establishment *per se.* And even those of us who hail from the Congregational heritage will want to recognize certain virtues in Establishment. Few have outlined them in such an even-handed way as John Habgood. In his *Church and Nation in a Secular Age*, the then Archbishop of York, notes that "To be conscious of belonging to a national church is to be given a broad sense of responsibility for all and sundry."[11] While it may be granted that some groups of "gathered" Protestants have those sectarian tendencies which make them decidedly parochial in a way that "parochial" churches might be expected to be outward looking and thus bear "responsibility for all and sundry," we all know of "gathered" churches which exercise committed community-based ministries as well as "parochial" churches which are indeed decidedly parochial. Bearing "responsibility for all and sundry" is not guaranteed by Establishment, but it is part and parcel of our Christian calling.

Habgood came to the contentious conclusion that "the overall case for disestablishment, now or in the foreseeable future, is not convincing."[12] But there is "Establishment" English-style but also Scottish-style. The idea that the Crown and Parliament should have the final say in deciding the forms of worship used in local churches remains problematical, as does the State appointment of diocesan bishops and cathedral deans. A clear distinction of the roles of State and Church is useful if two dangers are to be avoided: first, the muzzling of the church by political interests; and secondly, the removal of the clear blue water which enables the church to maintain, when required, a prophetic stance concerning the activities of the State. This is not to suggest that the State will always seek to influence let alone control an Established Church's worship and polity—it is only to point out that sometimes Britain manages to throw up Prime Ministers like Margaret Thatcher who do attempt so to influence things. Nor am I suggesting that non-Established churches have a perfect track-record of being the Christian conscience that challenges governments which adopt sub-Christian policies. What I am claiming though is clearly stated in the "Statement concerning the Nature, Faith and Order of the United Reformed Church": "The United

---

11. Habgood, *Church and Nation,* 98.

12. Habgood, *Church and Nation,* 109.

Reformed Church declares that the Lord Jesus Christ, the only ruler and head of the Church, has therein appointed a government distinct from civil government and in things spiritual not subordinate thereto, and that civil authorities, being always subject to the rule of God, ought to respect the rights of conscience and of religious belief and to serve God's will of justice and peace for all humankind."[13]

Thirdly, therefore, the Great Ejectment was very much to do with Christians asserting their right to be wholly free from State intervention in religious matters. The idea that the Crown or Parliament should determine how a local church worships on a Sunday remains for many of us theologically absurd. But this does not mean that Christians are free to do what they like. Nothing in the theology of the early Nonconformists could ever justify the atomistic Independency which has so bedeviled Congregational patterns of being the church. When at their best, Nonconformists possess a view of "catholicity" which pulls Christians together in common causes rather than grants them a license to do whatever they want within the comfort zone of any small gathering of the saints.[14] Nor is there anything in the first Nonconformist theologies which supports the kind of rugged individualism that so dominates the contemporary West, where now truth tends to be reduced to personal opinion, and there has emerged an extensive intellectual tradition which eschews the once common-sense view that truth carries universal intentions. We must always remember that the Nonconformist "objection to royal tyranny was not that it constrained personal autonomy but that it impeded godly religion."[15] Indeed, the early Dissenters would have been rather surprised at the amount of freedom all churches and Christians enjoy today.

When it comes to how churches worship and who play leadership roles in the church, who decides? Those who left the national church in 1662 passionately believed they had the only sustainable answer to that question: it was not the Crown or Parliament; rather, it was the gathered church or its representatives meeting to discern God's will under the guidance of the Holy Spirit. This understanding of church governance is essentially grounded in spirituality. The Puritan spirit which drove the first Nonconformists convinced them that all that is needed for a full catholic expression of Christianity can be found in local gatherings of Christians due to God's gifting of those who gather and are open to the Holy Spirit. It has been said that "Puritans monitored the state of their souls much as later generations

13. Found in the URC *Manual.*

14. For a Reformed account of catholicity see Jenkins, *Nature of Catholicity.*

15. Rosman, *Evolution,* 100.

watched their weight, blood pressure, or cholesterol levels."[16] And what they did individually they applied to their collective ecclesial activity, looking beyond themselves for guidance regarding doctrine and polity—but not to the Crown, rather to God through the Holy Spirit. This led to Christian decision making understood as a spiritual activity, rooted in biblical exploration and communal prayer. It is the tradition of the Church Meeting.

Fourthly, the 1662 Act of Uniformity necessitated that only those ministers who had been ordained by a bishop standing in the so-called historic, apostolic succession of bishops were to be allowed to hold office. There were many examples of ministers however who had not been so ordained exercising distinguished service in congregations which were benefitting from their ministry. So episcopal ordination was not accepted by early Nonconformists as anything other than a not so subtle attempt by the State through the bishops it appointed to establish conformity in religion by riding roughshod over central Reformation principles. I feel sure that God does not judge our competence as Christian ministers according to whether or not we are episcopally ordained. Nor is there much evidence to suggest that episcopal ordination is a guarantee of an orderly church. But what hurts me greatly is that some among those for whom Christ died do not accept me fully as a minister within the church to which we all belong—and it also hurts many a Roman and Anglican colleague with whom I have collaborated in Christ's service. Then there is the vexed matter of being excluded from the Lord's Table. At the bottom of these offences lies an idolatrous denial of what God has already done for us, namely, through the work of Christ and in the power of the Spirit calling us out of the world into the *one* church and then sending us back into the world to be a sign and sacrament of his love for all. As Sell notes: "It is [the gracious, prevenient, work of God the Holy Spirit] that underpins the ecclesiology of historic orthodox Dissent, epitomized by the Separatists, the rejected and their heirs."[17]

INDIVIDUAL LEADERSHIP AND CONCILIAR TRADITION

From the perspective of a high Nonconformist ecclesiology all God's saints have been called and gathered in one church, no matter what denominational

16. Rosman, *Evolution*, 61.

17. Sell, "Doctrinal and Ecumenical Significance," 228. Elsewhere Sell claims that "All that is required [for unity] is the joyful recognition of what the gracious God has done for us in the Cross-Resurrection, and the celebration of this together at the table of the Lord." ("Holy Spirit," 87).

label they now adorn. It follows that we are called to display that this is so, and that involves so ordering our ecclesial life that it is genuinely inclusive of others, even those others who drive us to theological distraction or whose ethical behavior disturbs us. Under Word and around Table all distinctions vanish—doctrinal, ecclesiological or ethical, since what we have is shared: we are all sinners for whom Christ died. One of the great lessons to be learned from 1662 is that all the distinctions we so much cherish are what Sell has called "interpretative afterthoughts to the gospel of God's grace savingly active at the cross and brought home to us by the Holy Spirit who has made us one in Christ."[18] As a fellow heir of the Dissenting tradition I sympathize with Sell when he declares that it is "the height of arrogance to suppose that our agreements or our disagreements ought to be more precious to us than the grace that has made us one already (whether we like it or not)."[19] He boldly asserts that "Wherever the ecclesiastical-sectarian spirit rears its head we need to take the pneumatological drill and dig it up."[20] The problem though is that there are different pneumatological drills!

Any attempt to authorize matters of faith and order on pneumatological grounds *alone* runs the risk of subjectivity. While theologians like Alan Sell and I follow our heritage in regarding Christ's gift as the calling into being of the gathered saints, that is the church *qua* body of believers, others suggest more extensive pneumatological gifting. That very ecumenical Roman Catholic Jean-Marie Tillard, for example, argues that the Papacy and the Episcopacy come with the divine gift of the Church, not as secondary add-ons but as essential to it. He says that "the very roots of the ecclesial institution—the apostolic function and its derivatives—are in the strictest sense a gift of Christ to the church of God, given, guaranteed and supported by a *charisma* of the Holy Spirit."[21] It is a given Spiritual gift that "the whole ecclesial institution—including the primacy of Rome . . . is built around the episcopacy, which comes from the Spirit sacramentally."[22]

A pneumatological approach to ecclesiology obviously can generate quite different doctrines of the church. It is very difficult not to conclude somewhat skeptically that when working out our ecclesiologies most of us most of the time do little more than rationalize the positions we have grown up with or have subsequently taken. Just as people outside the church will often remind those within it that just about any belief or practice can be

18. Sell, "Doctrinal and Ecumenical Significance," 268.

19. Sell, "Doctrinal and Ecumenical Significance," 268.

20. Sell, "Doctrinal and Ecumenical Significance," 252.

21. Tillard, "Episcopacy," 68.

22. Tillard, "Episcopacy," 69.

justified by the Bible, so it sometimes seems that a reasonable case can be made for most patterns of being the church through arbitrarily asserting that the essential features of a particular pattern are "gifts of the Spirit."

I do not happen to think that episcopacy is of the essence (*esse*) of the church. For me to think so would involve me un-churching the congregations of the early church, which historically were not episcopally governed in the way we understand episcopal government today. In this respect, I find myself agreeing with the official theology of Anglicanism, for, as Stephen Sykes affirms:

> It is . . . not a part of any historic formularies of Anglicanism to insist that episcopacy belongs to the *esse* of the church. More-over, the official Roman Catholic response to the Final Report of ARCIC (1991) insisted that "the Roman Catholic Church recognizes in the apostolic succession both an unbroken line of episcopal ordination from Christ through the apostles down through the centuries to the bishops of today and an uninter-rupted continuity in Christian doctrine from Christ to those who teach in union with the College of Bishops and its head, the Successor of Peter." Though certain Anglicans may believe some or even all of these propositions, none of them is embedded in Anglicanism's authoritative, traditional material.[23]

Roman Catholic opinion notwithstanding, history reveals churches without episcopacy which have shown just as much evidence of being true and faithful churches as the Roman Catholic Church, and arguably on certain occasions more so.

Nevertheless, an unfortunate experience of episcopacy encountered by our dissenting forebears ought not to be a reason against our considering whether or not some form of *episcope*, beyond that exercised by a minister within a local church, might be profoundly worthwhile and, hence, for the church's *bene esse*. After all, a great many of the non-episcopally structured churches have not only felt the need for "translocal ministry" but taken steps to appoint individuals to exercise it.[24] And, quite often they have done so against protests that they were taking episcopacy into their system.[25] The pattern of such ministries has come under review at a time when there is a similar discussion within episcopally ordered churches about the nature,

23. Sykes, "*Episkopé* and Episcopacy," 100.

24. I first came across the term "translocal ministry" in Stuart Murray, *Translocal Ministry*.

25 This was the case with the introduction of Superintendent Ministers and Mod-erators in the Baptist and Congregational worlds respectively. See my *Story of the Moderators*.

purpose, and function of the episcopate. When we bring all these reviews and discussions together we find a growing consensus which could, if there was a will, support the adoption of a translocal ministry incorporating the strengths—and eliminating the weaknesses—of the ministries presently undertaken by people like Bishops, Moderators, Regional Ministers, Chairs of Districts etc.

Within the "growing" consensus are the following points. (1) No single pattern of *episcope* can be authorized by Scripture. (2)There were different models of translocal ministry being exercised in the pre-Constantinian church. (3) A single continuous succession of ministers from Peter onwards cannot be demonstrated historically. (4) The pipeline view of grace which undergirds classical accounts of the so-called historic succession changes a deeply personal gift into a cold, mechanistic transaction. (5) Biblical scholarship has demonstrated that there is little evidence of Christ formally handing on authority to the first apostles as has been traditionally maintained by some churches. (7) Translocal ministries, like all ministries, need exercising in "a personal, collegial and communal way."[26]

There has been a tendency for translocal ministries to become impersonal due to the size of the areas being covered and the way in which a managerial mindset in the church has transformed an essentially pastoral ministry into one of administration and management.[27] When at their best, translocal ministries offer a sign and symbol both of "the connectedness of apostolic faith and life through time and space" and of the unity of the church; but given the humanness of those who exercise them there is no "'guarantee' of fidelity."[28] Recognition of this suggests that there is much to be said for an ecumenical approach to translocal ministry which accepts that all our current examples of it are to a greater or lesser extent deficient. Then instead of working with the principle that the central issue at stake is getting everyone to endorse and accept *one particular form of* translocal ministry the task becomes one of devising, inaugurating, and developing a brand new form which gathers up the strengths and avoids the weaknesses of our existing patterns.

The question I need to hear is not: Will you take episcopacy into your system? That question carries an impertinent assumption, namely, that the URC does not have episcopacy. It also begs the question whether one would want to adopt something of which those who have it are often so critical.

---

26. See *Baptism, Eucharist and Ministry*, 25–26.

27. For an Anglican perspective see Pickard, *Theological Foundations*, 169–88; and for a URC perspective see my *Story of the Moderators*, esp. 49–110.

28. Pickard, *Theological Foundations*, 196.

So a more radical ecumenical question would be: Will you join with us in fashioning a common form of *episcope* which draws together all the gifts from our current models of episcopacy and creates a new form of oversight that is pastorally earthed and missionary minded?

This proposal draws upon several rich theological resources. One of them is the proposal which has arisen out of Anglican-Reformed discussions on at least two occasions for a translocal ministry of "Bishop-in-Presbytery."[29] The very title suggests a drawing together of personal and conciliar patterns of *episcope*. What might be expected of my own tradition is outlined by the report of the Anglican-Reformed International Commission (1984):

> We think that Reformed Churches should accept the fact that, at every level, oversight needs to be exercised in a way that is both personal and corporate. Personal oversight apart from the wisdom of a corporate body is apt to become arbitrary and erratic; oversight by a corporate body without a personal pastor is apt to become bureaucratic and legalistic.[30]

But what has the Reformed world to contribute? Among other things, reference can be made to the collaborative nature of translocal ministry in a conciliar setting, the experience of women having held such offices for many years with distinction, the principle of timed appointments and designated appraisal regimes (as well as recognition of the hopeless messes in which our Moderators sometimes end up!). All this bears witness to "the episcopate as sign and symbol [being] a challenge for *all* churches rather than a problem to be solved by the non-episcopal churches."[31] What 1662 teaches us most of all is that rather than craving for uniform patterns of Christianity we need to receive more wholeheartedly one another's gifts.

29. See Church of Scotland, *Relations Between Anglican and Presbyterian Churches* and Anglican–Reformed International Commission, *God's Reign and our Unity*.

30. *God's Reign and our Unity*, para. 112.

31. Pickard, *Theological Foundations*, 197. Italics mine.

8

Education for the Art of
Christian Ministry

THIS CHAPTER EXPLORES THE methodology and content of educational programs that aim to prepare men and women for ordained roles within the Christian church. It is grounded in personal experience of such programs, first as a student,[1] and later as one responsible for their delivery.[2] My experience spans denominational and ecumenical contexts, North American as well as English, and it involves the preparation of both non-stipendiary (self-supporting) and stipendiary ministers for Christian service. I shall, first, outline a series of principles I believe should underpin all ministerial education programs. Then, secondly, I will use these principles to illustrate what such programs ought to look like in conversation with Alan P.F. Sell, whose views help us to focus on key features of them.[3]

1. I was a Hostelman at New College, London (1968–71), prepared for ordination in the URC at the Congregational College, Manchester (1971–74), and undertook post-graduate work at Perkins' School of Theology, Dallas, Texas (1974–75).

2. My roles in theological education have been Tutor, Northern College (United Reformed and Congregational) 1988–93, Principal, Northern College (United Reformed and Congregational) 1993–2003, Director of Academic Development and Traditional Theology, North East Oecumenical Course 2003–6, Development Strategy Officer, URC Northern Synod (2003–6), and Educational Training Officer, URC Northern Synod (2006–9).

3. For an earlier discussion with Sell on the subject of ministerial education see my "So Last Century?—Review Article"; Sell, "So Last Century?—A Response"; and my "Still so Last Century?"

PRINCIPLES FOR MINISTERIAL EDUCATION

Keep the Aim Firmly in View

The purpose of the educational programs we are considering is one of preparing men and women to be ordained ministers of Word and Sacrament within, in this case, the URC. Nothing should be allowed to divert the deliverers of such programs from that clear task. They are not aiming to produce academic theologians, though they will be failing if they produce ministerial candidates devoid of genuine theological acumen; neither are they intent on producing pastoral counselors, though counseling skills are invaluable to ministers when undertaking pastoral work; and they are not ultimately concerned with producing spiritual directors, though spiritual maturity should be an important feature of every minister. Their fundamental aim, always to be kept in view, is that of ensuring that the men and women sent to them leave their educational programs fit and ready for ordination.

This raises an obvious question: "What knowledge, skills and attitudes do ministerial candidates need to possess if they are to show that they are fit and ready for ordination?" And that, in turn, raises an important subsidiary question: "Whose role is it to decide upon the required competences for ordination candidates?" Acute problems arise when colleges or courses are perceived by the churches to be producing candidates with an inadequate mix of competencies. The nature of Christian ministry though is contextual: new occasions require fresh patterns of ministry. It is conceivable therefore that candidates and/or churches may conclude that a college or course is not providing them with the right set of knowledge, skills, and attitudes for their *contemporary* roles as ministers of Word and Sacrament. Tensions are also generated if there is a lack of clarity on *both* sides concerning what the educational program concerned is aiming to achieve. It follows that churches owe it to colleges and courses to be absolutely clear about what they are expecting them to achieve; and also that colleges and courses need to develop their programs in ways that both respect and meet church requirements.

It makes educational sense for curriculum design to be carried out collaboratively with representatives of both church and college/course being involved. That requires, first, coming to a common mind about the knowledge, attitudes, and skills expected of ordinands upon completion of their educational program; secondly, it entails devising modules of learning which meet the resulting educational aims and objectives; and, thirdly, it necessitates deciding how attainment in each module is to be assessed. Good practice suggests that the over-all program needs reviewing about every five years, with each module being open to revision annually following a staff-student evaluation. Both program and module review ought to be carried out against a backcloth of the original program/module aims and objectives, with the likelihood of those aims and objectives needing revision always an open question.

Educate the Whole Person

All education involves the development of three areas of the human personality: mental, attitudinal, and practical. There is knowledge to be grasped, attitudes to be cultivated, and skills to be acquired. Courses which prepare people for ordination therefore inevitably will have to be three dimensional. They will be inadequate if they leave any of the three elements under-developed. First, it is essential that ordained ministers of Word and Sacrament have an adequate knowledge base. This ought to include a personal credo which has been constructed out of an encounter with the various expressions of the Christian faith that have occurred during the church's rich history. It will also involve an awareness of the ordinand's Christian ethos as that now finds its place in the wider ecumenical context. Involved in all this will also be a clear understanding of what constitutes an appropriate Christian approach to contemporary personal and social ethics. If ministers are to play an effective leadership role in the church's encounter with society they will need to possess a level of sociological and political understanding which enables them to understand the context within which they are ministering. Secondly, colleges and courses need to ensure that students have their hearts in the right place. Ordinands should be encouraged to undergo a spiritual discipline that enables them over time continuously to be shaped by the grace of God. This involves the enrichment of personal prayer every bit as much as the sustenance of communal worship. It entails growing spiritually and keeping in touch with God. Thirdly, attention should be given to acquiring the necessary skills for ministry, whether that involves the craft of preaching or the ability to chair a meeting, lead a congregation in extempore prayer or meet a church member's pastoral needs. The work of the minister of Word and Sacrament involves a set of skills which can be learned and or developed.

There is little doubt that education for Christian ministry has tended to prioritize the mental and attitudinal dimensions over the practical. It has reflected thereby a common failure in other branches of professional education, where, as Donald A. Schön has shown, a hierarchical ordering of curriculum content is often found in operation: "The rule is: first, the relevant basic and applied science; then, the skills of application to real-world problems of practice."[4] It leads to "the normative idea of a curriculum which places general principles and methods before the skills of application."[5] All too often it involves a clear "ladder of status," with universities who are dedicated to delivering principles and methods being regarded as superior to professional schools that are incorrectly perceived as mainly giving attention to the delivery of a skills component of learning.[6] Schön argues that "The greater one's proximity to basic science, as a rule, the higher one's academic status."[7] In the case of education for Christian ministry the "science" in question is the traditional subset of disciplines which constitute Christian theology. Many students preparing for ordination have wondered, though, about the *relevance* of some of the "science" they have been expected to learn. Even those attending to their academic learning in a whole-hearted way have sometimes found a thought crossing their minds concerning the usefulness to their future ministries of the learning being required by them. Their beleaguered teachers meanwhile often find themselves trapped in what Schön calls "the rigor-or-relevance dilemma": they try to maintain the rigor of what they teach all the time knowing that there are a host of *practical* topics that warrant places in the curriculum.

The "relevance" issue is not resolved simply by ensuring the required amount of skill training is in the curriculum. Also required are dedicated efforts to ensure the *art* of ministry is explored. I use the word "explored" quite deliberately to emphasis that some dimensions of what I have in mind when speaking about "the art of ministry" cannot be taught—rather, they are "caught." Ministers of Word and Sacrament share the traditions of a calling whose knowledge base is sometimes *implicit* in the way they go about their practice. The know-how of ministry therefore is often discovered *in* ministerial practice. Schön reminds us that "Although we sometimes think before acting, it is also true that in much of the spontaneous behavior of skilful practice we reveal a kind of knowing which does not stem from a prior intellectual operation"[8] An intellectual bias though has tended to make us blind to "the non-logical processes which are omnipresent in effective practice."[9] But, as Schön argues, "knowing-in-action" is "*the* characteristic mode of ordinary practical knowledge."[10] Our descriptions

---

4. Schön, *Reflective Practitioner*, 27.

5. Schön, *Reflective Practitioner*, 30.

6. See Schön, *Reflective Practitioner*, 37.

7. Schön, *Educating*, 9.

8. Schön, *Reflective Practitioner*, 51.

9. Schön, *Reflective Practitioner*, 52.

10. Schön, *Reflective Practitioner*, 54. Italics mine.

of knowing-in-action are always *"constructions,"* since we are seeking "to put into explicit, symbolic form a kind of intelligence that begins by being tacit and spontaneous."[11] We can only arrive at such descriptions through "reflection-in-action," where "the rethinking of some part of our knowing-in-action leads to on-the-spot experiment and further thinking that affects what we do."[12] Not only do ordinands learn how to be ministers by exercising ministry and then reflecting upon what they have done and are doing, but it is also fundamental to good practice that critical self-reflection is at the heart of the ordained minister's work.

Utilize Appropriate Educational Methodology

It is clear that there is a large amount of necessary learning that the ordinand can undertake in a traditional academic setting through lectures and seminars: there are books to be read, texts which require careful attention, and classroom discussions that need to take place. Some of the more practical aspects of Christian ministry are also profitably addressed in a "safe" classroom setting where students are enabled to learn from observing practice. The use of "sermon class" in homiletic courses is well-established, while role-play is widely used in many pastoral studies courses. Theory gets tried out in practice, and practice is subjected to critical reflection in order that future practice can be improved. The academy therefore is an important context in which ordinands are enabled to undertake a significant amount of intellectual development and technical training.

But robust courses that prepare ordinands for their future ministries are never totally class-room bound. The benefit of placement learning in local churches is well established. Through their church membership ordinands are prevented from being educated totally out of a congregational setting; but when they work on placement in local churches under the supervision of an experienced minister their learning takes on a fresh hands-on dimension. Apprenticeship models of education of course are well attested, but in education for ministry they depend very much on successful collaborations between colleges/courses and local churches, as well as supervisory ministers possessing an appropriate skill set. The best supervisors usually have benefitted themselves from capable supervision in their own preparation for ministry. It is important to remember also that placement contexts are just as capable of encouraging "bad" as well as "good" habits in students.

11. Schön, *Educating*, 25.

12. Schön, *Educating*, 29.

Reference was made earlier of the need for ordinands to gain a sufficient level of sociological and political understanding. Classroom learning plays its part in accomplishing this, but there is a great advantage when a community placement can be included in the student's course, one that particularly takes the student out of their comfort zone. To work alongside people involved daily with those on the underside of history is a salutary learning experience for ordinands who are highly likely to find themselves later working in quite comfortable middle-class settings. It provides ordinands with an illuminating lens through which to view the society in which they will soon be ministering, but the value of community placements, like those in church settings, largely depends upon the quality of the student's reflection upon their experience while on placement. That must be enabled through an interaction between placement supervisors, college/course staff, and fellow students, who each in their own way take on the role of "coaches." Coaching plays an important role in preparing ordinands for their ministry. It helps them become initiated into a community of practitioners. The main activities of coaches are "demonstrating, advising, questioning, and criticizing."[13] Not the least significant element of learning on placement then is the often unconscious "background learning" achieved by students through an experience in which supervisors, college/course staff, and their peers play a crucial and skilful role.[14] Such learning takes place in a way that it is usually only recognized with hindsight, but quite often it is of major significance in ministerial development.

One Size Does Not Fit All

Ordinands are a diverse cohort of humanity. Long gone are the days when most candidates for ministry of Word and Sacraments were young persons arriving at theological college straight from secondary school. While there are still some young candidates most today fall in the mature student category. This means that ordination courses need to have part-time as well as full-time patterns of delivery, with the likelihood that few will avail themselves of hitherto traditional residential courses. The advent of non-stipendiary ministry has spawned an array of non-residential courses. Most of them are ecumenical in ethos and exhibit a style far removed from that of the traditional theological college, although changing demographics have meant that the latter now has a creative mix of non-residential and residential students.

13. Schön, *Educating*, 38.
14. Schön, *Educating*, 38.

It follows that students arrive at ordination having followed different educational pathways. If all ordained ministers of Word and Sacraments are to be treated as equals—whether stipendiary or non-stipendiary, full-time or part-time—a question is then raised concerning the *minimum* educational requirements of candidates for ordination. In the URC that has been set at under-graduate diploma level. In a few instances that minimum requirement regrettably has been treated as a maximum goal by those who want to be fast-tracked to ordination. It is a pity that a minimum requirement intended to maintain educational standards ends up, in a small minority of cases, lowering them. Also it is clear that when a denomination avails itself of different educational providers for the education of its ordinands the question of "quality control" is an ongoing issue which needs addressing.

Good practice suggests that at the outset of an ordinand's course every effort should be made to encourage the student to take responsibility for his or her learning. Through discussion and negotiation between sending denominations, educational provider, and ordinand "a personal learning plan" should be constructed that fits the ordinand's needs, gifts, and circumstances. In the broad scheme of things there will be a large degree of overlap in the content of such plans, although the differences between them will testify to their "tailor-made" nature. Each plan will reflect what is best both for the student and the church given each particular unique set of circumstances. When the plan gets reviewed and revised as the ordinand's course enfolds, opportunities open up for courses to be "tweaked" to allow students not only to address weaknesses that become evident but also to build on strengths that are obviously apparent.

It is very helpful sometimes to view the practice of Christian Ministry alongside that of professions like law, medicine, and teaching. Each profession sets its appropriate entrance requirements, but within the educational pathways that lead into the profession there is an opportunity to specialize in one of several ways, e.g. the educational pathway into the medical profession can lead to a variety of specialisms, whether in general practice or hospital consultancies. It ought to be possible within education for ordination and through the personal learning plan approach to set those who have the potential to exercise specialized ministries in the church upon an appropriate educational track, e.g. theological teaching or chaplaincies. An ordination course will fail if it does not provide the flexibility to enable the small number of ordinands who show particular aptitudes and abilities in the early part of their ordination course to specialize in ways that make it possible for them to practise one of the specialized ministries in the church sometime in the future.

Often the pathway to such specialized ministries leads in the first instance to a ministry within a pastorate. The final qualification for the specialized ministry then takes two forms: first, the demonstration of proven ability within the pastorate; and, secondly, the completion of in-service education. We are reminded therefore of the centrality of in-service education for ministers of Word and Sacrament whose on-going educational needs require meeting if they are to exercise ministry to their full potential. They will need periodic up-dating on current theological trends and best practice: if burn-out is to be avoided time away from ministry will be required to find refreshment and discover a greater perspective on their work; they will want to avail themselves of newly emerged approaches to ministry; and they will require opportunities to undertake any preparation required for the next phase of their ministries. A commitment to life-long learning therefore is at the heart of good ministerial practice.

The organization of in-service education for ministers of Word and Sacraments, though, has not been a straight-forward matter. A commitment to life-long learning does not actually seem to be a universal part of our ministerial culture. It is unheard of in, say, law, medicine or teaching however for practioners to operate on the basis that the education they received when qualifying for their profession is sufficient for a life-time of service in that profession; but for some ministers such myopic attitudes are common-place. Perhaps the financial incentives which come from salary rises within the professions provide mammon's incentive to take seriously in-service education? None of us I venture to suggest want to be treated by a doctor who has the approach to life-long learning that seems endemic among some ministers! Ministers receive flat-rate stipends rather than incrementally rising salaries, thus leaving their Church with no financial incentives to place before its ministers when it comes to in-service education. Also it is very difficult for churches to organize in-service programs centrally that meet the felt needs of ministers whose pre-ordination education has been undertaken on a multitude of different courses. Nothing is more frustrating for ministers than being summoned to take an in-service training course that either fails to meet their needs or duplicates what they actually did pre-ordination, but some have had to face such experiences. It does not promote a serious attitude to life-long learning when post-ordination "one size fits all" approaches to learning still hold sway. The personal learning plans which ought to play such an important part of ordination learning have a continuing place in a minister's career post-ordination. Continuity between pre- and post-ordination learning is essential so there is some merit in placing the final responsibility for the delivery of post-ordination education with the college/course which provided the education for ordination.

ALAN P.F. SELL ON 'EDUCATION FOR MINISTRY'

Although Alan Sell was in pastoral charge for only nine years,[15] he possessed notable credentials to be a voice worth listening to on the subject of education for ministry. He viewed his entire vocation as an outworking of his calling to be a disciple of Jesus Christ, whether he was involved in pastoral ministry, ecumenical bureaucracy, teaching, or scholarship. His ministry involved significant periods in settings other than pastorates; but its composite whole provided him with his own perspective on the preparation of ministers of Word and Sacrament. He talks of having "the quite unexpected privilege of ministering in a variety of ways in many parts of the world"; he notes that he "had opportunities of teaching students, some of them destined for ministry, in both church and secular institutions at home and abroad"; he testifies to having "learned much from discussing the nature and content of ministerial education with those responsible for providing it in five continents"; and he reminds us that he "participated in numerous ecumenical discussions of ministry."[16]

In 1964 we find Sell "mapping" what the universities were providing at the time as "the staple diet of many an ordinand's *academic* training."[17] That he wanted to draw together all the relevant information on this was testimony to his belief that at the time there was "A widespread concern for adequate and relevant ministerial training."[18] He tells us that he is not suggesting "that university courses alone are all that is required in the training of ordinands."[19] After providing an analysis of what the universities then offered by way of "first *honours* degrees, further Arts degrees where these may be taken in theological subjects, and Divinity degrees,"[20] Sell expressed his regrets that "more universities do not make Comparative Religion compulsory," along with a note of surprise that, "in view of the widespread interest in things liturgical," the universities had been rather slow to provide courses in liturgy—as they also had been concerning "ecumenical studies," all coupled with a wish that students should face "the

---

15. Sell's ministries were at Sedburgh and Dent (1959–64) and Worcester, Hallow and Ombersley (1964–68). For a biography see my *Crucicentric*, 1–33.

16. Sell, *One Ministry*, 1.

17. Sell, "Theological Education by Degrees," 196.

18. Sell, "Theological Education by Degrees," 196.

19. Sell, "Theological Education by Degrees," 196n2

20. Sell, "Theological Education by Degrees," 196. Representatives of the Universities of Bristol and Hull subsequently offered corrections to Sell's analysis. See Sell, "Letter: Theological Education buy Degrees," 70.

techniques of the Philosophy of Religion in the shape of linguistic analysis.[21] In keeping with many others who have proposed additions to a curriculum, Sell fails to mention what would have to give way to accommodate the additions! This is very apposite in Sell's case since, as we shall soon see, he is very critical of the way modern programs for education for ministry have included new elements in the curriculum at the expense of subject matter he regards as essential.

Sell's last two books were concerned with theological education.[22] They reflect the way in which a pattern of education for ministry that had prepared Sell for his varied ministry became for him a veritable model for others to revere, and a yardstick by which contemporary ordination courses can be shown to be wanting. Those who knew Sell well will recognize Andrew Atherstone's portrait of him: "It is easy to imagine him as a mischievous and eccentric tutor, or a sagacious grandfather treating the younger generation to pearls of theological wisdom gained over half a century."[23] But when his discussions of education for ministry are considered objectively the important points we all need to hear from him are in danger of being lost as we recoil at some of his ill thought-out "back to the future" opinions. Not only is his reverence for his own preparation for ordination the exception to his opinion that "theological students seldom consider that they have been adequately trained,"[24] but his prescriptions for contemporary education for ministry often do not pay enough attention to contextual changes over the last fifty years which have driven theological educators to devise fresh patterns of ordination preparation. It leaves to him sometimes sounding like "an old man airing his complaints about the church,"[25] rather than a fellow practitioner engaging in a positive dialogue about educational patterns and possibilities that are actually viable today.

Sell's Preparation for Ordination

There were four components in the ordination course when Sell studied at Lancashire Independent College.[26] The first was delivered by the University

21. Sell, "Theological Education by Degrees," 200.

22. See Sell, *Theological Education of the Ministry* and *One Ministry.*

23. Atherstone, *Review of Enlightenment,* 68.

24. Sell, *Commemorations,* 208.

25. Sutcliffe, Review of *One Ministry,* 37.

26. Sell speaks about the content of the course and the teachers who delivered it at various points in his writings. See *One Ministry,* 98–104; *Theological Education of the Ministry,* 265–89; and *Philosophy, History, and Theology,* 3–4. See also my *Crucicentric,*

of Manchester. The vast majority of candidates for ministry in those days were young. Several routes through university courses were possible for them depending initially upon their educational qualifications upon entry. Those who entered with qualifications that gained university matriculation took a BA arts degree followed by BD, which, unlike that, say, at the University of London, was (and still is) a second degree. For those who didn't have university entry requirements two options were available. Students who were perceived to have academic potential were encouraged to work towards matriculation by taking appropriate GCSE "A" levels and/or the university's Certificate in Biblical Knowledge. This was the route followed by Sell who started the BA degree in his second year before completing the formidable BD in two years, making six years of study overall. Those perceived to have less academic potential than Sell studied for the Certificate in Biblical Knowledge followed by the Certificate in Theology. Quite often ministerial candidates of mature years took this educational pathway. A fourth option was available to candidates who, upon College entry, were already graduates in subjects other than theology. They proceeded straight to the BD, a pathway which involved a lot of preparatory work (e.g. learning the biblical languages and basic church history) for courses that assumed pre-requisite knowledge. A fifth pathway was available to the small minority of candidates who entered College with a theological degree. It involved a selection of BD courses before moving to a Master's level program.

Two things ought to be clear from this brief survey of what was available for ministerial students at the University of Manchester during the 1950s and 1960s, the period viewed so favorably by Sell. First, there was a clear recognition that "one size does not fit all."[27] Several educational pathways were available to suit different needs. However much Sell revered his own preparation for ministry and advocated something like it for younger candidates, he fully recognized that it was not suitable for other candidates, e.g. those of mature age and/or lower academic ability. Secondly, the university regime of courses ensured that Manchester ordinands worked at high intellectual levels. In 2004 we find Sell wondering whether, compared to his era, "present-day universities are in danger of ceasing to be the centres of enlightenment that the best of them had become."[28] Whatever the truth of that, the demands placed on ordinands at the University of Manchester were high. Hard work was involved. Those whose preferred learning styles did not equip them for lots of essay writing and all that is

6–8.

27. See *One Ministry,* 80

28. Sell, *Philosophy, History, and Theology,* 117

involved in end-of-session unseen examinations did not on the whole have as happy a College experience as Sell.

The second component of the ordination course at Manchester in Sell's era involved courses of study mounted by and assessed by the College. All students were examined while at College on the English text of the Bible. Sell admits that sitting Bible examinations at the start and end of every College term was a bit of a bind, but with hindsight, like many of his colleagues, he came to be thankful for the extensive if basic biblical knowledge that resulted from the private study involved. The College scheme ensured that by the end of his six years as an ordinand Sell covered and was examined on "the contents and contexts of all the books of the Bible (not only on the texts in Greek and Hebrew set for the BD, or the texts in English set for the University Certificate)."[29] Also delivered by the College was a "Worship and Preaching" course at the center of which sat a Sermon Class in which annually students had one of their sermons critiqued by their peers and a member of staff. Knowing that one day their turn would come round to be in the hot-seat students quickly learned to be temperate critics of their compatriots' homiletic endeavors! College "Pastoral Studies" courses meanwhile were seldom examined, so they tended to be treated less seriously by students than the university courses that had to be passed if the Degree or Certificate concerned was to be gained. The curriculum as a result—at least in the eyes of many students—was undoubtedly skewed towards the intellectual aspects of learning.

The third component of the ordination course at Manchester involved the spiritual development of candidates. One of the ways this took place was through compulsory attendance at communal worship in the College chapel. It is significant that Sell does not dwell very much on the attention paid to spiritual direction in his accounts of his time at Lancashire Independent College. He makes no mention for example of attending sessions aimed at fostering a private prayer life. It would take a generation or so of ecumenical encounter for Free Church theological educators to discover the benefits of "spiritual direction." Meanwhile a diet of worship in College chapel does not necessarily guarantee that an ordinand's spiritual needs are met. It is difficult to avoid the conclusion that "spirituality" was very much the Cinderella of the curriculum during Sell's time in Manchester. All too often in ordination education the misplaced assumption is made that everything is going well in a ministerial candidate's relationship with God.

Sell also mentions a fourth component of his ordination course, namely, the practical experiences of ministry which contributed to him being fit and

29. Sell, *One Ministry,* 98.

ready for stipendiary service. Two examples stand out. First, most Sundays in term-time the College's students were sent out to meet pulpit-supply requests from churches, not only in the Manchester area but also further afield on both side of the Pennines. The norm was to take morning and evening worship at a church that either didn't have a minister in pastoral charge or shared one with others in a group pastorate. The churches visited by the student itinerant preachers had often seen their better days, but some more lively churches came up on the weekly Preaching List, particularly if students were invited to lead "College Sundays," when the work of the College was the focus of attention, leading to a donation being made to the College to support its work. Over six years Sell would have discovered the unreliability of the North of England's public transport system as well as gaining valuable experience in leading public worship. He developed particular bonds with certain congregations who invited him back for repeat engagements. But itinerant preaching among often weak, run-down congregations can be a soul-destroying experience for a young ordinand. Negative experiences seldom make for good learning. And all too easily the pressure to write essays, prepare for seminars, and revise for examinations strips the itinerant student-preacher of the time to prepare adequately for the weekly preaching assignments: many sermons get preached but few are written. As valuable as Sell's experience was therefore it would have been even more instructive for his future ministerial practice had there been built into the Preaching List arrangements a more formal opportunity for his craft as a worship leader and preacher to be critiqued and evaluated. The accent most of the time was on the College, through its students, serving local churches, with a lack of concern to ensure that the students learned as much as they might have done. From many an ordinand's point of view though the preaching fees received from churches were a much needed source of income.

Secondly, the long university vacations provided ample opportunity for students to undertake student pastorates in churches with or without a resident minister. A longer exposure at the coal-face of ministry, with adequate time to prepare worship and educational material, became for many students a rich introduction to the privileges and duties of Christian ministry. Feedback on performance in a supportive setting also led to significant learning. About the time Sell was working as a Summer Pastor at Macedonia Congregational Church, Failsworth, Lancashire, New College, a sister theological college in London, was developing a practice involving final year students being placed as assistants to senior ministers in local churches. The obvious merit of ordinands "learning on the job" therefore was being extended at New to a more lengthy period of apprentice style learning. The embryo that grew into adulthood with the Internship Training of which Sell was so critical was already in its infancy in the shape of student summer pastorates of the type he richly benefitted from in Failsworth.

Whither the "Scholar-Pastor"?

It was Sell's conviction that a fully adequate ordination course seeks to enable a ministerial candidate to carry out *four* core tasks: "the conduct of worship, the preaching of the gospel through word and sacramental action, and the pastoral care and Christian education of the people."[30] But it is important to bear in mind what this actually means in practice. Sell argues that "it is asking too much of theological educators to provide whatever knowledge may be useful to a minister three or four decades hence."[31] This does not however lead Sell to argue powerfully in favour of a rigorous program of in-service education for ministers post-ordination. Instead, he follows the advice of Robert Franks:

> It is too often forgotten that the ideal of ministerial education is not to send a man out with some knowledge of every subject he will afterwards find useful. It is to send him out with a mind that can tackle with success any subject as need arises. The opposite leads to self-confident shallowness.[32]

But Frank's advice arguably over-intellectualizes what is involved in the personal development of ministers during their service to the church. It is correct to recognize that an ordination course cannot be expected to cover everything a minister might need to know or practise in ministry. But this need not also entail the expectation that what the course has provided will be totally sufficient to enable the minister to get by without serious attention being paid to a pattern of in-service education involving practical, attitudinal, and theological learning. Sell can even give the impression that he is following earlier advice than that of Franks. He recalls that Richard Alliott (1804–63) "argues in a calmly defiant way that if any changes are to be made in the theological college curriculum they should be designed to make the students more thorough scholars and philosophers."[33] However much I may have wished that my students would become "scholars and philosophers" I hope that I fully realized that many of them were actually gifted by God in other ways. Our task in ordination education is to prepare

30. Sell, *One Ministry*, x–xi.
31. Sell, *One Ministry*, 96.
32. Quoted by Sell in *One Ministry*, 96.
33. Sell, *Hinterland*, 204.

men and women to be *ministers*, only *some* of whom will be called to become outstanding academics.

Robert Pope has accurately summed up Sell's "approach to ministerial education" as emphasizing "the importance of immersing candidates for ministry in the theological disciplines in order to nurture a genuinely *theological* mindset which, he believed, would cope with those situations in ministry which can never be predicted and for which no amount of practice—and skills—based training can equip ordinands."[34] Although I share with Sell the aim of enabling students to acquire "a genuinely *theological* mindset," a more holistic aim in education for ministry should give greater weight to the attitudinal and practical dimensions of an ordinand's personal development.[35] But, in fairness to Sell, it is incumbent upon us to remember that the burden of a lot of Sell's thinking is his belief that "we face a crisis in high-calibre theological leadership in many churches in the West."[36] He maintains that "as far as ministers are concerned some at least of the denominations do not have the 'critical mass' of scholarship that they once had."[37] Conversations with Sell left me in no doubt that he believed that one of the allegedly impoverished denominations was the URC of which we both were members and ministers. When due allowance is made for the decline in the number of ministers over the life-time of the URC, however, it is possible to show statistically that in the last thirty years the URC—affiliated colleges have actually increased "the 'critical mass' of scholarship" within the URC by encouraging, enabling, and supporting younger ministerial candidates in their acquisition of "higher" degrees. But in his Didsbury Lectures we hear Sell's concern that the churches were not then producing sufficient numbers of ministers proficient in the core theological disciplines. He implores that "the churches would do well to encourage in all possible ways those ministerial candidates whose gifts take them in these directions, and whose academic lungs can withstand prolonged immersion in extensive and sometimes choppy waters."[38] Well, to its credit, the URC at that time was already doing what Sell was advocating. Few things annoy educational practitioners more than being told to do things they are already doing with some measure of success—often against the odds!

Lest there are still those who, blinded by the anti-intellectual mindset so prevalent in the contemporary church, do not sense the need

34. Pope, "Alan Philip Frederick Sell," 525.

35. See n3.

36. Sell, *Testimony*, 9.

37. Sell, *Nonconformist Theology*, 189.

38. Sell, *Nonconformist Theology*, 191. See also *Hinterland*, 626–27.

for education for ministry courses providing the churches with "scholar-pastors,"[39] a further exploration of Sell's thinking on the matter is apposite. At the outset we need to remember that Christian ministers are endowed with different God-given gifts and aptitudes. There is no such thing as *a* model minister. So when Sell advocates that the creation of "scholar pastors" is important for a flourishing church he is light years away from suggesting that such a ministerial vocation ought to be every ordinand's aim. In the wider scheme of Christian ministry the "scholar-pastors" will inevitably be somewhat in the minority—not just because a large proportion of contemporary ministerial candidates are mature students embarking upon a second career and therefore will not have time to devote to the education involved to become one, but also because the intellectual demands involved will be beyond some candidates' abilities. What then separates "scholar-pastors" from the more numerous "pastors"? It certainly is nothing of a hierarchical nature; it is more a matter of fulfilling different tasks. Sell, for example, envisages that from the body of "scholar-pastors" there will emerge "competent staff for our remaining theological colleges, expert participants in theological and ecumenical discussion, and those who can in local and regional contexts train and encourage elders and others in their several ministries."[40] The spheres of ministry that require "scholar-pastors" are not so numerous that huge numbers are involved in meeting demands for them. I have occasionally learned of some ministers who belong to the category of "scholar-pastors" actually feeling that their gifts and talents are under-used in the URC. This prompts the suspicion that more "scholar-pastors" than Sell thought perhaps already exist.

Sell is wise to counsel against going along with views of "theological education of ministers of the gospel" that advocate "the pragmatic supply of 'tricks for the trade.'"[41] To suggest otherwise would end any hope we still have of maintaining the ideals of a learned ministry. But, frankly, I have not come across any contemporary practitioner in education for ministry who believes in such absurdly utilitarian approaches to their work. Students whose age permit them to engage in the length of course required for the preparation of *learned* ministers and *scholar*-pastors are commonly given the opportunity to become thoroughly at home in what Sell regards as the core disciplines of "biblical, historical, theological and pastoral studies."[42]

39. Sell, *One Ministry*, 89.

40. Sell, *One Ministry*, 101.

41. Sell, *One Ministry*, 96.

42. Sell, *Testimony*, 8. Elsewhere Sell lists the "core disciplines" as "biblical studies, ecclesiastical history, philosophy, doctrine and systematic theology." See *Theological Education of the Ministry*, 4

Strident efforts continue to be made to meet Sell's wish that "younger candidates at least receive a full and rigorous academic course."[43] And that can be achieved without unduly undermining within the *entire* course the much needed integration of the intellectual component of education for ministry with its other more attitudinal and practical dimensions. But Sell is absolutely correct to remind us that, *at the level of scholar-pastor*, competence in biblical studies requires a working knowledge of the biblical languages; ethical wisdom presupposes grounding in moral philosophy; and apologetics require a sharpness that a serious excursion into the land of philosophy of religion will only provide.[44] Nevertheless, I suggest that the ministry of pastors at the coal-face will not be rendered impossible if their academic record reveals that they have not learned the biblical languages or delved *in depth* with moral philosophy and philosophy of religion. That needs saying on behalf of many whom God called to Christian ministry at a time in their lives when they did not have the opportunity to engage upon the length of preparation for ministry enjoyed by Sell and the present writer.

Changing Times and Current Constraints

It is tempting to engage with Sell's views on education for ministry by way of an *argumentum ad hominem*: after all his own hands-on experience of ministry in pastoral charge of congregations was brief, and his knowledge of URC life was limited, due both to having worked overseas for a period and being a member of Churches other than those into which he was ordained a minister. But that would be a superficial way of critiquing a position which exhibits undoubted strengths as well as offering glaringly impractical suggestions. Sell tends to judge contemporary education for ministry on the basis of its worst examples; he fails to appreciate the best intentions of those who mount and deliver our ordination program curricula; and he does not take fully into account the constraints under which they now work. Nor does he face up to the fact that some of his contemporaries at Lancashire Independent College were not as enthusiastic as he was about the relevance of the course which prepared them for ordination. Their critical comments —positive as well as negative—were formative influences in driving the curriculum changes at Northern College of which Sell subsequently became so negatively critical.[45] In short, he is repeatedly in danger of giving the impression that he lacks understanding of why education for ministry has

43. Sell, *Nonconformist Theology*, 191.

44. See Sell, *Philosophy, Theology and History*, 181, 288–89.

45. See my "Still So Last Century?," 154

evolved in the way it has over the last fifty years, and he very easily can be accused of paying insufficient attention to the reasons that made changes both necessary and inevitable.

Before I deal with the major criticisms Sell launches at contemporary programs of education for ministry, it will be helpful to set the context by pointing out why theological educators decided the kind of ordination preparation Sell and I received in Manchester is unrealistic, inadequate, and unaffordable in our contemporary setting. First, it is unrealistic since it fails to address the way in which the URC has altered over its life-time, particularly due to the change in the demographics of its ministerial candidates and the arrival of non-stipendiary ministry. The major driver in all this was a profound change in the Church's profile mainly caused by numerical decline. The URC throughout its life-time has been hemorrhaging members at the rate of between three to four per cent per annum. This decline has not been caused by the departure of adult members as much as an acute inability to attract a younger generation. By the turn of the twenty-first century the presence of young people in many URC congregations was rare. The dearth of young candidates for ordination therefore is hardly surprising. This situation was not helped however by a prevailing prejudice over several years against encouraging young ordination candidates. The mantra that ordination candidates must have had "an experience of life" before entering upon an ordination course was often heard. But thankfully it was never found on Sell's lips. Like me, Sell was a *young* candidate for ministry with what some may have regarded as insufficient life-experience. I warmly welcome the way he argued forthrightly in favour of encouraging young ordination candidates. First, he notes that some contemporary young people get more experience of life in their early years than many from earlier generations had in their entire life-time. One thinks, for example, of the almost *de-rigueur* "gap-year" which can take modern youngsters around the world. Secondly, Sell correctly notes that "no minister can possibly have experienced everything likely to befall the saints," thereby reminding us humorlessly "to beware of the slippery slope at the bottom of which lies the claim "You cannot be a prison chaplain if you have not been a convict."[46] Then, thirdly, Sell delivers a clinching *theological* argument: "the call to ministry is of God, and while the call must rigorously be tested, the time of its arrival cannot be determined by us."[47]

Changing church demographics though does seem to have contributed to the inevitable limiting of God's call in recent years to mainly mature

46. Sell, *One Ministry,* 101.
47. Sell, *One Ministry,* 101.

adults, those who subsequently enter upon their ministries as a second career. It is unrealistic to think that all of them can be prepared for their ordination roles on traditional *college*-based courses. Nor is it in either the Church's or their best interests to take up a large portion of the time they would subsequently have available to serve the Church with an ordination course of the length that Sell and I enjoyed. Not surprisingly therefore shorter, part-time, non-collegiate ordination courses emerged in the URC, many of them "piggy-backing" on already existing regional Anglican ordination courses. Ecumenical co-operation is a very virtuous objective, part of the URC's very *raison d'être*, but in the case of education for ministry an important recognition that "one size does not fit all" regrettably led in some places to mixed standards of ordination course provision, both in terms of their duration and quality. The arrival of shorter—and in several senses cheaper—ordination courses may have been music to the ears of some ecclesiastical "bean counters," the small number of those always in danger of knowing the price of everything and the value of nothing. A threat to ministerial collegiality however became evident in some of the early inter-actions between non-stipendiary and stipendiary ministers. Lying underneath all this was the fact that non-stipendiary candidates had not only followed courses of a much shorter length but also been at different institutions to their stipendiary colleagues. It was not lost on Sell that his six year full-time course leading to BA and BD degrees was rather "different," to say the least, to the new three year part-time courses which at best reached university under-graduate Diploma standard. While the latter kind of course may well be more appropriate and perfectly acceptable for mature students, his fears that the longer programs of education for ordination would become terminally marginalized were quite understandable.

Secondly, the earlier programs for education in ministry were found to be inadequate on two accounts. Feedback from those who had been prepared for their ministries on them reported that, however much their college-based education had been beneficial, they had been found wanting when working in a rapidly changing church context, one which increasingly involved ministering in several congregations rather than just one and engaging in extensive ecumenical endeavor. Some regretted that their ordination course had not provided them with the skill-set required in their multi-congregational pastorates. Others, perhaps more worryingly, reported that their spiritual resources had been quickly drained when trying to address the challenges of contemporary pastoral ministry. Using the language of Schön, we can generalize their problems by saying that what was lacking in their ordination programs was an education in the art of "knowing-in-action," which can be cultivated through rigorous reflection on ministerial work undertaken on placement under expert supervision. It is central to good ministerial practice. Another way of putting the matter is to say that many ministers have not been adequately prepared to be good *practical* theologians.[48] They have not been coached in the art of integrating what they have learned intellectually with their spirituality and developing skill-base in ministerial practice. The problem is not one of ensuring that ordinands have "experience" of ministry prior to commencing full-time ministry. Most from the Sell era certainly had that, and in spades.[49] What needs attention is the reflection on placement work that truly makes it placement learning. That will certainly involve ensuring that ordinands learn good rather than bad habits, but, most important of all, it should lead to the ordinand developing a genuinely theological mind-set concerning ministerial practice.

Until relatively recently the Church's ordination programs relied heavily upon utilizing university Certificate and Degree courses. Just as the university supplied courses which the legal and medical professions used to train the next generation of lawyers and medics, they also provided a service to the churches in playing a part in the education of their ordinands. But, as the churches slowly started to decline numerically, the number of ordinands needing a university education decreased to such an extent that the market for university theological courses became depleted, with universities increasingly constructing their courses to meet the requirements of a teaching profession in need of RE teachers. Not surprisingly some universities deliberately started to write their theological degree courses in ways that fitted in with what the school "A" level syllabus required, namely, a focus on world religions rather than Christian theology. An encroaching secular emphasis also made it increasingly difficult for those in charge of ordination preparation in the Churches to get universities to maintain theological courses appropriate to their needs, let alone offer new modules to meet their contemporary requirements, e.g. in the areas of liturgy, ecumenism, and missiology. Over time the inadequacy of the courses some universities offered therefore became increasingly obvious: it led to consortia of ordination program deliverers mounting their own courses and

---

48. For an account of what is involved methodologically in strategies that set "knowing-in-action" at the centre of good ministerial practice see the early pioneering work of Whitehead and Whitehead, *Method in Ministry*. For an English account of the "action-reflection-action" model for theological exploration in practical contexts see Reader, *Local Theology*.

49. Sell waxes eloquently about the "wide range of experience" he had during his time as an ordinand and that it was gained "without detriment to rigorous academic, and supplementary, college courses." See *One Ministry*, 102–3.

then seeking "validation" of them by a university. The university remains in charge of "quality control" in these arrangements, but the colleges and courses gain greater autonomy in the area of curriculum design. A major down-side of many current patterns of education for ministry though is the way in which some candidates for ministry may then miss the robust intellectual atmosphere of the university.[50] The *credibility* of any ordinand's theology needs to satisfy not only Christians within the churches, but also those in the wider society and the academic world.[51] That will not happen if seminary-style education promotes inward-looking attitudes.

Thirdly, some ordination programs are unaffordable. A very forward-looking College treasurer I once knew saw his role as one of enabling those who directed his college's program to get the finance they needed to meet their aims and objectives. But his ability to see through a financially ill-thought out proposal was notable. Whenever he opened up with: "But, you know, from a financial point of view I am not sure whether it is prudent to . . ." we knew we had problems! And there are times when Sell's proposals on education for ministry warrant a less sensitive recall to financial reality. In a numerically declining denomination, within a society that has radically reduced the amount of money it is prepared to set aside for tertiary education, it is unrealistic to contemplate full-time ordination programs of six years duration. And it is going to be difficult convincing a denomination strapped for cash that a reasonable number of candidates can be supported for four full-time years of study. Also, whatever the merits of Sell's repeated proposal for a two-year probationary and stipendiary period for ministerial candidates prior to ordination, the simple fact of the matter is that on financial grounds alone it is a non-starter.[52] There are a lot of things we might want to do, but sometimes we have to recognize that we cannot afford to do them.

Targets of Straw?

I move on now to consider Sell's critique of contemporary ordination programs. He is concerned that "calls for the increasing 'professionalization' of ministerial education which have led here to time-consuming internship methods of training, there to a smorgasbord of modules which encourage tasting rather than digesting or, to change the metaphor, courses which, by

50. See Sell, *Testimony*, 17–18.

51. Sell, *Enlightenment*, xvi.

52. For Sell's proposals see *Testimony*, 8; *Nonconformist Theology*, 191; and *One Ministry*, 104–5.

prescribing such small doses, threaten to inoculate students against particular disciplines for life."[53] This raises three issues. The first concerns whether or not it is actually helpful to view a Christian minister as a "professional" person akin to, say, a doctor or a lawyer. I believe that it is. It seems perfectly reasonable for different professions to learn from one another about the best ways of educating their practioners; and it is also appropriate that churches should have a clear idea about what a minister of the gospel requires by way of knowledge, attitudes, and skills to carry out their calling, and then go on to develop programs of learning to enable their ordinands to reach the point where they are fit and ready for ministry. I have found it instructive to learn how the medical profession builds upon what might be called "academic" learning in areas such as anatomy and pharmacology through extensive hands-on engagement with *clinical* practice under supervision.

This leads me to suggest, secondly, that Sell's pejorative characterization of "internship methods of training" as "time-consuming" suggests he hasn't fully grasped the purpose of placement-based learning under supervision. Would the British Medical Association countenance the idea that their doctors should learn their clinical practice in a largely unstructured way? My complaint about internship is not that it prevents students from engaging in what Sell believes is more important learning for a budding scholar-pastor, but rather that a student's placement work ought to be spread out rather more during the ordination program, thereby enabling the art of integrating theory and practice to be nurtured and developed during shorter blocks of time, rather than left to the penultimate or final academic year. A modular structure of education organized by those who manage the ordination program makes it quite easy to arrange this.

The very mention of "modular" education will remind Sell's readers that, thirdly, he is prone to point out its *possible* pit-falls without ever fully acknowledging its benefits. Sometimes he is simply disingenuous. Perhaps he had just emerged from the difficult task of writing up "learning objectives" for his courses when he suggested that "our contemporary scrutinizers of higher education who go in quest of 'measurable outcomes' at the end of twelve-weeks of modular 'input' have somehow failed to grasp what the theological disciplines are about."[54] It was surely the case that he would have marked exam papers in pre-modular days having in mind as he did so a basic idea of what he expected the students he was examining to have learned from his teaching. What therefore other than bad practice stands in the way of making *explicit* the "measurable outcomes"? I fail to

53. Sell, *Nonconformist Theology*, 190.
54. Sell, *Enlightenment*, xvi.

see how that in itself misses the point of the theological disciplines. On other occasions when Sell has modular education in his sights he makes mountains out of mole-hills. Two examples illustrate what I have in mind. First, he points out that "the very brevity of modules *can* mean that students do not have time to become truly immersed in the disciplines and thus, by giving them a small dose all we have done is to inoculate them against the subjects for life."[55] Setting aside the ill-chosen metaphor which carries a somewhat difficult—even dangerous—perception of the nature and purpose of education, one wonders why Sell does not consider the exciting possibility that the early modules of a theological curriculum might serve as "tasters" for subjects students are then motivated to go on to study at further length and in greater depth later in their course. Let us not forget that passage through a modular degree course from Level 1 to Level 2 to Level 3 creatively allows ample opportunity and time for students "to become truly immersed in disciplines"—not *every* discipline, of course, but then the older degree programs never actually enabled students to be "truly immersed" in *all* of them. By way of a second example, Sell tells us that, "It would seem that in many places seed corn disciplines—particularly linguistic and logical ones—have suffered death by modular choice, with resulting "gappiness" in the intellectual experience of students."[56] Let us assume that Sell is correct in claiming that there is such a "gappiness" in some students' "intellectual experience." Is it not the case though that the likely cause of this is not the adoption of modular patterns of education but rather the fact that, compared with former ordinands, they are likely to have undertaken much shorter ordination programs? My experience of modular education programs in ordination provision testifies to the way staff carefully plan with the student an appropriate pathway through the program. Usually the modules on the program are split into the categories of "prescriptive" and "elective" courses, with Level 1 and much of Level 2 belonging to the former category. Provided ordinands are given enough time to prepare for ministry, I can see no reason why, *in principle,* modular education prevents ordinands from becoming competent pastors, with some of them going on to be "scholar-pastors." Sell gets nearer to actual practice when he adds the following qualification: "I do not say that coherence and progression cannot be achieved with a modular regime, or that modules have no place in full-time, extension or in-service courses; but where degree courses are concerned, careful organization is needed to ensure that students are guided through a coherent course, and

55. Sell, *One Ministry,* 97. Italics mine.
56. Sell, *Convinced,* 48–49 n75.

that the pitfalls I have indicted are avoided."[57] While it would be a counsel of perfection to suggest that "pitfalls" will always be avoided, contemporary practitioners do actually provide the guidance Sell advocates. But, given the shortness of some courses, the range of options open to many students is smaller than Sell suggests. Their courses end up being wholly made up of prescriptive modules.

Fourthly, Sell sounds a warning concerning the way in which education for ministry programs recently have been heavily influenced by *contextual* approaches to theological understanding, with their theological agenda largely being set by the issues, questions, and problems raised by contemporary society. Reflections on the Christian approach to that agenda then provide the intellectual and practical backbone for a relevant Christian praxis. There are clear echoes here of Tillich's "method of correlation":

> Symbolically speaking, God answers man's questions, and under the impact of God's answers man asks them. Theology formulates the questions implied in human existence, and theology formulates the answers implied in divine self-manifestation under the guidance of the questions implied in human existence. This is a circle which drives man to point where question and answer are not separated.[58]

Theological thinking therefore is perceived to take place at the interface between the Christian witness of faith and the context in which Christians are called to live and serve. Contextual approaches to theology also often draw on the methodology of the liberation theologians, which displays a robust preoccupation with practical concerns about action and justice in a divided and hurting world. Or, to make the point in another way, liberation theology emphasises this-worldly humanitarian concerns— often, it is sometimes claimed, at the expense of devoting enough attention to the spiritual and perhaps ethereal concerns of Christian believing. An adequate contextual theology however should give equal attention to both sets of concerns, since essentially they are two sides of the same coin. The basic aim of theology is to speak of God whose saving activity "comprises two quite different, even if closely related, processes that can and must be distinguished respectively as redemption and emancipation, God himself being understood correspondingly as both the Redeemer and the Emancipator."[59] We can confidently affirm that Sell attends to the *redemptive* aspect of God's work. He also recognizes the importance of Christian

57. Sell, *One Ministry*, 97.
58. Tillich, *Systematic Theology*, 1, 69.
59. Ogden, *Faith and Freedom*, 36.

theology being grounded in "the particular circumstances in which we are set" since "we cannot communicate effectively if we pay no heed to these."[60] But there remains a clearly *asymmetrical* relationship between context and tradition in his theology, with the Christian gospel being understood by him in such a way that, of the two components of God's liberative activity, "redemption" is give more attention than "emancipation." While he is committed whole-heartedly to "our explorations" not being "confined to the Christian tradition then and now," and to our ongoing requirement to "investigate the intellectual and general human environment in which we are called to proclaim the message today," he nevertheless insists that "our hearing of the world must be tempered by our hearing of the tradition."[61] It is not insignificant that Sell had little time for the thinking of either Tillich or the various theologies of liberation, pointing out the way in which contextual theologies can become so focused on a particular context that they become dangerously *this*-worldly and, hence, unfortunately parochial.

> In the deepest sense our context as Christians is life within the orbit of the triune God. Our life, thinking and witness are to be reflective of, as they are sustained by, God's grace and mercy. Often when people think of context they have in mind the par-ticular circumstances in which we are set . . .the fact remains that we are, by grace, recipients of revelation, not devisers of a theory constructed by ourselves out of ingredients supplied by our physical or intellectual environment.[62]

Sell's emphasis is seldom on the troubles and strife involved in this life. His primary focus seems to be on a very otherworldly promise: "We have received a word from God which no earthly context could by itself have provided."[63] But is it not the case that central to that world is a two-fold commandment which casts our eyes heavenwards in equal measure to the way it directs our earthly activity to the needs of others? (Mark 12: 28–34). Or, to put the matter another way, God speaks to us not just through *special* revelation to us in the Christ event but also in a more *general* way through the plight of the least of the members of Jesus' family (Matt 25: 31–46). An adequate ordination program must indeed be rooted theologically in the fact that we are "recipients of revelation," but it also must be one which

---

60. Sell, *One Ministry*, 78.

61. Sell, *Testimony*, 3; 14.

62. Sell, *One Ministry*, 78–79.

63. Sell, *One Ministry*, 78.

recognizes that the revelation in question concerns not just the work of God: the Redeemer but also God: the Emancipator.[64]

Fifthly, Sell makes a very important point concerning the content of pastoral care courses in the ordination program. During his time on the staff of the West Midlands College of Higher Education he was responsible for setting up a Counseling Service for the entire College. The experience taught him that pastoral counseling provides important components of a minister's pastoral care-set.[65] Nevertheless, Sell was concerned about the tendency of some of the pastoral care courses on ordination programs becoming merely counseling courses. He believed they should always exhibit a realistic *theological* understanding of the human person. We moderns, he wisely insisted, need to recover the essential truths underpinning what our Christian forebears meant by pastoral care. They spoke of it being centered in the "cure of souls," thereby explicitly testifying to it having a crucial theological dimension and implicitly implying that it involved spiritual and prayerful emphasis. Sell expressed his unease as follows:

> The slightest acquaintance with counselling literature, much of which has found its way into what are announced as courses in pastoral theology, will reveal that it is innocent of the language of the 'cure of souls', and that the doctrine of humanity underlying these tomes is seldom articulate and still less frequently exposed to criticism. Christians, having swept their house clean of their native vocabulary, should not be unduly surprised if seven Carl Rogerses rush in to take its place.[66]

The teaching of pastoral care is one of those many places on the curriculum where the need to integrate theology and practice is very obvious. Its style and content must be shaped by an adequate *theological* understanding of human beings, one which takes the phenomenon of what the Christian tradition has called "sin" with due seriousness, along with all the best insights from psychology.

---

64. For a further discussion of Sell's one-sided stress on the redemptive side of God's liberative activity see my *Crucicentric*, 153–56.

65. See my *Crucicentric*, 16.

66. Sell, *Nonconformist Theology*, 179.

CONCLUSION

P.T. Forsyth, Sell's great theological mentor, declares that "The Church will be what its ministry makes it."[67] He is firmly of the view that "the first test of an efficient ministry is its effectiveness on the Church; effectiveness on the world is a test of the Church which the ministry makes."[68] Forsyth therefore had a high view of both ministry and the church: ministers have an important role in the church, which in turn has a mission to and in the world. He had no time for a ministerial strategy that finds the church's ordained servants "acting directly on the world with the Church for a platform, instead of acting directly on the Church, and on the world through it."[69] But in the light of years of incremental numerical decline in our mainstream Churches, can this strategy be deemed successful? And, following on from this important question, is it right that ultimately the blame for Church decline should be focused firmly on the failure of ministers to equip their congregations adequately for their mission? As one of those ministers I cannot help but import some old wisdom in defense of my devoted colleagues: "You can take a horse to water, but you cannot make it drink."

The above thoughts certainly raise a raft of issues and questions beyond the scope of this chapter, not least concerning the more systemic forces involved in the Church's recent demise. But what is clear is that if the Churches are to re-discover, or even have to re-construct, a Christian narrative to stir the minds, hearts, and wills of the un-Churched in a largely secular society, it is going to have to be *theologically* confident and articulate. Sell's emphasis upon the necessity of the church having a suitable number of "scholar pastors" is very apposite. It need not be understood in terms of a hierarchical view of who does theology in the Church's life. In fact, Sell speaks of them being "a leaven of deeply learned theologians."[70] They should work within a theological community of pastors and church members, at the bottom of an inverted pyramid supporting, equipping, and motivating the pastors and members above them in their ministry and mission. And, running throughout the body of Christ, all ministers ought to be modeling an approach to learning which enables the whole congregation to increase in theological literacy. As Sell emphasises, to fulfil this task ministers will need to be *formed* as well as *informed*, if they are "to fulfil their primary

---

67. Forsyth, *Lectures*, 121.

68. Forsyth, *Lectures*, 122.

69. Forsyth, *Lectures*, 122.

70. Sell, *Nonconformist Theology*, 189.

obligation of leading the people of God to the throne of grace."[71] But, if they are to become fully rounded ministerial practioners, they will also have to acquire those practical skills which, rooted in "knowing-in-action," are essential for competent ministerial practice.

71. Sell, *Enlightenment,* 236. Italics mine.

Postscript

Reviewing the Direction of Travel

IN THIS SHORT POSTSCRIPT I offer a brief reflection on my theological journey. The journey is not yet over, so what I offer is provisional. But it is informative as well as interesting to delineate bedrock convictions and trace major changes of thought.

THE DRIVING FORCES OF THEOLOGY

My theology is inevitably parasitic upon the specifically Christian journey I have been following since birth. Where I have now arrived has been the result of an intriguing mixture of total chance, personal decision, and divine guidance. Things could and most probably would have been different if I had been born at a different time and place, or if I had belonged to a non-Western culture. My Christian family upbringing set the scene for much that has followed in my life. The inevitably contextual nature of my theology is consequently one of its undeniable features. During my journey I have increasingly recognized a need to widen my horizons and engage not only with Christian theologians but other religious thinkers whose backgrounds and cultures are different from my own. I know I have to live with relativities rather than trade in absolutes.

But where I stand theologically is not only a product of chance: I am far from being a victim of fate. Nor do I advocate theological relativism. The scientist in me tells me that all truth-claims have universalizing tendencies.

There is a fundamental difference between "relativity" and "relativism." Choices have to be made between rival truth claims and we are all ultimately responsible for the intellectual decisions we make. I sometimes wonder nevertheless whether the decisions I have made would have been different if my background had been in arts rather than science, or if I had studied theology in Oxford rather than Manchester, and then undertaken post-graduate studies at *Reformed* Princeton rather than Southern *Methodist* University, Dallas. It seems clear that the earlier choices in life's sequence of opportunities largely determine all our subsequent decisions. We hardly ever go back to first principles, thereby running the risk of constructing our little theological systems on soft sand rather than firm rock. I now find it more important than I once did to read in equal measure theology which challenges as well as massages my prejudices.

Looking back on my Christian journey I testify to having felt the hand of God in it, but I cannot report having had any dramatic revelatory experiences. While I have missed out on the wind, earthquake, and fire, my life nevertheless has been challenged by the "sound of sheer silence" (1 Kings 19: 11–12): I *felt* called to be a Christian minister; I *felt* guided back to England when an attractive post-graduate opportunity became available in the USA; I often *felt* God's direction when serving the churches to which I was called to minister; and I *felt* God drawing intellectual gifts out of me to equip me for a teaching role in the church. Not only accidents of birth and personal choices but also divine guidance therefore have shaped my theology. With hindsight I sense having been caught up in what Gordon Kaufman calls "a serendipitously creative process."[1] God works wonders through an evolving universe in which the future is being fashioned by the interaction of creaturely choices with divine creative and redeeming activity. To be a part of this is very humbling and rewarding. It also brings with it opportunities for Christian discipleship carrying tremendous responsibilities.

THEOLOGICAL COMMITMENTS

The genesis of my theological journey resides in my teenage years when I felt the need to bring together my understanding of the Christian witness of faith with what I was learning in my science studies. I assumed from the start that any conflict between them is resolvable; but I also accepted that a radical revision of the supernatural theism on which a large number of traditional Christian statements have been based would most likely

---

1. Kaufman, *In Face of Mystery*, 279.

be required. "Faith" and "reason" are not enemies: I believed then and I maintain now that they can and should be brought together in composing a narrative which (1) explains God's relation to the world; (2) makes clear the importance for world history of the life and teaching of Jesus, viewed from the perspective of the Easter event; and (3) provides freedom and hope to those who commit their lives to it.

My theological commitments have not altered in any drastic way during my theological journey, but I certainly now deploy theological resources in a more sophisticated way. Three examples spring to mind. First, I am now less cavalier about what philosophy can contribute to the theological task. During the early days of my attempt to integrate the Christian witness with science I assumed it was possible to produce a kind of theological equivalent of the physicists' much sought after grand unified "theory of everything" (TOE). How absurd it now seems that I should have thought it possible to achieve what physicists have failed to accomplish, not least when scientists, unlike theologians, never have to deal with the complications arising from the logical oddness of the concept of God. My youthful audacity needed a note of Pauline caution: "For now we see in a mirror, dimly . . ." (1 Cor. 13: 12). As my URC colleague Alan Sell once testified: "By grace my hope is secure, but my knowledge is partial."[2] Colin Gunton, another URC colleague, issues the following warning in his comparative study of the doctrine of God in the work of Charles Hartshorne and Karl Barth: "theology that wishes to stand on the intellectual feet of a philosophy is likely to remain a cripple."[3] The book in question set in motion a glittering theological career tragically terminated by Gunton's early death in 2003. Its argument was clear: Barth's position is to be preferred since Hartshorne's neoclassical theism leaves God "in metaphysical chains."[4] But it left Gunton with an unfortunate two-fold legacy. On the one hand, he joined a line of British theologians whose criticism of neoclassical theism is based at best on a pejorative appreciation of process thinkers' achievements, or at worst on the basis of misunderstandings of their theological positions. When interpreting Hartshorne he had criticized a straw man.[5] Then, on the other hand, Gunton's critique of Barth was so laudatory that a Barthian label inevitably was attached to him, rather unfairly I think since his subsequent work exhibits evidence of much wider influences, e.g. Samuel Taylor

2. Sell, *Spirit Our Life*, 82.

3. Gunton, *Becoming and Being*, 222.

4. Gunton, *Becoming and Being*, 52.

5. See Ogden, "Christian Theology and Neoclassical Theism." For a discussion of the way Sell and other British theologians exhibit similar problems of interpretation see my *Crucicentric*, 71–92.

Coleridge and the Cappadocian Fathers. He went on to become a powerful voice in British theology, particularly noted for the way he championed fresh understandings of the doctrine of the Trinity.

While my expectations concerning the possibilities opened up for theology by metaphysics have been lowered I still find neoclassical theism's conceptuality useful for theology, especially its dipolar structure of the concept of God and panentheistic description of the God-world relation. One can accept the limitations of any metaphysical system without eschewing the benefits of all its conceptuality. I find a statement of Dorothy Emmet's therefore very persuasive: "The light given to our minds may not give us a 'total explanation', or 'map of the world'; it may nevertheless help us to see in their true character certain features of the landscape through which we must pass."[6] And, of course, scratch theology's anti-metaphysicians and we eventually reach a redundant metaphysics. I continue to search for conceptual precision in theology, now seeing much more clearly how God-talk invites in addition to philosophical concepts the use of analogical, symbolic, and metaphorical modes of speech in the construction of our theological narratives.

Secondly, from an early age I have *felt* God's presence through the natural world. It is hardly surprising therefore that "experience" has been an important resource for my theology. Schleiermacher, unsurprisingly, helped me develop my thinking in a way that makes me less vulnerable to the charge that I am simply a mere romantic. Brian Gerrish particularly helped me understand Schleiermacher, liberating the so-called "founding father" of liberal theology from the usual charge of emotional subjectivism. For Schleiermacher, "feeling" involves an intellectual component. I now recognize more fully the balance that needs to be struck between "feeling" and "intellect"; each requiring the other in a robust theology. While I now can see how I might once have been designated as a "mere romantic," today I am more than happy to be labeled a Neville Cardus type romantic: "To me, a romantic is someone who puts beauty and feeling . . . before intellect and reason; though I *insist* that the expression of romantic feeling must be controlled by the intellect."[7]

Thirdly, my approach to the Bible has become simpler but less simplistic. In the URC's *Basis of Union* we are told that the Church's life "must ever be renewed and reformed according to the Scriptures, under the guidance of the Holy Spirit."[8] All who enter upon a recognized sphere

---

6. Emmet, "The Philosopher," 538.

7. From Daniels, *Conversations*, 262.

8. Thompson, *Stating The Gospel*, 249.

of ministry within the URC—whether elder, minister, or church-related community worker—acknowledge "the Word of God in the Old and New Testaments, discerned under the guidance of the Holy Spirit, as the supreme authority for the faith and conduct of all God's people."[9] There is no reference in those statements to any specific theory of biblical inspiration; no claim is made that the biblical text is inerrant; and a clear distinction is made between "the Word of God" and "the words of the Bible" insofar as the former is to be discerned from the latter "under the guidance of the Holy Spirit." If it had been otherwise I could not remain associated with the URC. My sympathies with "fundamentalism" are minimal.[10] I have always been committed to studying the scriptures with the aid of historical critical methods and to using contemporary ways of reading the biblical texts. The Bible has been a constant source of insight, admonition, challenge, and motivation. I maintain that the major significance of the Bible for Christians lies in its being the source for all we can ever know about Jesus, set in the context of the claims of witnesses, evangelists, and disciples concerning the significance of Jesus for their lives and the world. Our understanding of the Christ event is marginal without the Old Testament, the Jewish scriptures which provide us with important insights into the history, culture, and religion which Jesus inhabited and without which our understanding of him is bound to be superficial.

ECCLESIOLOGY

How I think about the church has certainly altered, largely as the result of reflecting upon two factors: the reshaping of the ecumenical adventure and the numerical decline of Britain's mainstream denominations.

Ecumenism

The URC is a union of Churches committed to taking, "wherever possible and with all speed, further steps towards the unity of all God's people."[11] At my ordination I resolved "to pray and work for such visible unity of the whole Church as Christ wills and in the way he wills."[12] With many others in the early

9. Thompson, *Stating The Gospel,* 262.

10. On "fundamentalism" see Barr, *Fundamentalism* and *Escaping from Fundamentalism.*

11. From the *Basis of Union* found in Thompson, *Stating The Gospel,* 249.

12. From "A statement concerning the Nature, Faith and Order of the United Reformed Church" found in Thompson, *Stating The Gospel,* 263.

years of the URC I was carried along on a wave of ecumenical enthusiasm. I shared a widespread belief that the URC's birth was a harbinger of further visible union of the mainstream denominations in England and Wales. In retrospect we were proved to be idealistic and naïve. By the mid-1980s the URC had lost a major element of its *raison d'être*: it was never going to be a front runner in the quest for further visible union. When the C of E General Synod rejected the "Covenanting for Unity" scheme in 1982, ten years after ensuring the demise of an Anglican-Methodist union scheme, the curtain came down on a search for a certain style of church union. We entered what has been called "an ecumenical winter." Former Congregationalists within the URC could be forgiven for wondering whether the schism within the CCEW that occurred when the URC was created in 1972 had been a price worth paying in the cause of wider church union.[13]

My own disillusionment was tempered by the way in which church relations had nevertheless altered for the better. Failure at denominational level cannot hide the advances made in the relationships between many local congregations, where longstanding hostilities and competition have largely been put aside. Local ecumenical *experiments* became local ecumenical *projects*, and "*councils* of churches" morphed happily into "churches *working together.*" While a sense of weariness, even boredom, was evident concerning the highly bureaucratic top-down attempts to achieve organic, visible union, it was not unusual to find those who displayed it being genuinely enthusiastic about more local collaboration and engagement. Not only does this reflect the "localism" so typical of our time, but it also belongs to a culture which increasingly finds that it can cope with difference, even to the point of exalting its virtues. From being committed to one style of ecumenism, I found myself supporting another. As local churches engaged together in diverse mission projects the old mantra that "doctrine divides but service unites" found some renewed traction. In a manner similar to the way people are apt to blame government for our social ills—often quite rightly—it was commonplace to hear Christians enthusiastically engaged in local ecumenical activities contrasting their local, positive inter-church experiences with the perceived failures of their church leaders. Lay-people committed to ecumenism could even be found suggesting behind the backs of clergy that the major ecumenical problems rested with the church's ordained servants, thereby perhaps reminding us of the ecumenical contribution made to enabling positions of leadership to be opened up to lay-people—and particularly to women in the Church of England. A

13. For a discussion of the way in which the URC's early ecumenical dreams were shattered see Camroux, *Ecumenism in Retreat.*

style of ecumenism was thus born which takes for granted what is already held in common by different churches, but also is genuinely interested in discovering more about the beliefs and practices unique to each church tradition. As Owen Chadwick says, "What is vigorous and worthwhile in the various traditions is precisely what is not in common."[14]

The decisions of the Second Vatican Council brought the Roman Catholic Church more fully into the ecumenical arena. Catholics very quickly were found playing active roles in grass-roots ecumenical activity, but Vatican doctrinal red-lines limited the extent of their involvement. This becomes painfully real for them (and us) when it comes to participation at the Lord's Table. While the barriers to structural unity are seemingly insurmountable, Roman Catholic theologians arguably have been responsible for the most significant recent ecumenical initiative. "Receptive Ecumenism" is a new strategy for ecumenical engagement led in the UK by Paul Murray at Durham University's Centre for Catholic Studies.[15] It has two working presuppositions: first, a recognition that "the hope for structural unification in the short to medium term is, in general, now widely recognized as being unrealistic"; and secondly, the belief that further progress in contemporary ecumenism is possible "only if each of the traditions, both singly and jointly, makes a clear, programmatic shift from prioritizing the question "What do our various others first need to learn from us?" to asking instead, "What is that we need to learn and can learn, or receive, with integrity from our others?"[16] This new ecumenical strategy suggests that if everyone involved in ecumenical encounter asks this question fresh possibilities for convergence emerge with partners each moving forward in ways that deepen their ecclesial identities as well as create more intimate Christian fellowship.

Seven methodological principles guide Receptive Ecumenism.[17] First, the Christian churches are called into being by the Trinitarian communion of God and forever embraced in God's love. The origin of ecumenism therefore is found in God's calling of the separate churches "to grow ever more deeply and more visibly together in this communion and to come to express the union-in-relation it implies in appropriate structural and

---

14. Chadwick, *Michael Ramsey*, 66.

15. For an explanation of the aims and objectives of Receptive Ecumenism see Murray and Murray, "Roots"; Murray, "Receptive Ecumenism"; and Murray, "Introducing."

16. Murray, "Introducing," 1.

17. I am grateful to Paul Murray for giving me sight of the titles of the "key principles" as they are described in his forthcoming monograph entitled *Healing the Wounds of the Church: The Theology and Practice of Receptive Ecumenism*. They draw together a long list of key points about Receptive Ecumenism found in "Roots," 86–89.

sacramental unity."[18] Ecumenism is not "any merely human project of our own creation, possession and control";[19] it is rather a Godly project into which we are drawn. The driving force of ecumenism also lies essentially with God. We must maintain an "active trust that we *are* being resourced by God" for the ecumenical pilgrimage, as well as a "patient recognition that any real receptive ecclesial learning necessarily takes time to be realized."[20] The journey "is one of long, slow learning into greater life and maturity . . . a time of grace for the eventual unfolding and present anticipation of God's success, not a time of irredeemable failure."[21] The goal of ecumenism—"the full flourishing of difference in communion"[22]—ultimately also lies in God's hands.

Secondly, the church is subject to change and development. Driven by the winds of the Spirit it is not subject to the treadmill of endless repetition, but rather is called ever anew to renew itself by returning to its "core calling . . . to ask what fresh performances of this, with dynamic integrity, are appropriate to the specific challenges and opportunities of our times and contexts."[23] Fresh occasions invite new ecclesial responses. There is a requirement therefore "to resist exclusively past-orientated views of tradition and exclusively problem-solving understandings of the ecumenical task relative to such past articulations" as well as a challenge "to engage also future-orientated understandings of the tradition . . . relative to the saving purposes of God in Christ and the Spirit."[24] Traditions are not inflexible structures but more akin to living, dynamic webs.

Thirdly, the experience of churches that live outside "full and visible structural, sacramental, and ministerial communion" with other churches is one of finding themselves "in a state of profound lived contradiction, rent by wounds and tears in the ecclesial body of Christ."[25] The Johannine Jesus' high-priestly prayer challengers the divided churches: "I ask not only on behalf of these, but also on behalf of those who will believe in me through their word, that they may all be one. As you, Father, are in me and I am in you, may they also be in us, so that the world may believe that you have sent me" (John 17: 20–21). All churches have skeletons in their ecclesial cupboards,

18. Murray and Murray, "Roots," 86–87.

19. Murray and Murray, "Roots," 88.

20. Murray and Murray, "Roots," 88.

21. Murray and Murray, "Roots," 89.

22. Murray, "Introducing," 2.

23. Murray and Murray, "Roots," 87.

24. Murray and Murray, "Roots," 87.

25. Murray, "Introducing," 2.

evidence that "our traditions are limited as well as life-giving, wounded as well as grace-bearing."[26] A fundamental feature of Receptive Ecumenism consequently is that it "represents an ecumenism of the wounded hands: of being prepared to show our wounds to each other, knowing that we cannot heal or save ourselves; knowing that we need to be ministered to in our need from another's gift and grace; and trusting that as in the Risen Lord in whose ecclesial body these wounds exist, they can become sites of our redemption, jewels of transformed ecclesial existence."[27]

Fourthly, Receptive Ecumenism involves the challenges of attending to the truth of the other. Truth is lived and not just thought. Receptive Ecumenism therefore also involves learning from the examples of good practice in other traditions. Whether at theological or practical levels we need to be open to conversion as we pay attention to the thinking and practices of others: "the call to graced conversion is always the call to greater life and flourishing, never, fundamentally, to diminishment."[28] Each party in ecumenical dialogue should worry less about the learning their partner needs to do and attend wholeheartedly to their own learning, "mindful of the adage that 'We cannot change others, we can only change ourselves but changing ourselves will enable change in others.'"[29]

Fifthly, there is clear unilateralist intention in Receptive Ecumenism. It involves "a move away from the presupposition of mutuality—'we'll move if you move'—to the embrace of a certain unilateral willingness to walk the path of ecclesial conversion for the sake of the greater flourishing (sic) one's own tradition's (sic) and regardless, to some extent, of whether others are also currently prepared so to do."[30] The primary aim has less to do with *inter*-denominational unification, more with *intra*-denominational conversion and growth.

Sixthly, the issues that divide Christians are deeply held and heartfelt. Receptive Ecumenism therefore involves theological reflection on emotive differences of ecclesial praxis. It is committed to "a move *away* from ideal theorized, purely doctrinally driven ecclesiological constructs in ecumenical dialogue" and also "a definite move *towards* taking the lived reality of traditions absolutely seriously, together with the difficulties and problems, tensions and contradictions to be found there."[31]

26. Murray and Murray, "Roots," 87.

27. Murray, "Introducing," 5.

28. Murray and Murray, "Roots," 88.

29. Murray and Murray, "Roots," 88.

30. Murray and Murray, "Roots," 88.

31. Murray, "Introducing," 4.

Lastly, Receptive Ecumenism accepts that we are now on a long-term ecumenical journey. It is "a time of grace for growth towards the goal by the only route possible: that of patient, grace-filled learning of how each is called to grow to a new place where new things become possible."[32] Although some of the contemporary ecumenical problems seem insurmountable this is not a time for ecumenists to throw in the towel. They must not give up on whole-heartedly responding to their God-given calling to be one; nor should they settle for a life in the household of God which only involves engaging with fellow Christians at odd moments on the landing; they should rather live boldly and imaginatively with and for others. Receptive Ecumenism is an invitation "to 'lean-into' the promise of God's purpose and the presence of God's Spirit" to heal the church's brokenness "through the sustained passion of love."[33]

It may be correct to say that Receptive Ecumenism is "a way of thinking and acting that has long been incubated in the ecumenical movement and which has, in part at least, been assumed in all good ecumenical work throughout."[34] And it is true that "If Receptive Ecumenism is indeed fruitful for our times, it represents the coming of age and to full voice of a gift born within and given by all *that* has and all *who* have gone before in the ecumenical movement."[35] That said, its effectiveness will largely depend upon the extent to which it moves away from being confined to the level of experts and academics towards being owned and practiced by church leaders and members on-the-ground at a congregational level.

When I started out my theological journey I never expected that in the early part of the twenty-first century a major driving force in ecumenism would come from a Roman Catholic source. Nor would I have believed that some of the major divisions within the Christian family are now *intra* rather than *inter*-denominational: this is particularly the case concerning issues in personal and social ethics. I now often feel more at home with Christians beyond the URC than I do with some within it. We live at a time when for some of us attending a church in which we feel comfortable increasingly is more important than denominational loyalty.

My studies in early Christianity suggest that from the very beginning diversity was a feature of the Christian movement. Part of its genius, to use a biological metaphor, came with its ability to mutate into variants that gave it an evolutionary advantage. It began as a sect within Second Temple

32. Murray, "Introducing," 4.
33. Murray and Murray, "Roots," 89.
34. Murray and Murray, "Roots," 94.
35. Murray and Murray, "Roots," 94.

Judaism, adapted to a *Hellenistic* cultural environment, and then became the designated religion of the *Roman* Empire, with the story going on to embrace many cultures far and wide. Based on this evidence a powerful case can be made for a postmodernist perspective which argues that the differences within the various branches of the Christian church are not so much existential weaknesses as vital expressions of a rich, Spirit driven movement. The necessary ecumenical mindset therefore is not one which primarily views differences negatively as challenges to be overcome and ironed out but treats them instead as opportunities to be celebrated and often embraced. Today, in an era when the importance of inter-faith dialogue is pressed upon us, a wider ecumenism also beckons when world peace depends upon our ability to handle clashes of religious cultures and religious disagreements. And, to be sure, we will not succeed if we maintain a philosophy which assumes that *they* ought to become like *us*. Learning to live with God-given difference becomes a task which takes us well beyond traditional ecumenism, but without belittling its importance.

The Numerical Decline of the Church

Throughout my pilgrimage there has been a depressing undercurrent in church life caused by the exponential decline in churchgoing, regular church closures, and ageing congregations. When I was ordained I did not fully appreciated the gravity of the situation. Rather arrogantly I believed that the tide of decline could be reversed through the hard work of ministers. Forsyth had convinced me that "The Church will be what the ministry makes it."[36] In one sense I still think he is correct, but application of the law of cause and effect condemn many devoted and competent ministers as failures if we follow Forsythian logic to the letter. The reason for the Western churches current plight can hardly be wholly put down to the churches' ministers. A more collective responsibility needs discerning. I will restrict my analysis to Congregationalism and the URC.

The great heyday of nonconformity was in the 1880s, near the end of the Victoria's reign. We know that Forsyth was offering stinging rebukes to the Congregational churches, concerning their lackluster lives and misplaced practices when lecturing to his students before the Great War. His concerns were hardly about numbers; it had more to do with the churches' woolly theology and the lack of attention to spiritual matters. "A Church is made by what it believes," he thundered,[37] not by the quality of its social life!

36. Forsyth, *Lectures*, 121.
37. Forsyth, *Lectures*, 20.

There was insufficient attention being paid to the basic essentials of church life—worship, preaching, Bible study, and prayer, activities which equip God's gathered saints for their daily lives. Forsyth's prophetic voice went unheeded. Between the two world wars the Congregational moderators also give plenty of evidence that many congregations were ailing; but in their annual reports they convey an impression that if the churches could only get the "right" ministry their fortunes could be reversed. Since they were in charge of enabling the settlements of ministers in the pastorates of the CUEW one is tempted to retort that "they would say that wouldn't they!" Then in the 1960's with the churches hemorrhaging members at an increased rate the blight of decline became more obvious. Two numerically declining denominations eventually united to form the URC which year on year has lost members at the rate of about 4% per annum.

As we noted earlier sociologists and social historians have spawned a burgeoning literature about the contemporary state of religious Britain, often focusing on an assessment of the future possibilities for the churches in the post-Christendom world of a secular society. Their diagnoses for religious decline are varied and they differ concerning whether the current dismal trends can be reversed. One undoubted fact however runs through the literature: many churches seem unable to present a narrative that grips people, cuts ice in current society, and draws people into membership of Christian communities. To be sure, in some places the Christian story is actively being told and some people are responding to it; but overall churches are not adding new members at a rate which replaces those who are being lost through death. And what is the Christian narrative or story, if it is not a considered *theological* account? R.H. Tawney once said that "the church ceased to count when she ceased to think."[38] He had the C of E primarily in mind, but his observation has a wider application. I share David Thompson's view that there was "an underlying theological and intellectual poverty in twentieth-century Congregationalism which played a direct part in its decline."[39] Churches with a theological deficit have little worthwhile to say or do; they consequently lose their *raison d'être*.

In one sense Nonconformist congregations have been victims of their own success. Victorian confidence, often bankrolled by wealthy philanthropists, produced an era of chapel building and extension which left subsequent Congregationalism with church property its declining congregations found difficult to maintain. The energy required simply to keep the institution going resulted in many a congregation losing sight of

---

38. Quoted by Preston in Elford and Markham, *Middle Way*, 271

39. Thompson, *Decline of Congregationalism*, 27.

the role they had been called to play in their community, that of being a sign, embodiment, and foretaste of God's kingdom. Radical theological analysis of the nature and function of the church reminds us that it is essentially a *movement* within society called to promote and display a societal praxis earthed in *kingdom* values. When true to its calling it offers society a distinctive and often alternative way of living. It promotes what my long-time friend Tony Addy has called "conviviality," a way of "living a good life together."[40] Our Christian engagement within society therefore should encourage us to "move firmly away from the concept of working *for* other people, or of the church *for* others, to working *with* other people and the church *with* others," a way of being church liberated from the constraints currently imposed by a redundant ecclesiastical culture, along with a "move away from simply well-meaning, pre-defined actions for other needy people towards sharing life, based on empathy, reciprocity and presence."[41] It requires a process of de-institutionalization and missionary reconfiguration.

Many years ago I had a revelatory experience while rock-pooling with our children at Boulmer in Northumberland. The context was one of those privileged moments that naturalists, whether professional or amateur, have on very rare occasions: we watched a hermit crab "moving house." Having grown too big for its shell it slowly but purposefully left its former "residence" for the comfort of a more appropriately sized empty whelk shell. Would that churches could naturally move so easily to new life. Some congregations find it relatively easy to adapt their institutional framework to accommodate numerical growth, but it is less easy to shed when it becomes inappropriate. We can continue to expect to find some examples of church renewal from within our current churches, but in many cases any worthwhile future will involve new adventures in Christian discipleship free from the current constraints of the predominant ecclesial culture.

40. Addy, "Seeking Conviviality," 161.
41. Addy, "Seeking Conviviality," 168.

Bibliography

Addy, Tony. "Seeking Conviviality—A New Core Concept for the Diaconal Church." In *The Diaconal Church,* edited by Stephanie Dietrich, et al., 158–70. Oxford: Regnum Books, 2019

Anglican-Reformed International Commission. *God's Reign and Our Unity: the Report of the Anglican-Reformed International Commission, 1981–1984.* London: SPCK, 1984.

Atherstone, Andrew. Review of *Enlightenment, Ecumenism, Evangel: Theological Themes and Thinkers 1550–2000* by Alan P.F. Sell. *Modern Believing* 48.1 (January 2007) 68.

Baelz, Peter. *The Forgotten Dream: Experience, Hope and God.* London: Mowbrays, 1975.

———. *Prayer and Providence: A Background Study.* London: SCM, 1968.

Baillie, D.M. *God was in Christ: A Essay on Incarnation and Atonement.* 2nd ed. London: Faber and Faber, 1961.

Barbour, Ian G. *Religion in an Age of Science. The Gifford Lectures 1989–1991. Vol 1.* London: SCM, 1990.

Barnes, Simon. *The Meaning of Birds.* London: Head of Zeus, 2016.

Barr, James. *The Bible and the Modern World.* London: SCM, 1973.

———. *Escaping from Fundamentalism.* London: SCM, 1984.

———. *Explorations in Theology: The Scope and Authority of the Bible.* London: SCM, 1980.

———. *Fundamentalism.* 2nd ed. London: SCM, 1981.

———. *Holy Scripture: Canon, Authority, Criticism.* Oxford: Clarendon, 1983.

Barth, Karl. *Church Dogmatics.* Edinburgh: T & T Clark, 1936–77.

Barton, John. *People of the Book? The Authority of the Bible in Christianity.* London, SPCK, 1988

Bauckham, Richard. *The Theology of Jürgen Moltmann.* Edinburgh: T & T Clark, 1995.

Berger, Peter L. *A Rumour of Angels: Modern Society and the Rediscovery of the Supernatural.* Harmondsworth: Penguin, 1970.

Binfield, Clyde. "P.T. Forsyth as Congregational Minister." In *Justice the True and Only Mercy: Essays on the Life and Theology of Peter Taylor Forsyth,* edited by Trevor Hart, 168–96. Edinburgh: T & T Clark, 1995.

Binfield, Clyde and John Taylor eds. *Who They Were In The Reformed Churches Of England And Wales 1901–2000.* Donnington: Shaun Tyas, 2007.

Bonhoeffer, Dietrich. *Letters and Papers from Prison.* 2nd ed. edited by Eberhard Bethge. London: SCM, 1971.

————. *Sanctorum Communio: The Dogmatic Inquiry into the Sociology of the Church.* London: Collins, 1963.

Bosch, David J. *Transforming Mission: Paradigm Shifts in Theology of Mission.* Maryknoll: Orbis, 1991.

Brown, Callum G. *The Death of Christian Britain: Understanding Secularisation 1800–2000.* London: Routledge, 2000.

————. "What was the Religious Crisis of the 1960s?" *Journal of Religious History.* 34.4 (December 2010) 468–79.

Bruce, Steve. *God is Dead: Secularization in the West.* Oxford: Blackwell, 2002.

————. *Religion in Modern Britain.* Oxford: Oxford University Press, 1995.

Brueggemann, Walter. *The Prophetic Imagination.* 2nd ed. Minneapolis: Fortress, 2001.

Bultmann, Rudolf. *Essays: Philosophical and Theological,* London: SCM, 1955.

————. *Existence and Faith: Shorter Writings of Rudolf Bultmann.* Selected, translated and introduced by Schubert M. Ogden. London: Fontana, 1964.

————. *Faith and Understanding: Collected Essays.* London: SCM, 1969.

————. *New Testament and Mythology and Other Basic Writings.* Selected, edited and translated by Schubert M. Ogden. London: SCM, 1985.

Calvin, John. *Institutes of the Christian Religion.* Edited by John T. McNeill and Translated and Indexed by Ford Lewis Battles. Philadelphia: Westminster, 1960.

Camroux, Martin. *Ecumenism in Retreat.* Eugene, OR: Wipf & Stock, 2016.

Capetz, Paul E. "Theology and the Historical-Critical Study of the Bible." *Harvard Theological Review* 104.4 (2011) 459–88.

Cardus, Neville. *Second Innings.* London: Collins, 1950.

Carroll, Robert P. *Wolf in the Sheepfold: The Bible as Problematic for Theology.* 2nd ed. London: SCM, 1977.

Chadwick, Owen. *Michael Ramsey: A Life.* 2nd ed. London: SCM, 1998.

Church of England. *Mission-Shaped Church: Church Planting and Fresh Expressions of Church in a Changing Context.* London: Church House, 2004.

Church of Scotland et.al. *Relations between Anglican and Presbyterian Churches: Report of the Discussions between the Church of Scotland, the Scottish Episcopal Church, the Church of England and the Presbyterian Church of England, 1954–57.* London: SPCK, 1957.

Clayton, Philip and Arthur Peacocke, eds. *In Whom We Live and Move and Have Our Being: Panentheistic Reflections on God's Presence in a Scientific World.* Grand Rapids: Eerdmans, 2004.

Cobb, John B. Jr. *God and the World.* Philadelphia: Westminster, 1969.

Congregational Union of England and Wales. *Congregational Praise.* London, Independent, 1951.

Cornick, David. *Under God's Good Hand: A history of the traditions which have come together in the United Reformed Church in the United Kingdom.* London: United Reformed Church, 1998.

Cranfield, C.E.B. *The Bible and Christian Life: A Collection of Essays.* Edinburgh: T & T Clark, 1985.

Cunliffe-Jones, H. "P.T. Forsyth: Reactionary or Prophet?" *Congregational Quarterly* 27 (October 1950) 344–56.

Cupitt, Don. *Taking Leave of God.* London: SCM, 1980.

Daniels, Robin. *Conversations with Cardus.* London: Gollancz, 1976.

Davie, Grace. *Religion in Britain since 1945: Believing without Belonging*. Oxford: Blackwell, 1994.

Drane, John. *The McDonaldization of the Church: Spirituality, Creativity and the Future of the Church*. London: Darton, Longman & Todd, 2000.

Eagleton, Terry. *Reason, Faith, and Revolution: Reflections on the God Debate*. New Haven: Yale University Press, 2009.

Ekblad, Bob. *Reading the Bible with the Damned*. Louisville: Westminster John Knox, 2005.

Elford, R. and Ian S. Markham, eds. *The Middle Way: Theology, Politics and Economics in the later thought of R.H. Preston*. London: SCM, 2000.

Emmet, Dorothy. "The Philosopher." In F.A. Iremonger, *William Temple, Archbishop of Canterbury: His Life and Letters*, 521–39. London: Oxford University Press, 1948.

Farmer, Herbert H. *Experience of God: A Brief Enquiry into the Grounds of Christian Conviction*. 2nd ed. London: SCM, 1929.

———. *The Healing Cross: Further Studies in the Christian Interpretation of Life*. London: Nisbet, 1938.

———. *The World and God: A Study of Prayer, Providence and Miracle in Christian Experience*. 2nd ed. London: Nisbet, 1936.

Fiddes, Paul S. *The Creative Suffering of God*. Oxford: Clarendon, 1988.

———. *Participating in God: A Pastoral Doctrine of the Trinity*. London: Darton, Longman & Todd, 2000.

———. *Past Event and Present Salvation: The Christian Idea of Atonement*. London: Darton, Longman & Todd, 1989.

Fiorenza, Elisabeth Schüssler. *Jesus: Miriam's Child, Sophia's Prophet. Critical Issues in Feminist Christology*. London: SCM, 1994.

———. *In Memory of Her: A Feminist Theological Reconstruction of Christian Origins*. 2nd ed. London: SCM, 1994.

Forsyth P.T. *The Cruciality of the Cross*. 2nd ed. London: Independent, 1948.

———. "A Holy Church The Moral Guide Of Society." In *The Congregational Year Book 1906*, 15–56. London: Congregational Union of England and Wales, 1906.

———. *The Justification of God*. 2nd ed. London: Independent, 1948.

———. *Lectures on the Church and Sacraments*. London: Longmans, Green and Co., 1917.

———. *The Person and Place of Christ*. London: Hodder & Stoughton, 1910.

———. *Positive Preaching and the Modern Mind*. London: Independent, 1962.

———. *Revelation Old and New: Sermons and Addresses*. Edited with a Preface by John Huxtable. London: Independent, 1962.

———. *Rome, Reform and Reaction: Four Lectures on the Religious Situation*. London: Hodder & Stoughton, 1899.

———. *The Work of Christ*. 2nd ed. London: Independent, 1938.

Foust, T. F. "Lesslie Newbigin's Epistemology: A Dual Discourse?" In *A Scandalous Prophet: The Way of Mission after Newbigin*, edited by T. F. Foust et al., 153–62. Grand Rapids: Eerdmans, 2002.

Foust, T. F. et al. eds. *A Scandalous Prophet: The Way of Mission after Newbigin*. Grand Rapids: Eerdmans, 2002.

Fox, Richard Wightman. *Reinhold Niebuhr: A Biography*. New York: Pantheon, 1985.

Garvie A. E. *The Christian Belief in God*. London: Hodder and Stoughton, 1932.

———. *The Christian Doctrine of the Godhead*. London: Hodder and Stoughton, 1925.

———.*The Christian Ideal for Human Society.* London: Hodder and Stoughton, 1930.

Gerrish, B.A. *Continuing the Reformation: Essays on Modern Religious Thought.* Chicago: University of Chicago Press, 1993.

———.*The Old Protestantism and the New: Essays on Reformation History.* Chicago: University of Chicago Press, 1982.

———. *A Prince of the Church: Schleiermacher and the Beginnings of Modern Theology.* London: SCM, 1984.

———.*Tradition and the Modern World: Reformed Theology in the Nineteenth Century.* Chicago: University of Chicago Press, 1978.

Gibbs, Mark and T. Ralph Morton. *God's Frozen People: A Book for—and about—Ordinary Christians.* London: Fontana, 1964.

———. *God's Lively People: Christians in Tomorrow's World.* London, Fontana, 1971.

Goheen, Michael. "The Missional Calling of Believers in the World: Lesslie Newbigin's Contribution." In *A Scandalous Prophet: The Way of Mission after Newbigin,* edited by T. F. Foust et al., 37–54. Grand Rapids: Eerdmans, 2002.

Goodman, Frank. *The Great Meeting.* Kettering: Toller Congregational Church, 1962.

Green, S.J.D. *The Passing of Protestant England: Secularisation and Social Change, c. 1920–1960.* Cambridge, Cambridge University Press, 2011.

Gunton, Colin E. *The Actuality of Atonement: A Study of Metaphor, Rationality and the Christian Tradition.* Edinburgh: T & T Clark, 1988.

———. *Becoming and Being: The Doctrine of God in Charles Hartshorne and Karl Barth.* Oxford: Oxford University Press, 1978.

———. *The One, The Three and The Many: God, Creation and the Culture of Modernity. The Bampton Lectures 1992.* Cambridge: Cambridge University Press, 1993.

———. "The Real as the Redemptive: Forsyth on Authority and Freedom." In *Justice the True and Only Mercy: Essays on the Life and Theology of Peter Taylor Forsyth,* edited by Trevor Hart, 37–58. Edinburgh: T & T Clark, 1995.

Guttierez, Gustavo. *A Theology of Liberation: History, Politics and Salvation.* Maryknoll: Orbis, 1973.

Gyrs, Alan Le. *Preaching to the Nations: The Origins of Mission in the Early Church.* London: SPCK, 1998.

Habgood, John. *Church and Nation in a Secular Age.* London: Darton, Longman & Todd, 1983.

Hamilton, Duncan. *The Great Romantic: Cricket and the Golden Age of Neville Cardus.* London: Hodder & Stoughton, 2019.

Hampson, Daphne. *Theology and Feminism.* Oxford: Blackwell, 1990.

Hart, Trevor, ed. *Justice the True and Only Mercy: Essays on the Life and Theology Peter Taylor Forsyth.* Edinburgh: T & T Clark, 1995.

———. "Morality, Atonement and the Death of Jesus: The Crucial Focus of Forsyth's Theology." In *Justice the True and Only Mercy: Essays on the Life and Theology of Peter Taylor Forsyth,* edited by Trevor Hart, 16–36. Edinburgh: T & T Clark, 1995.

Hartshorne, Charles. *Creative Synthesis and Philosophic Method.* London: SCM, 1970.

———. *The Divine Relativity: A Social Conception of God.* New Haven: Yale University Press, 1948,

———. *The Logic of Perfection.* La Salle, IL: Open Court, 1962.

———. *Man's Vision of God and the Logic of Theism.* Hamden, CT: Archon, 1964.

———. *A Natural Theology For Our Time.* La Salle, IL: Open Court, 1967.

————. *Omnipotence and Other Theological Mistakes.* Albany: State University of New York Press, 1984.

————. *Reality As Social Process: Studies in Metaphysics and Religion.* New York: Hafner, 1971.

Hartshorne, Charles and William L. Reese. *Philosophers Speak of God.* Chicago: University of Chicago Press, 1953.

Hastings, Adrian. *A History of English Christianity: 1920–1985.* London: Collins, 1986.

Hick, John and Paul F. Knitter, eds. *The Myth of Christian Uniqueness.* London: SCM, 1987.

Hilton, Donald. *To follow truth, and thus . . . An elliptical faith.* London: United Reformed Church, 1993.

Hull, John M. *Mission-Shaped Church: A Theological Response.* London: SCM, 2006.

Hunsberger, G. R. *Bearing the Witness of the Spirit: Lesslie Newbigin's Theology of Cultural Plurality.* Grand Rapids: Eerdmans, 1998.

Huxtable, John. *The Tradition of Our Fathers.* London: Independent, 1962.

Jantzen, Grace M. *God's World, God's Body.* London: Darton, Longman & Todd, 1984.

Jenkins, Daniel T. *The Nature of Catholicity.* London: Faber and Faber, 1942.

Käsemann, Ernst. *Essays on New Testament Themes.* London: SCM, 1964.

Kaufman, Gordon. *An Essay on Theological Method.* Missoula: Scholars, 1975.

————. *In Face of Mystery: A Constructive Theology.* Cambridge, Mass: Harvard University Press, 1993.

————. *God, Mystery, Diversity: Christian Theology in a Pluralistic World.* Minneapolis: Fortress, 1996.

————. *God The Problem.* Cambridge, Mass: Harvard University Press, 1972.

————. *Relativism, Knowledge, and Faith.* Chicago: University of Chicago Press, 1960.

————. *Systematic Theology: A Historicist Perspective,* 2nd ed. New York: Charles Scribner's Sons, 1978.

————. *The Theological Imagination: Constructing the Concept of God.* Philadelphia: Westminster, 1981.

Kellogg, Edwin H. "A Theologian for the Hour: Peter Taylor Forsyth." *Bulletin of Western Theological Seminary* 6 (April 1914) 204–43.

Kimball, Robert C. ed. *Theology of Culture.* New York: Oxford University Press, 1959.

Küng, Hans. *Christianity: Its Essence and History.* London, SCM, 1995.

MacIntyre, Alasdair. *After Virtue: A Study in Moral Theory.* 2nd ed. London: Blackwell, 1985.

Mascall, E.L. *Whatever Happened to the Human Mind?* London: SPCK, 1980.

McLeod, Hugh. *The Religious Crisis of the 1960s.* Oxford, Oxford University Press, 2007.

McFague, Sallie. *The Body of God: An Ecological Theology.* London: SCM, 1993.

————. *Metaphorical Theology: Models of God in Religious Language.* London: SCM, 1982.

————. *Models of God: Theology for an Ecological Nuclear Age.* London: SCM, 1987.

————. *Super, Natural Christians: How we should love Nature.* London: SCM, 1997.

Meeks, Wayne. *The First Urban Christians: The Social World of the Apostle Paul.* 2nd ed. New Haven: Yale University Press, 2003.

Moltmann, Jürgen. *The Church in the Power of the Spirit.* London: SCM, 1977.

————. *The Coming of God: Christian Eschatology.* London: SCM, 1996.

————. *The Crucified God.* London: SCM, 1974.

————. *God in Creation: An Ecological Doctrine of Creation. The Gifford Lectures 1984–1985.* London: SCM, 1985

————. *The Spirit of Life: A Universal Affirmation.* London: SCM, 1992.

————. *Theology of Hope.* London: SCM, 1974.

————. *The Trinity and the Kingdom of God.* London: SCM, 1981.

————. *The Way of Jesus Christ: Christology in Messianic Dimensions.* London: SCM, 1990.

Murray, Paul D. "Introducing Receptive Ecumenism." *The Ecumenist* 51.2 (Spring 2014) 1–8.

————. "Receptive Ecumenism and Catholic Learning." In *Receptive Ecumenism and the Call to Catholic Learning: Exploring a Way for Contemporary Ecumenism,* edited by Paul D. Murray, 5–25. Oxford: Oxford University Press, 2008.

Murray, Paul D. and Andrea L. Murray. "The Roots, Range and Reach of Receptive Ecumenism." In *Unity in Process: Reflections on Receptive Ecumenism,* edited by Clive Barrett, 79–94. London: Darton, Longman & Todd, 2012.

Murray, Stuart, ed. *Translocal Ministry: Equipping the Churches for Mission.* Didcot: Baptist Union of Great Britain, 2004.

Newbigin, Lesslie. "A Decent Debate about Doctrine: Faith, Doubt and Certainty." Plymouth, Devon: GEAR, 1993.

————. *A Faith for this One World?* London: SCM: 1961.

————. *The Finality of Christ.* London: SCM, 1969.

————. *Foolishness to the Greeks: The Gospel and Western Culture.* Geneva: World Council of Churches, 1986.

————. *The Gospel in a Pluralist Society.* London: SCM: 1989.

————. *Honest Religion for Secular Man.* London: SCM, 1966.

————. *The Household of God: Lectures on the Nature of the Church.* London: SCM, 1953.

————. *The Open Secret: Sketches for a Missionary Theology.* Grand Rapids, Michigan: William B Eerdmans, 1978.

————. *The Other Side of 1984: Questions for the Churches.* Geneva, World Council of Churches, 1984.

————. *Proper Confidence: Faith, Doubt and Certainty in Christian Discipleship.* London: SCM, 1995.

————. *Truth to Tell: The Gospel of Public Truth.* London: SPCK, 1991.

Niebuhr, H. Richard. *Christ and Culture.* London: Faber and Faber, 1952.

————. *The Meaning of Revelation.* New York: Macmillan, 1946.

————. *Radical Monotheism and Western Culture with Supplementary Essays.* New York: Harper & Row, 1970.

Niebuhr, Reinhold. *The Children of Light and the Children of Darkness: A Vindication of Democracy and a Critique of its Traditional Defenders.* London: Nisbet, 1945.

————. *Discerning the Signs of the Times: Sermons for Today and Tomorrow.* London: SCM, 1946.

————. *Moral Man and Immoral Society: A Study in Ethics and Politics.* New York: Charles Scribner's Sons, 1932.

————. *The Nature and Destiny of Man: A Christian Interpretation. Vol 1 Human Nature.* London: Nisbet, 1941.

————. *The Nature and Destiny of Man: A Christian Interpretation. Vol.2 Human Destiny.* London: Nisbet, 1943.

Nineham, Dennis. *The Use and Abuse of the Bible: A Study of the Bible in an age of rapid cultural change.* London: Macmillan, 1976.

Nurse, Paul M. *The New Enlightenment. The Richard Dimbleby Lecture 2012.* London: Royal Society, 2012.

Oman, John. *The Church and the Divine Order.* London: Hodder & Stoughton, 1911.

———. *Concerning the Ministry.* London: SCM, 1936.

———. *Grace and Personality.* Cambridge: Cambridge University Press, 1919.

———. *The Office of the Ministry.* London: SCM, 1928.

———. *The Natural and the Supernatural.* Cambridge: Cambridge University Press, 1931.

———. *Vision and Authority or The Throne of St Peter.* 2nd ed. London: Hodder & Stoughton, 1928.

Ogden, Schubert M. "The Authority of Scripture for Theology." *Interpretation* 30.3 (July 1976) 242–61.

———. *Christ without Myth: A Study Based On The Theology Of Rudolf Bultmann.* London: Collins, 1962.

———. "Christian Theology and Neoclassical Theism." *The Journal of Religion*, 9.2 (April 1980) 205–209

———. *Doing Theology Today.* Valley Forge, PA: Trinity Press International, 1996.

———. *Faith and Freedom: Toward a Theology of Liberation.* Nashville: Abingdon, 1979.

———. "Introduction" to Rudolf Bultmann, *Existence and Faith: Shorter Writings of Rudolf Bultmann.* London: Fontana, 1964, 9–13.

———. *Is There Only One True Religion or Are There Many?* Dallas: Southern Methodist University Press, 1992.

———. *On Theology.* San Francisco: Harper & Row, 1986.

———. *The Point of Christology.* London: SCM, 1982.

———. *The Reality of God and Other Essays.* New York: Harper & Row, 1963.

———. "Truth, Truthfulness, and Secularity: A Critique of Theological Liberalism." *Christianity and Crisis* 31.5 (April 1971) 56–60.

Page, Ruth. *Ambiguity and the Presence of God.* London: SCM, 1985.

———. *God and the Web of Creation.* London: SCM, 1996.

———. *God with Us: Synergy in the Church.* London: SCM, 2000.

———. *The Incarnation of Freedom and Love.* London: SCM, 1991.

Pailin, David A. *The Anthropological Character of Theology: Conditioning Theological Understanding.* Cambridge: Cambridge University Press, 1990.

———. "The Doctrine of Atonement. (2) Does it Rest on a Misunderstanding?" *Epworth Review* 18.3 (September 1991) 68–77

———. *God and the Processes of Reality: Foundations of a Credible Theism.* London: Routledge, 1989.

———. *Groundwork of Philosophy of Religion.* London: Epworth, 1986.

———. *Probing the Foundations: A Study in Theistic Reconstruction.* Kampen: Kok, 1994.

Pannenberg, Wolfhart. *Basic Questions in Theology.* London: SCM, 1970–73.

———. *Systematic Theology.* Edinburgh: T & T Clark, 1991–98.

Paul, Robert S. "P.T. Forsyth: Prophet for the Twentieth Century." In *P.T. Forsyth: The Man, The Preachers' Theologian, Prophet for the 20th Century: A Contemporary Assessment*, edited by Donald G. Miller et al., 43–70. Pittsburg PA: Pickwick, 1981.

Peacock, Arthur R. *Creation and the World of Science. The Bampton Lecutures,* 1978. Oxford: Clarendon, 1979.

———. *God and the New Biology.* London: J.M. Dent & Sons, 1986.

———. *God and Science: A Quest for Christian Credibility.* London: SCM, 1996.

———. *Theology for a Scientific Age.* 2nd ed. London: SCM, 1993.

Peel, Albert. *A Brief History of English Congregationalism.* London: Independent, 1931.

Peel, David R. "Alfred Ernest Garvie: Early Scottish Congregational Process Theologian?" *King's Theological Review* 12 .1 (Spring 1989) 18–22.

———. "Can You Not Read 'The Signs of the Times'?" *Faith and Freedom* 43.1/2 127/128 (Spring/Summer 1990) 43–50.

———. *Crucicentric, Congregational, and Catholic: The Generous Orthodoxy of Alan P.F. Sell.* Eugene, OR: Pickwick, 2019.

———. *Encountering Church.* London: United Reformed Church, 2006.

———. "Is Schubert M. Ogden's "God" Christian?" *The Journal of Religion* 70.2 (April 1990) 147–66.

———. "Juan Luis Segundo, *A Theology for Artisans of a New Humanity*: A Latin American Contribution to Contemporary Theological Understanding." *The Perkins School of Theology Journal* 30.3 (Spring 1977) 1–9.

———. "A learned ministry for a learning church." In *Renewing Reformed Theology: A collection of papers given at a conference in Autumn 2010 at Westminster College, Cambridge,* edited by Martin Camroux, 41–69. London: United Reformed Church, 2012.

———. "P.T. Forsyth on Ministry: A Model for Our Time?" In. *P.T. Forsyth: Theologian for a New Millennium,* edited by Alan P.F. Sell, 171–208. London: United Reformed Church, 1999.

———. *Reforming Theology: Explorations in the Theological Traditions of the United Reformed Church.* London: United Reformed Church, 2002.

———. Review of *Confessing the Faith Yesterday and Today: Essays Reformed, Dissenting and Catholic* by Alan P.F. Sell. *Modern Believing* 57.2 (2016) 189–91.

———. Review of *Nonconformist Theology in the Twentieth Century* by Alan P.F. Sell. *JURCHS* 8.1 (January 2008) 49–54.

———. Review of *The Theological Education of the Ministry: Soundings in the British Reformed and Dissenting Traditions* by Alan P.F. Sell. *Friends of the Congregational Library Newsletter* 5.3 (Spring 2016) 16–19.

———. "So Last Century?" A Review Article of *Nonconformist Theology in the Twentieth Century* by Alan P.T. Sell. *JURCHS* 8.1 (January 2008) 49–54.

———. "*Sola Scriptura* The Achilles Heel of Reformed Theology?" A Free to Believe Booklet. Sutton: Free to Believe, 2012.

———. "Some Unfinished Business from the Great Ejectment of 1662." *JURCHS* 9.3 (November 2013) 171–184.

———. "Still So Last Century?" *JURCHS* 9.9 (November 2016) 149–55.

———. *The Story of the Moderators: The Origin, Development and Future Office of the Moderator in Congregationalism (1919-1972) and the United Reformed Church (1972-2010).* London: United Reformed Church, 2012.

———. "The Theological Legacy of Lesslie Newbigin." In *Ecumenical and Eclectic: The Unity of the Church in the Contemporary World. Essays in Honour of Alan P.F. Sell,* edited by Anna M. Robbins, 128–48. Milton Keynes: Paternoster, 2007.

Pickard, Stephen. *Theological Foundations for Collaborative Ministry.* Farnham: Ashgate, 2009.

Pittenger, Norman. *Picturing God.* London: SCM, 1982.

Plant, Raymond. *Hegel.* London: George Allen & Unwin, 1973.

Pope, Robert. "Alan Philip Frederick Sell (15 November 1935—7 February 2016)." *JURCHS* 9.9 (November 2016) 519–26.

Polanyi, M. *Personal Knowledge: Towards a Post-Critical Philosophy.* London: Routledge & Kegan Paul, 1958.

Preston, Ronald H. *Explorations in Theology 9.* London: SCM, 1981.

———. *The Future of Christian Ethics.* London: SCM, 1987.

———. *Religion and the Ambiguities of Capitalism.* London: SCM, 1991.

———. *Religion and The Persistence of Capitalism. The Maurice Lectures for 1997 and other studies in Christianity and Social Change.* London: SCM, 1979.

Price, L. "Churches and Postmodernity: Opportunity for an Attitude Shift." In *A Scandalous Prophet: The Way of Mission after Newbigin,* edited by T.F. Foust et al., 238–42. Grand Rapids: Eerdmans, 2002

Rack, Henry D. *Reasonable Enthusiast: John Wesley and the Rise of Methodism.* London: Epworth, 1989.

Rahner, Karl. *Theological Investigations* Vol 5. London: Darton, Longman & Todd, 1966.

———. *Theological Investigations* Vol 6. London: Darton, Longman & Todd, 1969.

———. *Theological Investigations* Vol 14. London: Darton, Longman & Todd, 1976.

———. *Theological Investigations* Vol 16. London: Darton, Longman & Todd, 1979.

Ramsay, Ian T. *Models for Divine Activity.* London, SCM, 1973.

———. *Religious Language: An Empirical Placing of Theological Phrases.* London: SCM, 1957.

Reader, John. *Local Theology: Church and Community in Dialogue.* London: SPCK, 1994.

Robinson, John A.T. *Honest to God.* London: SCM, 1963.

Robinson, John A.T. and David L Edwards. *The Honest to God Debate.* London, SCM, 1963.

Rodd, C.S. Review of *Lesslie Newbigin: A Theological Life* by G. Wainwright. *Expository Times* 112.11 (August 2001) 365.

Rosman, Doreen. *The Evolution of the English Churches 1500-2000.* Cambridge: Cambridge University Press, 2003.

Ruether, Rosemary Radford. *Sexism and God-Talk: Towards a Feminist Theology.* 2nd ed. London, SCM, 2002.

Sanders, Jack T. *Charisma, Converts and Competitors: Societal and Sociological Factors in the Success of Early Christianity.* London: SCM, 2000.

Schleiermacher, Friedrich. *The Christian Faith.* Edinburgh: T & T Clark, 1928.

———. *On Religion: Speeches to its Cultured Despisers.* New York: Harper Torchbooks, 1958.

Schön, Donald A. *Educating the Reflective Practitioner: Toward a New Design for Teaching and Learning in the Professions.* San Francisco, CA: Jassey-Bass, 1987.

———. *The Reflective Practitioner: How Professionals Think in Action.* New York: Basic Books, 1983.

Segundo, Juan Luis. *The Liberation of Theology.* Maryknoll: Orbis, 1975.

———. *A Theology for Artisans of a New Humanity.* Maryknoll: Orbis, 1973-4

Sell, Alan P.F. *Commemorations: Studies in Christian Thought and History.* Aberystwyth: University of Wales Press, 1993.

———. "The Doctrinal and Ecumenical Significance of the Great Ejectment." In *The Great Ejectment of 1662: Its Antecedents, Aftermath, and Ecumenical Significance,* edited by Alan P.F. Sell. Eugene OR: Pickwick, 2012.

———. *Enlightenment, Ecumenism, Evangel: Theological Themes and Thinkers 1550–2000.* Milton Keynes: Paternoster, 2005.

———. *Hinterland Theology: A Stimulus to Theological Construction.* Milton Keynes: Paternoster, 2008.

———. "The Holy Spirit and Ecumenism: Some Catholic Ruminations of a Reformed Theologian." In *The Holy Spirit, the Church, and Christian Unity: Proceedings of the Consultation held at the Monastery of Bose, Italy (14–20 October 2002),* edited by D. Donnelly et al., 75–92. Leuven: Leuven University Press, 2005.

———. "Letter: Theological Education by Degrees." *Expository Times* 75.7 (April 1964) 196–200.

———. *Nonconformist Theology in the Twentieth Century.* Milton Keynes: Paternoster, 2006.

———. *One Ministry, Many Ministers: A Case Study from a Reformed Tradition.* Eugene OR: Pickwick, 2014.

———. *Philosophy, History, and Theology: Selected Reviews 1975–2011.* Eugene OR: Pickwick, 2012.

———. "So Last Century?—A Response." *JURCHS* 8.1 (January 2008) 55–59.

———. *The Spirit Our Life: Doctrine and Devotion.* Shippensburg, PA: Ragged Edge, 2000.

———. *Testimony and Tradition: Studies in Reformed and Dissenting Thought.* Aldershot: Ashgate, 2005.

———. "Theological Education by Degrees." *Expository Times* 75.7 (April 1964) 196–200.

———. *The Theological Education of the Ministry: Soundings in the British Reformed and Dissenting Traditions.* Eugene OR: Pickwick, 2013.

Spencer, Nick and Denis Alexander. *Rescuing Darwin: God and Evolution in Britain Today.* London: Theos, 2009.

Sproxton, Vernon. *Teilhard de Chardin.* London, SCM, 1971.

Stark, Rodney. *The Rise of Christianity: A Sociologist Reconsiders History.* Princeton: Princeton University Press, 1996.

Suchocki, Marjorie. "The Question of Immortality." *Journal of Religion* 57.3 (July 1977) 289–94.

Sutcliffe, John M. Review of *One Ministry, Many Ministers: A Case Study from a Reformed Tradition* by Alan P.F. Sell. *Reform* Dec 2015/Jan 2016, 37.

Swinburne, Richard. *The Coherence of Theism.* Oxford: Clarendon, 1997.

Sykes, Stephen. "*Episkopé* and Episcopacy in some recent Bilateral Dialogues." In *Episkopé and Episcopacy and the Quest for Visible Unity. Two Consultations,* edited by Peter C. Bouteneff and Alan D. Falconer, 99–105. Geneva: World Council of Churches, 1999.

Taylor, Michael H. "Afterward." In *A Scandalous Prophet: The Ways of Mission after Newbigin,* edited by T. F. Foust et al., 238–42. Grand Rapids: Eerdmans, 2002.

Tertullian. *The Apology.* In *The Ante-Nicene Fathers,* edited by Alexander Roberts and James Donaldson, Vol. III, 17–55. Edinburgh: T & T Clark, 1997.

Te Selle, Sallie. *Speaking in Parables: A Study of Metaphor and Theology*. London: SCM, 1975.

Thompson, David M. *The Decline of Congregationalism in the Twentieth Century*. London: Congregational Memorial Hall Trust, 2002.

————. ed. *Stating The Gospel: Formulations and Declarations of Faith from the Heritage of the United Reformed Church*. Edinburgh: T & T Clark, 1990.

Thompson, John Handby. "A History of the Coward Trust: The First Two Hundred and Fifty Years, 1738–1988." *JURCHS* 6 (May 1988). Supplement No.1.

Tillard, J.M.R. "Episcopacy: A Gift of the Spirit." In *Episkopé and Episcopacy and the Quest for Visible Unity. Two Consultations*, edited by Peter C. Boutenoff, and Alan D. Falconer, 65–79. Geneva: World Council of Churches, 1999.

Tillich, Paul. *The Boundaries of Our Being*. London: Fontana, 1973.

————.*The Interpretation of History*. New York: Charles Scribner, 1936.

————. *The Shaking of the Foundations*. Harmondsworth: Pelican, 1962.

————. *Systematic Theology*. Combined Volume. Digswell Place: Nisbet, 1969.

————. *Theology of Culture*. New York: Oxford University Press, 1959.

Tracy, David. *The Analogical Imagination: Christian Theology and the Culture of Pluralism*. London: SCM, 1981.

————. *Blessed Rage for Order: The New Pluralism in Theology*. New York: Seabury, 1979.

————. *Plurality and Ambiguity: Hermeneutics, Religion, Hope*. London: SCM, 1988.

United Reformed Church. *The Manual*. London: United Reformed Church. Updated Annually.

————. *Rejoice and Sing*. Oxford: Oxford University Press, 1991.

Wainwright, G. *Lesslie Newbigin: A Theological Life*. Oxford: Oxford University Press, 2000.

Walls, Andrew. "Enlightenment, Postmodernity and Mission." In *A Scandalous Prophet: The Way of Mission after Newbigin*, edited by T. F. Foust et al., 145–52. Grand Rapids: Eerdmans, 2002.

Ward, Keith. *Holding Fast to God: A Reply to Don Cupitt*. London: SPCK, 1982.

————. *Rational Theology and the Creativity of God*. Oxford: Blackwell, 1982.

Welch, Claude. "Samuel Taylor Coleridge." In *Nineteenth Century Religious Thought in the West*, Vol II, edited by Ninian Smart et al., 1–28. Cambridge: Cambridge University Press, 1985.

Whitehead, James D. and Evelyn Eaton Whitehead. *Method in Ministry: Theological Reflection and Christian Ministry*. New York: Harper Collins, 1980.

Wiles, Maurice. *God's Action in the World*. London: SCM, 1986.

Willmer, H. "The Collapse of Congregations." *Anvil* 18.4 (2001) 249–60.

World Council of Churches. *Baptism, Eucharist and Ministry: Report of the Faith and Order Commission of the World Council of Churches*. Geneva: World Council of Churches, 1982.

General Index

Paternoster:
thinking faith

The 'Theological Legacy of Lesslie Newbigin' chapter is taken from the book *Ecumenical and Eclectic: Studies in Honour of Alan P.F. Sell* published by Paternoster.

Paternoster is the theological imprint of Authentic Media, and publishes books across a wide range of disciplines including biblical studies, theology, mission, church leadership and pastoral issues.

You can sign up to the Paternoster newsletter to hear about new releases by scanning below:

Online:
authenticmedia.co.uk/paternoster

Follow us:

Printed in Great Britain
by Amazon

11939656R00129

C000281552

NOIR

NOIR

Charlotte Gann

HAPPENSTANCE

By the same author:
The Long Woman, Pighog Press, 2011

Acknowledgements are due to the editors of the following publications where some of these poems, or versions of them, first appeared: *And Other Poems, Antiphon, Bridgewater & Other Poems, Compass, The Echo Room, Envoi, Fanfare, The Frogmore Papers, Ink, Sweat & Tears, The Interpreter's House, Lighthouse, Magma, The North, Poetry & All That Jazz, Poetry South East 2010, The Rialto, Sentinel Literary Quarterly, Smiths Knoll, Under The Radar, Ver Prize 2009.*

Several poems also appeared previously in *The Long Woman* (Pighog Press, 2011).

Thanks to John O'Donoghue, Clare Best and the 'New Zealand Poets',
Mimi Khalvati and her Saturday afternoon Lewes Live Lit groups, Andrew Staib,
Alex Gann, Francesca Hume, Julia O'Brien, Pete Burden, and Will and Joe.

An Arts Council England Award in 2014 assisted the author with the writing and shaping of this collection.

First published in 2016
by HappenStance Press
21 Hatton Green, Glenrothes KY7 4SD
www.happenstancepress.com

ISBN: 978-1-910131-35-0

Paperback edition printed and bound in the UK
by Martins the Printers Ltd, using acid free paper
sourced from mills with FSC chain of custody certification
www.martins-the-printers.com

Contents

About the Author

For my father,
A.S. Gann 1927-1989

*Who among us has not at one time or another felt overwhelmed
by the sensations from within our own minds?*

—Daniel Siegel, Mindsight

*Thought and warmth must give place to action in cold streets—reality,
buses, tubes, booking-offices, life again, electric-lit London, endless terrors.*

—Patrick Hamilton, Hangover Square

SURVEILLANCE

PUZZLE

If I look closely I can see just how these
red-roofed houses slot together—where
to unclip the lid on each, lift it gently
and peep inside. In this one, a lad with his back
to a box-room door plays Space Invaders.

Next door, a lonely widower stares out
at the jutting bones of a climbing frame.
In Number 3, two women sit at a kitchen table,
a bottle of red open between them. One cries,
shakes her head, talks heatedly in a whisper.

Here a teenage couple undress each other
in a large bay-windowed bedroom. A man
lurks in shadows on the stairs outside their door.
Meticulously, I chalk an outline wherever
I see a body fall. I plot my own route through—

between houses, head down, hurrying—yank
a red thread taut around drawing pins.
It's only occasionally a roof won't click back
neatly—I leave it tilted. Have to hope this
won't upset the whole. Or that it will.

NEIGHBOUR

When I take the rubbish out, there's a woman
coming in through my gate. The wind's
blowing so hard her hair's wrapped itself
around her face. She's speaking to me while
walking away. The news I've already
blurted out has changed her mind. She's
tucking a manila envelope back inside
her shoulder bag. She points a gloved finger
up at my neighbour's top casement window.
This has slipped its latch, is banging back
and forth in a shaky frame. *They're out all day,*
I try to tell her. *There's nothing I can do. Besides,*
the attic's a magnet for birds. Dave
can't touch them. They need a way out.
Helpless, we stand together in the small garden
gazing up at the wild window smashing itself
against a red-brick wall covered in roses.

SISTERS

We're at your small high window.
You stand. I kneel, rest my cheek
on the window sill.

You're reaching for the letterbox
of blue, I'm ducking down low.
The dark windowless wall

falls away beneath me, just
a knife-slice of view.
We're smoking together.

All I need is a visa, you say.

THIRST

All day she pads on bare cracked feet
nowhere, jug heavy,
in and out the kitchen door.

She's with the kids: feeds them
chicken, chips and ice cream;
hears the six-year-old say *thank you*

but she can't talk to any of the women who come:
she bears them orange mugs of tea, sits;
she is sealed.

She feels someone somewhere
may have seen her once

and her poor kids roll round their mattresses
in nothing but boxers and twisted sheets

until finally,
just as heads the size of moons
sink into crushed pillows,
the sky blinks

and she's gaping from her high window
for miles and miles, sees
the dark trees gather.

One moment fractures blue
and then the rain comes.

One two three, drops big as bullets

(Andy downstairs pantomimes
he's been wounded)
and suddenly every mouth turns upwards

and hers is the biggest
and the first

to drink and drink and drink.

NEXT DOOR

Always I see them—the handsome student
and his lover who arrives in nothing

but a fur coat—drifting by the thin
slow-moving curtain, wielding milk,

a box of cornflakes, blue naked flame
unattended on the hob behind them.

I worry they'll set fire to the flat—
whole street—if their passion, unabated,

drags them back to the bedroom.
It seems we are safe. Instead they potter,

fry eggs in butter, bare skin flitting by
the kitchen window—always open

so Mrs Smith's cat Jemima can squeeze
between the Fairy Liquid and dirty soap.

OLD GROUND

He's out there again this morning, raking
leaves. I see him from my upstairs window,
my red face pressed despite myself. A sheet
hangs heavily on the line. On the stone table,

forgotten tea grows cold. The garden
is triangular, folded. Goldfinches
visit to feed from tiny birdcages singing
in the trees. From here I could draw a plan

like a burial ground where he has turned
old soil in man-sized lines. His hair is white
but thick, his strong back bending. He thinks
he's alone. I shouldn't watch.

Every week this man appears, stooping over
our low garden. He travels like a familiar
shadow, rearranging light and darkness,
presses hands into the black earth, gathers up

the skeletons buried there. Lays them out
on his bare bed. Reads their rites.
Straightens things under a white tent. This ground
is cold and hard, ungiving. Still he rakes.

SUSPECT

This girl is laughing, pulling
a nylon uniform over her head,
bending forward. She's smiling,
but thin and pale. Look closer.
The light from the window shines
right through her pull-on dress.

Her laughing eyes are hollow
sockets. Peer right in—at the
black knot where a waist should be.
At the way she's pulled tight
on a small taut string: the hourglass-her
she knows nothing of.

See the black fire beneath the pin
she's fixed in place that reads
Here to Help in gold on blue.
The black scribble where brains
should work, to wake her up,
scream *Get out of here now!*

Out of this window frame. Out of
his camera lens. She can't hear any
of this. It's all she can do
to stand, pull a dress over her head,
rest one small hand on the
window sill, lean forward, grin.

DREAM (1)

She has to ring someone
but can't read the number.
Type melts into itself, dripping
from the directory's thin pages.

Her fingers miss the eyes of the dial,
slide off the phone's wet buttons.
The receiver slips from her grip.
Swings, like a dead man on a cable.

PRIVATE EYE

laurie trawls the beach   jayne knits jumpers
        everyone here watches their neighbours
through binoculars
              laurie trawls the seabed
i look up 'reassurance'
        you said something
                    once
i swear
about reassurance
      re·as·sur·ance
/ˌriːə'ʃʊ(ə)rəns/

eye a lad who cradles his motorbike helmet
              eyes me back
billy is mean
      though his eyes shine blue

NOUN
1. The action of removing someone's doubts or fears
             2. A statement or comment
that   removes
            someone's doubts or fears

he has a shotgun as well as noculars
        to watch the angular progress
of his last remaining daughter

           laurie trawls the seabed
for interesting drowned girls

'care'   (less)
/keə/
NOUN
The provision of what is   necessary
            for the health   welfare
            maintenance and protection
                                    of someone
or something

            he also wants me

one night laurie goes awol   i see jayne curved silently
            lemonlike

VERB
Feel concern or interest
                                    attach importance
to something
            at the upstairs hall window

PRISONER

Round the corner from the high street and the county court
where they bring their vans to linger,

two guards lead a female prisoner.

She's dressed all in grey,
head down, hair over her face,

tiny beside them, handcuffed
to a woman guard.

She climbs up into the van
and they lock her into the tiny box-like cubicle inside.

Then they step back out into the bright sunshine,

chatting and laughing,
taking five.

WITNESS PROTECTION

TUNNEL

She and I, two farmers' wives, sit together
drinking giant frosted lagers. Dotted around us
the specks of other lives.

The darkness is real, she says, leaning towards me.

I glance around the room. An old sod
in red trousers. A writer I know from the pub.
Various others.

These people are all in pain?

Oh yes, she murmurs, and smiles.

And we dig enthusiastically into our carbonara
as the dark tunnel opens, unzips the length of
our table, the room, the restaurant,

its lime-green tables-and-chairs, Charlie and Lola
wallpaper, pseudo-Italian staff, its rows
of optics and chrome bar stools, its black-and-white

swirling floor tiles.

The chasm swallows them all.

DAUGHTER

She's a summer one,
folded away like linen,
facing in.

At times, the thinnest moon
is her tiny seashell, clipping
in a pea-green sky.

See, she's a whisper of wool;
an empty swing swinging
in a big hay barn.

She meanders
round the rose garden,
her fingers lingering

on petal tips of pink and lemon,
even milk teeth
of thorn.

Just once we touched,
a butterfly kiss
of longing

but I was still a child myself,
too slight to bear
the brunt of her.

PERSONAL ASSISTANT

The table bows under the weight
of all the wine you've bought him.
That's how drunk he's instructed you
he needs to get them.

And later, when you tuck your tight
handbag under your arm,
leave quietly by the back stair, pass
beneath the steamed-up window,

what'll you think

as you turn your key in the smooth
ignition, slide your meal-for-one
into the microwave, settle in front
of the aquarium of your blue TV screen,

check his itinerary for tomorrow?

GIRL IN THE HALL

Let's call her Hetty,
this girl who isn't me,

this thin white one,
this bare-knuckled beauty,

who lives in the wallpaper,
thin as wallpaper,

this bruise-eyed darling,
this one I'm half in love with,

who lives in the wall,
tap-tapping her urgent warnings,

the ones I adhere to
in this narrow dark corridor

where she's stock still,
stuck still,

open mouthed,
shrunk into a skirting board,

fingering a crack,
this white-thighed girl,

darting now,
a shadow

naked down the hall,
searching for a shower—

his thin line of sweat,
early evening stubble—

when she shouldn't
even be here.

VICE

He holds her in his vice.
The place is soundproofed.
She's screamed and screamed
and no one's come.

When she stops the birds still sing.
Weather passes. Days
are days. The postman calls.
She hears the milkman whistle.

CLUSTER

He leaves home at five, snatching up
his battered briefcase, backing out of the drive,
swinging his steering wheel northward.

    She lies on the bed he left, staring upwards,
    curtains open. His car lights throw elongated
    window frames across the ceiling.

He stands at the podium in a crowded hall,
seats rising in tiers, students' faces
quiet and pale, swivelled towards him.

    She's up now. Has already broken
    a glass, watched blood and juice swirl
    together down the plughole.

*Dark matter is determined by the mass
of objects, minus their luminosity—stars,
gas, dust.* His voice wavers on the poetry.

    Soon she'll pour herself a drink, go
    and sit at her desk. Her tongue tingles,
    anticipating the first taste.

Do you know, he asks, clutching at the lectern,
*dark matter plus dark energy accounts for
95.1 per cent of all we are and know about?*

DREAM (II)

We're playing ball—as we always have.
But now the ball is big and black, a cold
shadow-thing that cuts out sunlight. My brother
and I have grown bowed from our long-playing.

We hang on tight each time we catch the ball,
stagger about, our arms stretched wide. Hold it
for longer and longer, then let it loose
to bound, lugubriously—almost in

slow motion, almost comically—across
the ground between us. The beach has shrunk, though
gained some sparkle. But, no, the ball has grown.
When it bounces my way now, it fills the sky.

OLD WIVES

come in off the dark street, narrow alleyway,
duck in under the smoking streetlight,

settle at her kitchen table, drink tea,
smoke, stain their mouths with wine.

She says nothing, keeps pouring
and the women keep coming, ducking through

her narrow doorway, under the small light,
gathering at her kitchen table

to knock back tumblers, start on their
inevitable *He's a terrible man, terrible*...

and the low-hanging light sways softly
in the thick air, and she never lifts a finger

and nothing, nothing ever changes—
just this endless stream of wives-and-mothers

gathering at her kitchen table
to weep and smoke and whisper secrets,

ducking in from the narrow alleyway,
coming in off the dark street to find her.

THE BLACK WATER

is lapping at your cup and saucer.
Do you really not see it? Ink sloshing
against fine-rimmed china.

My eyes are on your kindness, on
a vase of sweet peas in your alcove.
Quiet standard lamp by pale-blue armchair

casting its aura. But I can't not see
the cold dark water, can't not feel its oil
seep up through my boyfriend's jumper.

You pass a plate of small pink cakes
even as the black sea licks bookshelves,
light-shades, even as I hoist my body

out of this chair—toppling the delicate
oval table—back away across worn
grey carpet. Grope for the door.

CORNERS

Once he's done she makes him up a nice bed
for the night. Takes sheets and blankets, neatly
folded, from the linen cupboard outside
her bedroom and carries them down the stairs.
While he enjoys a final cigarette
and scotch in the small walled garden, she smoothes
the sheets out on the put-you-up mattress,
then tucks them tight in hospital corners.
Early next morning she cooks him breakfast:
tea, orange juice with bits in, soft boiled egg,
two slices of white toast and marmalade,
sweet black filter coffee boiled on the hob.
She walks him to the station, allowing
plenty of time for him to buy a bar
of chocolate and a newspaper, and still
be comfortably on the 9:23.
It's only after his late train pulls out,
and a passing friend, concerned, touches her
back gently, that she bends double on
the pavement outside the station, and cries out.

COLLECTED

Her shift over, she shimmies out of nylon skin, pricks
her finger hard on the badge-pin. Snaps shut
her locker door, like one life closing. The other waits

purring in shadows, slinking forward along the kerb.
She emerges from a narrow side street, slides
into his passenger seat without a word. As they pass

the infirmary, the cigarette factory, the museum
of Egyptian mummy heads in yellow bandaging, she leaves
each one in flames. He opens up on the motorway.

The sea is rising, black, choppy. Gone, the picture
postcard. 'Remember *The French Lieutenant's
Woman?*' he asks. She remembers only *The Collector.*

THE PROJECTIONIST

FULL MOON OVER THE FAIR

You lead me on a thin leash to the lip
of our small red town. I see your mouth twitch
as you ask, is it true, the thing you've heard?
Big pink candy flosses nod, faces
in a crowd. Your mouth keeps moving, words lost
on the wind. I slip my knot, head for the hills:
low chalk path climbing skyward, people
so near I can hear them breathe. I don't care.

I give him everything: panting, wordless,
long hair mingling, bodies white in the blue
grey grass.

               Later you come round to mine,
coffee in my parents' house. Somehow
you seem appeased. I peck goodnight, smile,
teeth bared as I close my door on the moonlight.

THE KING'S HEAD

She sits alone, swaddled
in a boy's black jumper
unravelling at the cuffs,

head bowed, eyes lost
in shadow, scratching one nail
fixedly along a dark crack.

Her yellowed finger will not
cease—now rolling a fleck
of wax back and forth

across the tabletop, while
the jukebox sings its heart out
and the pinball machine flashes.

When her older, anoracked
companion returns from the gents
she doesn't look up,

and when he leans in,
resting his hand on her knee,
she remains quite still.

LITTLE MATCH GIRL

Small, pointy, blue, I crouch, bare knees jutting
from rumpled socks. I'm hunched in the dust,
playing my game, intent on this, eyes bruised

in the half-light. I strike my matches one by one.
They flare yellow, die in my palm. What I don't do,
what I won't, is stand. Unfold my full-grown body.

Turn. See the lush green Downs replete with rain
and sun, the porous chalk. The big switched-on faces,
like lamps, burning at every window.

COUNSEL

Out front, a retired paedophile leans on
his push mower, resting in unexpected heat.

I'm scanning the dark outline of your face.
We can work through all this, you say

though your words mean little to me.
Beyond, a vast patio window looks out

over bleached school fields. Two boys crawl
like insects the length of this long window.

All of life has led me to this moment.
This L-shaped sofa. Sitting across from a man

whose face I can't make out, the window
white behind him. Those boys reach

the far side of their field. I catch the distant
flare of a match. What a long way back.

PICTUREHOUSE

Darkness is the wave that carries us crashing,
crashing onto this beach where scared young girls
wander barefoot, dressed in pale vests,
move like dancers with thumb-bruised arms.
Darkness is the wave that plunges us, lank-haired
and middle-parted, always staring straight ahead
at a family man gone bad/ loner with a grudge/
blinds lit from within, the mottled shape of butterflies.
Darkness is the wave that brings me here,
to the brink of her long tattooed back as she rides him
beneath a small high-bolted window.

Darkness is the wave that sends me spiraling
into lidless forest where someone hunted
hurtles always many miles from hearing.
Darkness is the wave that breaks, wet scarlet
on white plaster, in bedroom/ bathroom/ hotel room/
apartment/ in the ill-lit hallway beyond
the peephole, to the hectic rumble of a rising lift.
Darkness is the wave that sends us spinning out
onto this steep black-cobbled beach, lip-first,
to safely taste a woman, impossibly naked, in a room
frantic with wallpaper and lamp-thrown shadows.

ON THE TIDE

This long brown coastline is like a finger,
tongue lingering, hairs standing

on my naked forearm. I do not label this
'adultery'. Instead, I *want* those hands

to press against my back, to cup my belly,
to hold my coiled head of skin and muscle, bone

and blood. Shut eyed, curled tight, forehead
to forehead, I war with myself.

The sea washes up and away, up and away.

I am a broken shell, lying in the wet
grey sand, half in half out, half buried,

half alive. I am a creature of this earth,
for the moment safe. But one single boot

from a giant child could crush me.
I breathe in small cracked gasps,

red spots in my cheeks. *Fuck*
is the only word I speak.

The sea comes and goes, comes and goes.

I do not leave footprints in the sand;
the sand leaves footprints in me.

MOLECULAR BIOLOGIST

Great news! my brother cries, dimple jug
half raised to thin pink lips. *Turns out there's*

such a thing as cold mothers. Genetically
determined, I mean. I goggle wordlessly.

All I can see is my own face, drained
and strung, bulging in the white windows

of his specs. He leans forward,
thrusting a blunt finger, spindly pub table

rising like a ouija board to meet him.
Crisps skitter out of their silver purse:

pale faces on dark wood. *Cold mothers*
are the carriers of autistic genes,

he intones slowly, as if addressing
a conference. *Ah,* I flicker.

Yes, yes, exactly! he cries. *Mother*
was pleased too. 'I was your classic cold mother,'

she said when I told her. And he sinks
with a small smile into his hard hassock.

THE LETTER

This single A4 sheet
Typed by a doctor on a
Big black typewriter
Has been folded and

Unfolded more times

Than I can count now
I have pushed it under
Grilles into glistening
White reception-booths

Waited naked while

CRIMPLENE MATRONS EXTRACT IT

With clipped fingernails, scrutinise its contents under the surgi-
cal bulb of a table lamp, read it over half-moon glasses or with
their backs turned, shake their heads, fold the thing, slip it back
into its worn brown envelope. Slide it out to me.

I have traipsed a web of city streets, A-Z crumpled in my jacket,
turned bends where gusts of wind whip up, sweep me off down
black rain-sodden side roads. I have stood under a streetlight,
looked up, *prayed*, my face bathed in yellow.

Trudged on—down yet another wet pavement, under a suicide
bridge, past a 7-Eleven—

Envelope still clutched deep

Inside my pocket

NIGHTS OUT

The sweating ceiling leans in
to hear all the filth we're talking.
Our St Vitus fingers dance—

sculpting lurid figurines
from hot, dripping wax—grind
butts into an evening's ashtray

searching for gold dust.
He loves me, he loves me not.
My companion commiserates

as she always does,
Italian hair weighted by candlelight.
Her life carries other travails.

DREAM (III)

your wife comes to me
    talks earnestly
        procedural and compliance issues
    about
        how the body processes things

some nights
    small daughters hold your hands as you walk
others
    naked chested women flank your sides
                a teenager cries

your wife is thin dark beautiful
    nothing like me

for whole minutes we watch footage of
                what happened
headlights sweeping low across a seawall

    still you say   *she's in me*

THE BLOODY CHAMBER

COLUMN INCHES

Where are you getting your information?
My walls are papered with newspaper
cuttings—black and white on deep-red
plaster. Through one window I see
the red-brick houses I grew up in. Through
another, cliffs and sea and wild woodland.
Mostly, though, the cuttings I snip
from today's newspaper form the backbone
of my ongoing investigation.
Where are you getting your information?
I've pinned photos all around me—
marked each *Deceased*, or [the name
of a city]. Shoe boxes, stacked along
the hallway, bulge with extra details.
They're held together by elastic bands
a) snitched from my dad's old chest;
b) dropped on pavements by passing postmen.
Mostly, though, the cuttings I snip
from today's newspaper form the backbone
of my ongoing investigation.
Where are you getting your information?
You and I stopped once to embrace
at the side of a lake without either of us
knowing why. I have a carbon copy
of that exact moment, put through my usual
filters, then pinned here: see, the thick tight
brambles skirting the lake, the smooth
dark surface stretching away? How
close we stand together, and to the edge.
Mostly, though, the cuttings I snip
from today's newspaper form the backbone
of my ongoing investigation.

MRS COULTER'S SCISSORS

i
Small and fierce, she stands hands on hips
in the blue doorway of her windswept kitchen.

Enough is enough! she screams, into the fury
of wind. No one's listening.

She raises her hand, tiny bright blades glinting,
aims, strikes, finds a hacking, like severing dough.

Flesh is thick pomegranate.
The child's eyes shine.

ii
After, she reels the thing up by its feet.
It hangs three weeks from her Sheila's Maid.

The floor is mopped, table wiped.
Time soon passes.

One of the coal men swings it up, over
his shoulder, carries it off without a murmur.

The child's much quieter now; at times even pretty.
And who'd have thought it?

iii
On a far shore, crouching, people pause
from braiding hair, trading beer.

What is that creature lumbering along
the beach, half woman, thick

with matted hair like river reed, skin
the shade of mud and sun? And what is that?

As it blunders past, there's a flash
like silver fish leaping in an arc around it.

BUCKLE

He drove her to the coast once, so drunk
she stripped off and swam out
into the black sea, sea wall
smaller and smaller, until she
was just a dot.

Other teenagers he'd filled his car with
spilled out along the dark
beach, necking red wine,
and screaming like seagulls until
even that stopped.

DREAM (IV)

Small smudged faces loom from unlit stair.
I let myself in. Wait. Waif on a doormat.
Start the long walk along the long dark hall.

Leave behind white light, frost on trees, lick
of cold sun in my hair. One boot forward.
Small smudged faces loom from unlit stair.

On I go. Into the farthest shadows.
Trail fingers on wallpaper. Feel its flock.
Start the long walk along the long dark hall.

Past the dresser, bulbous with half-full
bottles, cream dial phone I never touched.
Small smudged faces loom from unlit stair.

I used to be alone here, quaking.
Now children press against the banister.
Start the long walk along the long dark hall.

Their deep eyes on me. Their pale tired nighties.
It's only now I see. Whole seas of them.
Small smudged faces loom from unlit stair.
Start the long walk along the long dark hall.

LOVE POEM

His iron gates stand shut. A murder
of plump crows hangs suspended from black
branches: charcoal thumbed into thick white fog.

Slip of a girl, caught in a trap, stares
up at the house from the edge of the wood:
loam eyes, hair wild, the way he likes it.

He buried this one years ago; churchyard
down the lane. Thick ankled and drunk she was.
Now she's back, pupils huge in the moonlight.

He licks dry lips, lamp at the window.
Stabs his nib deep in the inkwell. His new
young wife starts, cheeks paling, eyes watering.

Pauses at her stitch, but does not speak.
He's taught her about interrupting.

NO

Thank you so much for your invitation
I stand by my bed in the dark

I am very sorry but I have decided
I crouch by my bed in the dark

This is not a decision I have made lightly
I'm near the curtained window, crouched

I hope very much you don't feel
I'm by the curtained window, trembling

All I really want you to know is how
I shake by my bed in the dark

STATEMENT

One minute it was black and night-time and Jimmy
and me, we were inching forward along the edge of that
swimming pool wall to see what all the noise was,
who was that crying, and the next headlights flared

blinding and his car shot forward, and *thud* that silence.
We saw her sliding, and we ran like hell. Sat up all night
talking, round and round—what we'd seen, what he'd done,
was it really him. Jimmy and me stopped going out

after that, couldn't face each other, couldn't face what
we knew. All that summer it was hot, I was sick. Wait till she
gets back, I said to myself, and confront her. The papers
are only obsessed 'cause they like running her photo.

You think if no one's kicking your door in you got away
but when I close my eyes I see her in the headlights.
The next year I left—I pretended she left too.
I tried not to blame myself, I couldn't have saved her

even if I had told them everything that night before
she was even 'missing'. She's there all the time
in my mind, her white face rising rising in a rush.
Some nights I watch him turn her body on the dark grass.

THE CALL

Every evening I call you
from a phone box in the basement.
A queue is always forming.
The door slides closed, creating
a pocket of hot silence.

Pennies drop. *Hello? Are you
all right?* Me—crying—No . . .
We fold into handsets. *Here I am,*
you whisper, pushing your door to
with socked toe.

You say there's nothing wrong
with me. At the end of the corridor,
a figure mops, sloshing away
my year's intake of scum
with disinfectant.

Every evening I call.
I'm with you, you say. When
the pips go, the dark wave inside me
swells. I open
the door and drown.

THE OTHER GIRL

The one who came to see you earlier
trailed around these busy streets after
she left your building. Crept along
the inside edge of pavements. Steadied

herself with one hand to railings. Kept
her eyes down, except for glances over
her shoulders to check black-coated
others didn't walk too near behind her.

When doorways gaped, throwing warm
yellow arcs across the paving stones,
she snuffled close, snorting the scent
of overcoats draped over the backs

of armchairs, trays of bright sherry
and chocolates. She scuttled across stiff
Welcome mats while automatic doors
slid open. Closed again. Let no one in.

The Christmas lights dragged her free
of the ground. Loosed at last, she drifted
and bounced like a grey dust ghost
against the crowd's puffa jackets, bags

of late-night shopping. Listed along
between lanes of traffic. Hopped across
the central reservation, pulled on
a jerky silver thread towards the lanterns.

While you reversed out of the mews
and dipped your headlamps southward,
she climbed up on the rail, lifted her face.
Her eyes, they said, were shining.

ELEVENTH HOUR

NOIR

I only ever catch a moon-thin glimpse
of the projectionist's face as I wander down
my lonely aisle, glance back, before

he whips his curtain shut. In this deserted
auditorium, I park my own blunt
calf of body—let it sink, groaning,

into a rising trough of darkness. This is our
windowless home. Behind my head, nothing
but deep thick folds of milky black,

while my eyes, live though furtive creatures,
dart across the nuance of the piece
worn thin like hallway carpet. Inside this

bobbing car is where I touch the hidden seam—
as the last reel rolls, heroes rise before
the kiss—where my life and the darkness meet.

DREAM (V)

Always on that faint
horizon the white
rider is galloping
galloping in eerie silence.

Sent to overwhelm
her enemies, on
this raging, empty,
storm-swept, grey-lit

even-tide beach where
parched sand meets
black sea, he never
arrives, never arrives.

QUEUE

The idea is
    you stand here, shuffle along and
when your turn comes she'll
        sign your book, and hug you.
    Under these arches, though, even
the pigeons are freezing;
    the girls ahead and behind me
are both turned, facing others.
        The tide's coming in and it's
soaked my plimsolls.
        The queue stretches as far as I can
see in both directions.
I'm scared, of course, of losing
    my place but the woman
        in the distance, signing books
    is enunciating
        each person's name
    carefully, once,
through a tannoy.
        Of course, now I'm wishing
    I didn't hate *mine* so much—and
am killing time
    inventing others.
I yearn to be closer
    but the queue never gets shorter
and that woman stays
    small as a worry doll
        on the horizon.

ON NOT BEING ABLE TO SEE

The way the staircase is encased in glass.
The way the man in the white coat greets me gruffly.

The way the metal peepholes are set too far apart,
and my eyes are doorways on to darkness.

The way two flickering postage stamps loom:
      The lion.   *Its cage.*

The way these celluloid squares dip and judder.
The way these flickering blocks set sail from their corners.

The way I have to twist each hand towards the other.
The way things settle, the two lit squares only marginally closer.

The way I swallow, twist. How hard I have to try.
The way it all seems for the moment to be working.

The way the lion shudders, splits;
                      the cage shoots off into darkness.
The way everything is lost.

The way I twist and writhe; at long last, spot them.
The way I have to grit my teeth.

Occasionally, for one split-second, like something dreamt,
the way I glimpse the complete picture.

The way I cry out.
The way by then, of course, they've long since parted.
The way I end up where I started.

HER PUBLISHER

I love this time of year, time of day:
the light, pale-egg and misty; platform
almost empty. Malcolm says we'll wander,
find somewhere nice for lunch. We always do:
Italian spaghetti, a carafe
of red wine. I'll have to watch my frock.
I love all the bustle of Soho,
like another planet. The awards
don't start till 6. And, do you know, I don't
even mind meeting the Queen, the mood
I'm in. Plus, I put the milk bottles out
already, and extra food for Saturn.

Malcolm's eyes are the colour of clear sky.
I'm sure to make the 11:03.

FICTION

Later we'll go down to the water, watch
the locals race horses on the sand.

For now, I sit at my expansible keyboard
(neat, black, click clack)

on the verandah of The Sandcastle
drinking coffee

while Steve digs out flowerbeds,
a little Japanese bridge.

I sit on the verandah writing my novel,
London Windows, tanned legs

unrecognisable. I wear
a tiny cotton wraparound skirt, deep maroon

with golden flowers. I never in my life
wore such a thing—until now

on Golden Bay, sitting on the verandah,
drinking coffee,

writing my novel on the neat expansible
keyboard you bought me to travel

while Steve digs out flowerbeds,
a little Japanese bridge.

MISE-EN-SCÈNE

Crooked behind a broken sofa, I pray
to be disturbed before I turn
too many more pages in this yellowed
book I'll return to (time and again
like a moth to a flame): the diver,

clambering out of waves; the girl,
playing; the steep beach facing
the troubled sea, the girl not looking;
the sky heavy and dark as the fat
stone that rests among pebbles.

DREAM (VI)

I am swimming in the waves. My mother
and my sister are on dry land. I only see them
for a moment, when the black sea churns me
to its surface. I see a triangular slip of
white beach—like a handkerchief dropped
on rocks—and a cliff. Seagulls wheel:
my mother and sister are peeling hard-boiled eggs
on their slice of beach. I am in the black waves
and only see them for a moment. I think
my sister's eyes are stony? In my mother's—
a flash of love? This is new, or new for me
to notice. I think deep down she knows
the beach is getting smaller and the cliff is steep.
Someone has to swim out in the water.

DREAM (VII)

I've stood here too long, cramped and sad, and
suddenly I know it's time. Other folk
are shuffling round the busy room behind
me, their names being called—names I dimly
remember, like an old school register
to which I can no longer put faces.

Yes, I'm sure it's time. But when I turn to go,
I catch sight of a woman in a red dress.
Her eyes are averted. Still, in a flash,
I know I know her well, or could, or
yearn to. I too look down. Perhaps I blush.
I know I feel warm. Warmer than before.

I have to go. But the way to the door
now seems blocked by cloth and red wings.
I start across the linoleum, face down,
shoulders close, hands shoved deep in pockets.
The woman glides—now along the far wall,
now whispering to someone at the counter.

It's time to go. But my body has other news,
it crosses the waiting room suddenly, fast—
heads straight for this woman in red who
at the same time turns and rushes towards me.
When we collide it's with such force
you'd think we'd be broken or badly hurt

but we're not, we carry on, like clockwork toys,
walking into and into each other. I can't say how—
it feels like *through*—but of course
there's no way through another. Instead,
I find myself in the wardrobe of her:
fabric, skin, flesh. Rest.

MEETING

It grows dark without either of them noticing, sun
slipping below black cobbles. As they talk
details of her long journey here are forgotten.

Suddenly she says something so extraordinary
he lifts his face to meet her eyes in recognition.
She's all but gone, already, into shadows, her glow

a mere glimmer. He shifts arms, shivers.
They both blink. She leans across and—click—
switches on the desk lamp. Yellow light floods

the room, their faces. They shake hands warmly,
the future spread before them like a lain table.

IN THE CLASSROOM OF TOUCH

This is how you hold a person, Mr Farnham says
demonstrating. *Your touch needs to be light
but firm. Felt in the skin like a weight, a squeeze.*

No sudden movements, please. Still is best.
The pupil he's performing on closes her eyes,
head slightly folded like a bird's.

She's collapsed into his woollen front. *See how
my arms arc?* the teacher asks his class.
Hold each other like precious cargo.

*Never be too rough. Don't shove into
the person you love. Don't steal touch.
Be clear about this: we give a hug. Thanks Lydia,*

back to your seat now. Giles–? The boy
stares down at his feet, face pink. His worst subject.
Mr Farnham waits quietly, bends his head,

smiles. *C'mon Giles,* he says gently. The boy
staggers down the ragged aisle between assorted
classmates. Waits while this man

opens his arms. Falls forward, hiding his face,
his sobs. The teacher enfolds him carefully,
whispers, *You're doing well, Giles.*

AN ENDING

What might the end look like? An end to the playing
and replaying of the same old loops of grainy film.
Three shots pumped into the chest

of the man at the top of the stairs? Simple. Blood
on wallpaper, a sliding-down. Crumpled silence.
The end of misplaced love and loyalty.

Trap-doors slapping open onto the old ground.
Clambering up rickety steps out of these frozen cellars,
all of us emerging—dusty and blinking—

ducking under the trees, carrying children, who rest
their heads and sleep on our strong shoulders. All of us
free at last to walk up these hillsides into the white sunshine.

About the Author

Charlotte Gann studied at University College London and the University of Sussex. For some years she worked in magazine publishing. She was Managing Editor of Which?, and Editor of Health Which?. Today she freelances as a writer and editor. In 2012, her pamphlet collection, The Long Woman (Pighog Press), was shortlisted for the Michael Marks Award.